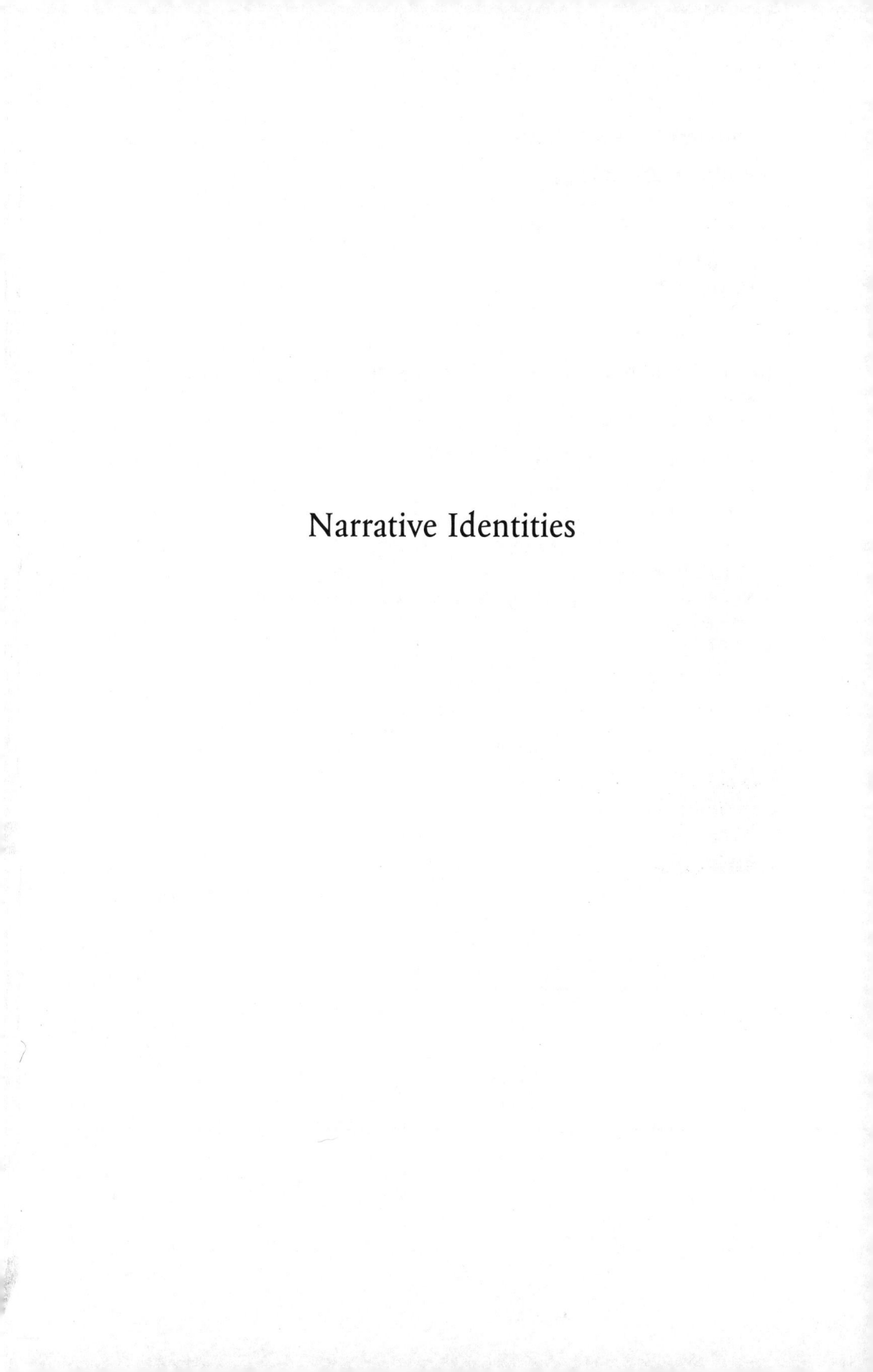

Narrative Identities

of related interest

Key Ideas in Psychology
Ian Stuart-Hamilton
ISBN 1 85302 359 0

Human Resilience
A Fifty Year Quest
Ann Clarke and Alan Clarke
ISBN 1 84310 139 4

Becoming a Reflexive Researcher – Using Our Selves in Research
Kim Etherington
ISBN 1 84310 259 5

The Psychology of Ageing
An Introduction 3rd Edition
Ian Stuart-Hamilton
ISBN 1 85302 771 5

Spirit and Psyche
A New Paradigm for Psychology, Psychoanalysis and Psychotherapy
Victor L. Schermer
ISBN 1 85302 926 2

The Dimensions of Dreams
The Nature, Function, and Interpretation of Dreams
Ole Vedfelt
ISBN 1 84310 068 1

Narrative Identities

Psychologists Engaged in Self-Construction

Edited by George Yancy and Susan Hadley

Jessica Kingsley Publishers
London and Philadelphia

First published in 2005
by Jessica Kingsley Publishers
116 Pentonville Road
London N1 9JB, UK
and
400 Market Street, Suite 400
Philadelphia, PA 19106, USA

www.jkp.com

Copyright © Jessica Kingsley Publishers 2005

The lyrics in Chapter 9 from 'Finale from Les Miserables' are reproduced with permission from Alain Boublil Music Ltd. © Alain Boublil Music Ltd. (ASCAP) Music by Claude-Michel Schonberg. Lyrics by Alain Boublil, Herbert Kretzmer, Jean-Marc Natel.
The extract in Chapter 12 from *Critical Psychology: Voices for Change* by Tod Sloan is reproduced with permission from Palgrave Macmilliam © Palgrave Macmillian 2000.

All rights reserved. No part of this publication may be reproduced in any material form (including photocopying or storing it in any medium by electronic means and whether or not transiently or incidentally to some other use of this publication) without the written permission of the copyright owner except in accordance with the provisions of the Copyright, Designs and Patents Act 1988 or under the terms of a licence issued by the Copyright Licensing Agency Ltd, 90 Tottenham Court Road, London, England W1T 4LP. Applications for the copyright owner's written permission to reproduce any part of this publication should be addressed to the publisher.
Warning: The doing of an unauthorised act in relation to a copyright work may result in both a civil claim for damages and criminal prosecution.

The right of the contributors to be identified as authors of this work has been asserted by them in accordance with the Copyright, Designs and Patents Act 1988.

Library of Congress Cataloging in Publication Data
A CIP catalog record for this book is available from the Library of Congress

British Library Cataloguing in Publication Data
A CIP catalogue record for this book is available from the British Library

ISBN-13: 978 1 84310 779 8
ISBN-10: 1 84310 779 1

Printed and Bound in Great Britain by
Athenaeum Press, Gateshead, Tyne and Wear

To our parents, siblings, and children

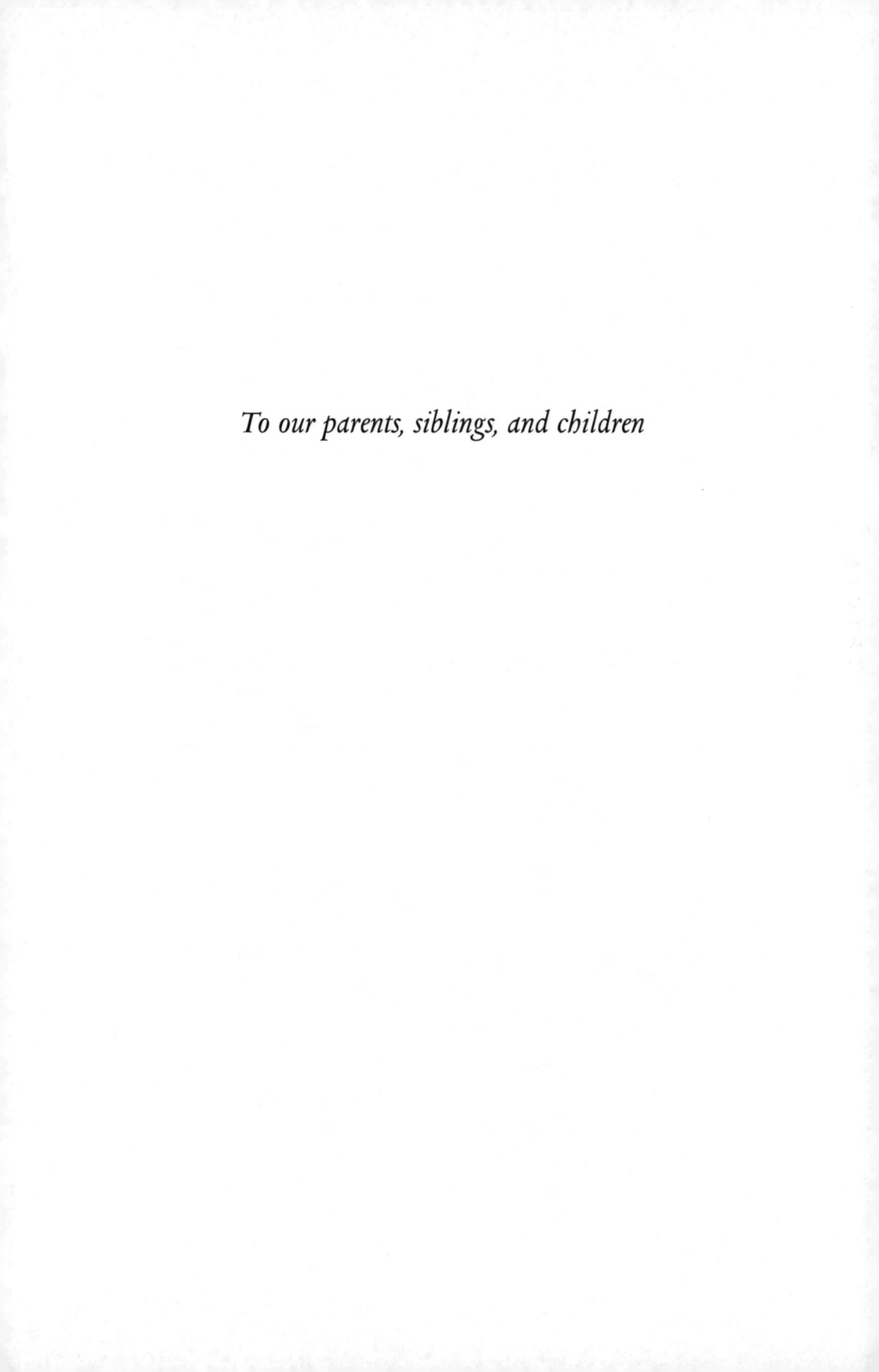

Contents

PREFACE   9
George Yancy, Duquesne University, and Susan Hadley, Slippery Rock University, Pennsylvania

1   The Poetics of My Identities   13
Theodore R. Sarbin, University of California, Santa Cruz

2   Lessons from Relics about Self and Identity   36
Karl E. Scheibe, Wesleyan University, Connecticut

3   Objects, Meanings, and Connections in My Life and Career   54
David E. Leary, University of Richmond, Virginia

4   From Poppies to Ferns: The Discursive Production of a Life   73
Gerald Monk, San Diego State University, California

5   Performing a Life (Story)   96
Lois Holzman, East Side Institute for Group and Short Term Psychothreapy, New York

6   A Psychologist without a Country, or Living Two Lives in the Same Story   114
Dan P. McAdams, Northwestern University, Illinois

7   Life as a Symphony   131
Christopher M. Aanstoos, University of West Georgia

8   Moving On By Backing Away   150
John Shotter, University of New Hampshire

9   Living with Authority in "The Between" 172
    Hendrika Vande Kemp, private psychotherapy practice,
    Annandale, Virginia

10 The Personal/Psychological and the Pursuit
    of a Profession 191
    Adelbert H. Jenkins, New York University

11 On Growing Up as a "Premodernist" 208
    Steen Halling, Seattle University, Washington

12 Life Reflections of a Nomadic Subject 228
    Tod Sloan, Lewis and Clark College, Portland, Oregon

13 Autobiography 245
    Ilene A. Serlin, Union Street Health Associates, Inc., San Francisco,
    California

    THE CONTRIBUTORS 261
    SUBJECT INDEX 265
    AUTHOR INDEX 270

Preface

The inspiration for this book grew out of our explorations of the interrelationships in life and work in our respective disciplines, our shared interest in psychology, and our conviction that human experiences are made meaningful through narratives. George Yancy's books *African-American Philosophers: 17 Conversations* (1998) and *The Philosophical i: Personal Reflections on Life in Philosophy* (2002) are the result of such explorations in the area of philosophy, while Susan Hadley's doctoral research, "Exploring Relationships Between Life and Work in Music Therapy: The Stories of Mary Priestley and Clive Robbins," similarly explores these themes within the field of music therapy. What we both found was that in the very process of engaging the narratives that were developed, we not only learned more about each person and the dialectical relationship between each person and the work that they do, but we also found ourselves transformed by them. This dynamic process of being transformed by these narratives speaks to the fluidity of selves and identities.

Knowing of our previous work, a friend of ours, Jerome Ruderman, suggested that this type of exploration would be intriguing in a range of disciplines. Given our shared interest in psychology, we began to consider how fascinating it would be to ask psychologists to turn their gaze toward who they have become/are becoming in terms of how they are situated within the complex interstices of social life. Indeed, we asked them to explore the dialectical relationship between their identities and their biographical context. Psychologists are known for the work they do exploring the lives of others. They help to weave and reweave meaning in the lives of individuals whose lives have been fractured in some way. This process of weaving and reweaving meaning is a co-authored journey; a journey of shared meaning, shared discourse, and shared insight. However, we rarely hear the psychologist's story. We were interested in the identities of psychologists that were not limited to the therapeutic relationship. We are/were interested in the personal and extrapersonal dimensions of the lives of a critical cadre of psychologists as autobiographically explored through various theoretical presuppositions held by each individual psychologist. This strategy is not only illuminating in terms of the theoretical side of the profession of psychology, particularly given the meta-theoretical reflections required of our contributors, but also in terms of how individual psychologists existentially breathe meaning into the theories that they have come to hold. Our working assumption is that theory also evolves within a context. We wanted to understand the relationship between theory and various epistemic self-graphs; how theory is related to and evolves out of lived experiences; how theory in turn comes to inform the lives of individual psychologists; how theory is mobilized to address problems that are themselves contextually pragmatic; and, how theory is linked to a discourse of praxis and societal transformation. These are crucial and important second-order reflections that psychologists have been asked to come to terms with in this text.

Narrative Identities: Psychologists Engaged in Self-Construction is not in search of an alleged transcendental ego or an ontologically self-subsisting entity, a thinking substance, that is said to exist beyond the dynamics of historical contingency. As the editors of this text we maintain that the ontological and epistemological status of the subject of modernity is deeply problematic. "The self" is often rendered as self-constitutive, completely transparent, and prior to the larger socio-cultural matrix of our being-in-the-world. We hold that it is the *lived* context of history, both immediate and distal, that constitutes the background of the self's intelligibility. Autogenesis is a fiction that supports a form of "individualism" that belies the manner in which the self is always already situated within a context of meaning, and is positioned by narratives and semiotic spaces. The self is *not* the absolute ground of its own meaning. In fact, by the time the self becomes critically self-reflexive it has already been shaped through various social processes, transversal relationships, and culturally encrusted meanings. It is within the context of the socially embedded, culturally ensconced, and existentially interpersonal sphere of sociality that a person evolves. On this reading, the very concept of "auto" in the term "autobiography" is called into question. As *homo narrans* and *homo significans*, we are not only positioned by history and culture, but we also position ourselves within history and culture. We *imaginatively* engage in processes of self-fashioning, making sense of our past, present, and future – which should not be reduced to an arbitrary and ad hoc formation of a pastiche identity. The process of being "positioned by" and "positioning ourselves within" bespeaks the "facticity–possibility" dynamic that each of us are as makers of meaning. Our "facticity" constitutes both obstacles later to be challenged and overcome, and the inherited, pre-interpreted framework of intelligibility within which the self becomes meaningfully grounded and is situated. Within the *subjunctive* mode, we exist as always already beyond ourselves, as *possibility*. In this sense, we are, in our historicity, *transcendent*. We are capable of re-narrating who we are, and signing for ourselves. This speaks to the agential and liberatory narrative dimensions of the self. Again, however, the narrative structure of the self always takes place already within a situated, shared dramaturgical matrix of lived embodied experience. We create as we are also created. To deny our being as a possibility, our ability to be, to deny our transcendence/agential capacity to narrate who we are is a form of bad faith; moreover, to deny our facticity, to deny the situatedness of our sociality, of being grounded inextricably within a lived situation, is also a form of bad faith.

The psychologists in this text are varied in terms of the theoretical orientations that they adopt. These include narrative, social constructionist, feminist, postmodernist, poststructuralist, hermeneutic, existential phenomenological, humanistic, critical, psychoanalytic, performative, and social therapeutic approaches. We were interested in the dynamics of these theoretical investments; how psychologists came to be the particular epistemic agents that they have become. So as to help shape the process of epistemic autobiographical self-reflection and exploration, we provided each contributor with a long list of questions, some generic and others that were tailored to the contributor's specialized work in psychology. Although such "guide questions" were provided, the first-person exploration and delineation of the self is by no means an easy task. After all, such significant issues as the appropriate narrative discourse in terms of which to narrate one's life and work, narrative coherence, selective memory, decisions regarding just the "right" self-image to project, and audience, are at stake. Storied selves are elusive, complex, and multicontextual. The contributors were cognizant of the fruits and difficulties faced by taking part in this project. Given the importance placed upon positionality and standpoint theory in philosophy and the social sciences more generally, and the conscious effort on the part of the book's contributors to delineate and engage their respective standpoints, the field of psychology will only benefit from the text that you have before you.

Narrative Identities: Psychologists Engaged in Self-Construction invites students and professional psychologists (and those outside the field of psychology) to journey with prominent psychologists as they delve into who they are as psychologists. As editors, we have opted to keep our voices to a minimum by limiting our remarks to this short Preface. The objective is to allow as much space as possible for our contributors. Moreover, we wanted to avoid overly mediating their reflections with our own theoretical orientation regarding issues of the self, self-construction, theory and practice, and so on. The storied lives within this text contain powerful evocative truths that encourage readers to embark on their own journeys of self-reflective meaning making within a broader context of always already historical and contextual received meaning. This invitation would not be possible, however, without the courage, honesty, and tenacity of our contributors. We thank them for providing such rich glimpses into their lived experiences, relationships between their life and work, theory and practice.

We are also thankful to Jessica Kingsley Publishers for overseeing this project from its proposal stage to its completion. A special appreciation goes to Jessica Kingsley for her immediate interest in this project, her availability when we had various concerns, and her wonderful personable qualities, particularly given the often impersonal nature of communication between potential authors/editors and publishing houses.

George Yancy and Susan Hadley
Pittsburgh, Pennsylvania

CHAPTER 1

The Poetics of My Identities

Theodore R. Sarbin

Introduction

In 1993, D. John Lee invited me, along with other scholars interested in narrative psychology, to contribute career autobiographies for a book, *Life and Story: Autobiographies for a Narrative Psychology* (Sarbin, 1993a). He asked the contributors to reflect on the effects of the process of rendering the autobiography. These reflections help to answer the social identity question that the current editors, George Yancy and Susan Hadley, have raised: Who is Ted Sarbin? After presenting the poetics of my identities, I will return to those reflections to illuminate a continuity that runs through the academic life span.[1]

I planned to focus this chapter on "the narrative construction of my identities," which conveys my general intent and is consistent with the use of "construction" in the social science literature. I find "poetics" a more apt descriptor than "construction," a word that calls up the activities of architects and carpenters. "Poetics" calls up imaginings of a person creating, shaping, and molding multidimensional stories. The use of "poetics" also reminds us that stories, in the main, are fashioned by means of spoken and written language.

Yancy and Hadley suggested that I discuss the "whoness" of Ted Sarbin. The word "who" is central to any exploration of identity. The pronoun "who" (and its cognates in other Indo-European languages) is employed to formulate a question the purpose of which is to establish the relationship between the questioner and a dialogue partner. Both participants implicitly entertain the reciprocal questions *Who am I?* and *Who are you?* The answers to the questions define the nature of the relationship. Establishing one's self-identity is concurrent with establishing the identity of the Other, which implies that identities are dialogical, and by implication, context-dependent. When interacting with a student, I am a teacher. When interacting with my son, I am a father. When interacting with my physician, I am a patient. When the question implies a more general positioning in the world of social institutions, I am a scholar. Hence, the response to the *Who am I?* question is the name of a status or position in formal or informal social orders, the validation of which is the enactment of the role that is coordinate with the position. Not only are my identities context-dependent with regard to the identities of the Others, but they are context-dependent with regard to time and place. The "whoness" of Ted Sarbin when I began my career was quite different from the "whoness" in midcareer, and still different at the present writing.

Recently much has been written about how persons establish their identities. Every time a person encounters another, the *Who am I?* question automatically comes up and is always answered in relation to the perceived identity of the other. Locating oneself in relation to others is a social survival mechanism parallel to the behavior of creatures in the wild wherein self-preservation depends on identifying the other as benign or malevolent. In like manner, establishing one's identity occurs simultaneously with establishing the identity of the dialogue partner. These questions and answers are not in the nature of automatic stimulus-response sequences of encapsulated individuals. It is the total context, including the time and place, that provides the ground for establishing identities in any particular interaction.

Beginnings of professional identities

I tender a brief statement to answer the editors' question about my entry into the field of psychology. My plan on entering the Ohio State University in 1934 at age 23 was to complete a program in social work in the interest of getting a job. It was during the Great Depression and there were jobs available in government relief agencies. My adviser in the social work curriculum suggested I first meet the general education requirements which included Introductory Psychology 401. My instructor was Frank Stanton, an advanced graduate student, later to become President of the Columbia Broadcasting System. During the discussion period following the second meeting of the class, he called on me to discuss a topic from the lecture. My response went beyond the contents of the assignment. After class, he asked me the source of my information. I had read *Seven Psychologies* by Edna Heidbreder (1933) as part of my informal reading before entering the university. The same book,

Stanton told me, was the assigned text in a graduate seminar. He decided that I should be in a more advanced class and arranged for me to take the previous quarter's final exam. I passed, was given credit for the course, and enrolled in Psychology 402.

This critical incident in my self-narrative started me on a career in psychology. I completed my undergraduate work in 1936, took a Master's degree at Western Reserve University in 1937, returned to Ohio State to enter the PhD program, completed all requirements except the dissertation, and accepted a job offer from the University of Minnesota in 1938. During my three years at Minnesota, I was engaged in student personnel work and in my free time worked on my dissertation. The Ohio State University awarded me the PhD in 1941.

My identity as a scientifically oriented psychologist

In the early part of my career, I was trying to establish my identity as a scientifically oriented clinical psychologist. The warrant for this identity took the form of a set of papers and a book dealing with clinical inference and prediction (Sarbin, 1941, 1943a, 1944; Sarbin, Taft and Bailey, 1960). I claimed that the clinician employed a probabilistic form of the syllogism in making judgments about his or her clients. My studies demonstrated, using accuracy of prediction as a criterion, that clinicians were no better and sometimes worse than a two-variable statistical prediction. My identity was shaped by work in the positivist tradition, supporting my claims with quantitative data. This identity was reinforced by Paul Meehl in his widely read book (1954) in which he devoted a chapter to my research and theoretical formulations. My identity as a scientifically inclined clinician was still perceived by others as late as 1985 when I was invited to participate in a symposium to evaluate the influence of the prediction controversy on subsequent theory and practice (Sarbin, 1986).

My identity as a role theorist

For most of my career I have been identified with role theory. It began when I was chair of the Psi Chi program committee at the University of Minnesota. I invited Norman Cameron, then Professor of Psychology and Psychiatry at the University of Wisconsin, to deliver an address to our monthly colloquium. His talk was a draft version of his later widely cited paper on paranoia (1943). A central category in his explanation was role taking. Cameron's exposition of role taking, the skill to take the role of the other, was an exciting and novel idea. The protagonists in his case studies were men and women who were inept role takers and, to make sense of their problematic worlds, constructed pseudocommunities, assigning the same ontological status to these constructions as to their social communities. Traditional psychiatry explained paranoia as happenings in the Cartesian mind. Cameron's emphasis on role taking moved me to think of people as actors engaged in intentional, purposeful actions in order to make sense of an imperfect, ambiguous, and sometimes confusing world of occurrences. Impressed with Cameron's contribution, I began to use role-taking conceptions in my own efforts to understand people who had been diagnosed as mentally ill.

I had had some significant preparation for a shift from traditional psychology to role-taking explanations. During my undergraduate years I was exposed primarily to the teachings of behaviorist psychologists. Behaviorist theories, flowing from a mechanistic ideology, were supposed to demonstrate the futility of mentalistic constructs. As an unsophisticated undergraduate seeking to become a scientific psychologist, I absorbed these teachings. The behaviorist credo encouraged the construing of people as complex machines. I became a convert to this secular religion, a movement in which John B. Watson and Ivan Pavlov were its prophets. Looking back, my identity as a behaviorist served as a comforting protection against the angst of living in a world full of ambiguities and uncertainties.

In the summer of 1936, toward the end of my undergraduate program, my earlier conversion to behaviorism was modulated by the writings and lectures of J.R. Kantor, a visiting professor from Indiana University, whose books on interbehavioral psychology supported much of the behaviorist program, but cautioned against accepting the notion that the mechanistic paradigm could contribute to understanding behaviors, such as thinking and imagining, that had been the province of mentalistic psychologists and philosophers. He pointed to the futility of regarding the mind as a source or resultant of the actions of mechanistic forces. He playfully referred to psychologists who espoused mentalistic theories as "spookologists," as assigning motivational force to "the ghost in the machine." What impressed me was his compelling arguments that constructs had to be related to concrete events – events that could not be divorced from historical, cultural, and biographical contexts. This was an unorthodox idea given that behaviorists worked from the entrenched belief that the secrets of behavior would be discovered in the rat laboratory. Also, Kantor rejected the claims of mentalistic psychologists who continued to follow in the footsteps of Descartes. Kantor's analytical, critical, and philosophical arguments had a great effect on me. Of all my teachers, he comes closest to having been my mentor. Among other things, he emphasized the role of language in human action, but more importantly, he was an exploder of myths, especially the myth of mind as advanced by Descartes and promulgated by generations of philosophers of mind. I trace my interest in exposing myths and undressing metaphors to his influence. I maintained contact with Professor Kantor until shortly before his death in 1987 at age 96. I am convinced that my early association with him had been a turning point in my self-narrative and in seeking a professional identity.

In 1941, opportunities arose to become more involved in role theory. I had moved to the University of Chicago on a Social Science Research Council Post-Doctoral Fellowship, dividing my time between the department of sociology and the psychiatric unit of the medical school. The distinguished urban sociologist, Ernest Burgess, was my sponsor. Associating with faculty and graduate students in sociology, I became immersed in the works of George Herbert Mead. Although Mead had died a decade earlier, his influence on social theory and research was very much alive. In the psychiatric ward of the university hospital, I was given the kinds of responsibilities usually given to faculty members. Most of the staff subscribed to psychoanalytic doctrine, a perspective that was unconvincing to me. However, my clinical contacts with inpatients and outpatients provided me with opportunities to employ role conceptions to interpret their personal stories.

Prior to my Chicago adventure, I had had some experience with hypnosis. During my graduate days at Ohio State, Joseph Friedlander, a fellow graduate student, asked for my help with his research. He had begun an effort to create a scale for measuring the depth of hypnosis. In the interest of friendship I joined him in the research effort. We subsequently published a paper describing the development and use of the scale (1938). Because the director of the psychiatric unit knew of my research in hypnosis, he asked me to work with a newly admitted patient who demonstrated the classic behavior of a fugue state. A college freshman, she had disappeared from her home in Chicago. When the police located her in a neighboring city a week later, she claimed not to know her identity. To get a job, she had invented a name. On being returned to her parents, she was taken to the family doctor who, unable to break through her amnesia, referred her to a neurologist who in turn referred her to the psychiatric unit. She failed to recognize her parents, siblings, or friends when they visited her in the hospital. After two or three hypnosis sessions, her memory and her identity were restored. News of the successful treatment spread through the hospital and I was asked to consult with physicians on various psychosomatic problems. I was invited to bring the patient to grand rounds and demonstrate to the assembled medical professionals both the nature of fugue states and also the hypnosis therapy.

Prior to these events I had not developed a theory of hypnosis that was substantially different from traditional theories: that the behaviors of the hypnosis subject reflected a special mental state. The beginnings of my turning to role theory as a way of accounting for the apparent mysteries of hypnosis followed a serendipitous discovery. I had begun a program of research in collaboration with Julian Lewis, a research professor in the medical school. It was a time of great interest in psychosomatic studies. We set up an experiment to measure the effects of hypnotic suggestion on gastric hunger contractions. The experiment required the subjects to swallow a balloon to which was attached a fine rubber tube. The balloon was then inflated. Hunger contractions compressed the balloon, the contractions being recorded on a kymograph. The subjects came to the laboratory in a fasting condition. During a hypnosis session, one of us suggested to the subject that he or she was being given preferred foods. The kymograph recordings showed that the subjects who were most responsive to the hypnosis induction were the subjects whose contractions were greatly modified or eliminated during the eating of a fictitious meal. We published the paper with little attention to theory, save that "hypnosis" was the antecedent condition for producing the physiological effects (Lewis and Sarbin, 1943). Our findings could have been cited as support for the special state theory of hypnosis.

After the publication of our research, a serendipitous event made it necessary to look into the phenomena more closely. Preparing for another study, I retrieved the notebook that contained qualitative notes written by Dr. Lewis describing the behavior of the subjects during their eating a fictitious meal. We had been so impressed with the findings as shown in the kymograph tracings that we failed to consult the qualitative notes. A belated review of the notes told us that the subjects who were the best responders had engaged in attenuated eating movements during the fictitious meal. Smacking of lips, swallowing, and chewing actions were noted for the responsive subjects but not for the unresponsive subjects. This serendipitous finding suggested that the agentive behavior of the subject was a more likely antecedent for the inhibition of gastric contractions than the undefined hypnotic trance. We speculated that the motoric acts set off peristalsis, a condition closely connected to the inhibition of gastric contractions. These qualitative findings influenced me to change my theoretical posture. The observed embodied imaginings that were performed by the subjects suggested that the inhibition of gastric contractions followed from a *doing* rather than a *happening* attributed to an undefined mental state.

Our published paper was consistent with the tradition of focusing on dramatic outcome variables, the end result of a complex social psychological sequence defined as a hypnosis episode. Our failure to incorporate the data contained in the behavioral notes was an unintended effect of the traditional practice of placing emphasis on the proximal features of the episode – in this case, the modifications of the gastric contractions – and not attending to the distal antecedent and concurrent conditions.

Immersed in George Herbert Mead's role conceptions as they were transmitted by faculty and graduate students in sociology, and attending to the serendipitous finding, I put together a theory of hypnosis that centered on the premise that hypnosis was an exemplar of role taking. To perform the behavior required of a subject was to enact a social role. I advanced some historical data to give warrant to my proposal that the role was a social construction and that the criterial behavior of the subjects reflected not a special state of mind but skill in imagining.

My identity as a theoretical social psychologist was taking form. At meetings of the American Psychological Association and at meetings of hypnosis groups, I was identified as the developer of a unique social psychological theory that accounted for hypnosis better than the Cartesian myth of special mental states. My later work in apparently unrelated fields stemmed from my early efforts to understand the antecedents to the individual differences in responsiveness to the hypnosis setting. My later work in imagining and hallucination, constructionism, contextualism, narrative, emotional life, believed-in imaginings, and dramaturgy stemmed in great measure from my earlier efforts to apply role theoretical conceptions to the phenomena of hypnosis.

My identity as a nonconforming clinical psychologist

After my post-doctoral fellowship, I did not return to Minnesota, but entered independent practice as a clinical psychologist. Although the work had many challenges, it was not consistent with my still partly formed identity as a scholar. In the spring of 1948, I was invited to the University of California at Berkeley to present a colloquium to the psychology faculty and graduate students. The colloquium was part of the procedure to consider me for a position in the fast-developing clinical psychology program. Rather than talking about diagnosis and therapy, I gave a summary of the psychology of role taking. I was offered the job. My identity was that of a nonconforming clinical psychologist.

During this period, most of the clinical psychologists who were called to teach had adopted Freudian conceptions. My focus was on role taking and the social self. At the end of my first decade at Berkeley, my identity had shifted from that of a nonconforming clinical psychologist to that of a social psychologist with an active research program to establish role theory as a way of exploring the complexities of human interaction.

I was given the responsibility for teaching the undergraduate course in abnormal psychology once or twice a year. This task allowed me to enlarge upon the use of role concepts to understand deviant and nonconforming conduct. An opportunity for a more complete development of role conceptions was afforded by an invitation to write a chapter on role theory for the *Handbook of Social Psychology* (Sarbin, 1954).

The narrative that supports my identity as a role theorist begins from a remote source. I read an article by Theodore Newcomb in 1947 in which he discussed the process of taking the role of the other. The contents of the article prompted me to write him a letter in which I pointed out certain features that were not consistent with G.H. Mead's formulations. Newcomb saw attitude as prior to role, I argued that role was prior to attitude. A decade later, after I had had a number of collegial contacts with him, Newcomb told me that he had recommended to the editor of the *Handbook* that I be invited to write the chapter on role theory. The chapter publicized role theory as a viable alternative to other theories expounded in the *Handbook*: field theory, psychoanalysis, learning theory, and cognitive theory. Unique was the description of the central variable: role enactment. Unlike the central variables in other theories, variables that were usually construed as context-free responses or as internalized dispositions, role enactment carried the meaning of action and that the appropriateness of the action was dependent upon social structural context. Thus, human social action had to be perceived as interaction. The story of my authorship of the role theory chapter in the widely used *Handbook* was an important validation for my identity development in that my name became associated with role theory.

In 1957, I was promoted to Professorship and appointed as chairperson of a newly organized research unit at Berkeley, the Center for Social Science Theory. It was a small faculty group, initially composed of two economists, a sociologist, and myself, later augmented by an anthropologist and another psychologist. The sociologist was Erving Goffman, at that time a junior member of the Berkeley faculty. Intensive discussions with Goffman steered me to a turning point in my identity narrative. My lectures in abnormal psychology were already organized along social psychological lines and were critical of the medical model, but it was not until I associated with Goffman on a one-to-one basis that I was able to give voice to the view that "abnormal conduct" could be accounted for with the same explanatory categories as "normal behavior." His dramaturgical approach to interactional conduct influenced me to enlarge my conception of role. Roles need not be stereotypes. Persons create and modulate roles in response to changing contexts.

My identity as a critic of the medical model of deviant conduct

In 1962 I was awarded a senior Fulbright Fellowship at Oxford University. I had ample time to study and to reflect on psychological theory. In response to an invitation from Michael Argyle, Reader in Social Psychology, I delivered eight lectures on abnormal psychology. I recast my lectures and developed a model of intentional conduct that brought into play the role-theoretical concepts that I had developed earlier. The model directed students to look for the existential and social antecedents of strain-in-knowing, and to observe the role behavior that people perform to resolve such strain. In the context of studying deviant persons it was important to recognize that we live in a moral order and there are always persons, usually more powerful than the targeted individual, who are ready to make moral judgments on an individual's public efforts to resolve his or her strain-in-knowing. These theoretical developments led to the conclusion that abnormal psychology was more properly a branch of social psychology, not a branch of medicine. It was more productive to speak of inept role players rather than sick minds.

In the course of showing the futility of the medical model for understanding deviant conduct, I collected case studies of men and women who had been diagnosed as schizophrenic. What impressed me in reviewing these histories was the great variability in the stories that led to the patients being hospitalized and inducted into the social role of mental hospital patient. Among psychiatric authorities, schizophrenia was (and is) a medical diagnosis. The variability of the behaviors of men and women who had been diagnosed as schizophrenic influenced my thinking about the whole diagnostic process. The only feature common to the patients I studied was the judgments made by others – spouses, parents, teachers, psychiatrists, social workers – the judgments that the target person performed unwanted behavior. The judgments were in the nature of moral verdicts.

In 1969, I transferred to the new campus in Santa Cruz. In 1970, James Mancuso, then Professor of Psychology at SUNY-Albany, came to Santa Cruz on sabbatical leave. We had previously engaged in collaborative work on public attitudes toward people diagnosed as suffering from mental illness. We shared the sentiment that psychiatric diagnosis, although presented as a feature of medical practice, was actually a moral judgment. We engaged in some preliminary search of the scientific literature to learn that many experimental efforts had been published that purportedly demonstrated that schizophrenics were inferior to normals, no matter what type of test used: problem-solving, motor control, perception, verbal comprehension, etc. Our preliminary search disclosed that the differences were invariably small – too small for aiding in diagnosis – and could be accounted for by differences in educational level, the effects of hospitalization, and the cognitive effects of medications. When the distributions of the schizophrenics and the "normals" were laid side by side, the overlap was so great that a radically different conclusion was warranted than that offered by conventional psychiatry. The performances on experimental procedures of most of the schizophrenics were like the performances of most of the "normals." This conclusion influenced us to analyze experimental reports in one journal over a 20-year period. The analysis confirmed our preliminary study and was the centerpiece of our book that appeared in 1980 under the title *Schizophrenia: Mental Diagnosis or Moral Verdict?* The fallout from the publication of the book had a significant effect on my identity: I had already published articles that became part of my self-narrative in support of my identity as a challenger of the dominant ideology, as an exploder of myths. The challenge to traditional theories of schizophrenia reinforced my identity as an iconoclast.

During my first years at Santa Cruz, I experienced an awakening to the fact that my lectures were primarily occasions for storytelling. In the teaching of abnormal psychology, for example, I had earlier discovered that reporting the results of research lacked interest for the students and, reciprocally, for me. Having had direct experience with both hospitalized patients and outpatients I used clinical case histories as the subject matter. My strategy involved showing that the people diagnosed as mentally ill employed the same kinds of solutions to their problems-in-living as others not so diagnosed. The difference was the judgments made by others as to the appropriateness of the target person's attempted solutions. My focus was primarily on the relationships of the people involved in the stories.

My identity as a narrative psychologist

This awakening to the fact that I had been a budding narrative psychologist was similar to Moliere's M. Joudain who discovered that he had been speaking prose all his life. I made some preliminary attempts to write an article that would justify using the narrative as a model for psychology. At a meeting of the American Psychological Association in 1979, I served as a discussant in a symposium on ecumenism in contemporary psychology. Although the four speakers each focused on different subject matters, I was able to discuss the papers as stories each of which contained, implicitly, a moral point.

My identity as a narrative psychologist did not spring full blown, but developed over time. I recall a discussion in 1973 with a graduate student, Robert Nation, during which I drew a distinction between doing psychology conceptually (the traditional way) and narrative. The conceptual mode directs psychologists to the hypothetico-deductive method, to the formation of concepts and to their testing, usually in the laboratory. The narrative mode directs psychologists and others to ask "What is the story?" The complexities of human biographies or autobiographies are such that staking out two, three, or more variables can give no more that a partial understanding of a life. The users of narrative approaches are like historians and biographers; they are free to look into all the complexities of being human, including the effects of differential contexts.

About the same time, Bruner (1986) made a similar distinction; he wrote of paradigmatic and narrative ways of doing psychology. The paradigmatic has been the dominant mode of discourse, closely associated with doing experiments, collecting data that can be quantified, and seeking general laws of behavior. The narrative mode is the form of doing psychology that is most like the art of the biographer, again asking "What is the story?"

Narrative psychology begins from the ontological perspective that we live in a story-shaped world; that our lives are guided by a narratory principle, i.e., the readiness to organize our experience, to interpret our social actions, and even to enact our roles according to the requirements of narrative plots. Among the warrants for this premise are experiences common to all of us. Daydreams are storied. They are sequences of interactions involving elements of the past, the present, and the still-to-be realized future. Night dreams are experienced and reported as narratives, often with mythic undertones. Rituals of daily life are organized as miniature dramas that, when told, reveal the multilayered nature of social process. Narrative themes are instrumental in forming and deforming our rememberings. The excuses and justifications that we offer for our lapses take the form of stories. Survival in a world of meanings would be problematic in the absence of skills to create and to interpret stories about interweaving lives and the places that serve as functional and symbolic backdrops.

Not any string of words constitutes a narrative. Borrowing from Aristotle, we can define a narrative as an account that has a beginning, a middle, an ending or at least the sense of an ending (Kermode, 1967) and, importantly, has a moral point. That is to say, to qualify as a narrative, a string of words would have to reflect a temporal dimension and also the recognition of, if not the solution to, one or more moral issues.

When persons attempt to articulate their sense of identity, they call up the gist of remembered stories in which they were participants. The participation could be as protagonists, antagonists, or involved spectators. The importance of remembering one's stories as a source of identity is nowhere better illustrated than in those occasions when we encounter a patient suffering from Alzheimer's disease – the principal feature of which is loss of personal memory. We are immediately aware that, unable to reconstruct personal stories, he or she can make no claims to having an identity.

A way station to developing a narrative psychology is the Quixotic principle, first advanced by the literary scholar Harry Levin (1970). He described numerous instances where novelists attributed the identity development of their protagonists to the influence of book reading. Don Quixote is the paradigm case. Involved in reading books of chivalry, he fashioned an identity for himself based on the exploits of knights errant of an extinct historical era. He constructed imaginings that replicated the heroic deeds described in tales of chivalry. In this respect, the protagonist is like other readers of adventure tales. Skill in imagining enables the reader to enter the pages of the book, sometimes as spectator, sometimes as actor. However, Don Quixote does more than participate in fantasy. To validate his imaginatively constructed identity, he takes the additional step of performing the social role of knight errant. Humor, pathos, and other novelistic tensions are created when his knight errantry impinges upon characters who belong to a 17th-century world far removed from the feudal institutions of the 12th century.

The Quixotic principle brings into sharp focus the observation that a person can construct his or her identity to conform to a fictional character's participation in a narrative plot (Sarbin, 1982). The principle applies not only to book reading but to other narrative sources of imaginative behavior: stories told about actual or fictional heroes, folktales, fables, movies, parables, sermons, opera, and other art forms.

My identity as a narrative psychologist was affirmed when I was invited by Brian Sutton-Smith to participate in a symposium on narrative during the convention of the American Psychological Association in 1983. At that time there were few, if any, publishing outlets for papers that were marginal to conventional psychology. I took upon myself the editorial responsibility for collecting a number of papers for inclusion in the book *Narrative Psychology: The Storied Nature of Human Conduct* (1986). Since then, writing and lecturing on narrative psychology has been the anchor for my professional identity. Papers written and books edited have been opportunities for elaborating the notion that we come into a world that is already storied; that we select, within limits, among the stories presented to us in our culture; and we transform our stories as demanded by social contexts.

My publications were influential in my being invited to present the narrativist viewpoint at conferences dealing with current issues in psychology. Such invitations took me into areas that required my taking some bold steps. For example, I was invited to present the narrativist point of view at a conference on "Emotions in Ideal Human Development" in 1986 at Clark University. My paper was later published in a book recording the conference (Sarbin, 1989). I had for many years been critical of the arbitrary separation of cognition, action, and emotion, a taken-for-granted separation inherited from the ancients. In earlier efforts to make sense of phenomena that have conventionally been subsumed under the title "the psychology of emotion," I had hoped to advance our understanding by enlarging the phenomena of interest to *emotional life*. Along with others, I saw the bankruptcy in the essentialist view of regarding emotions as thing-like entities. A review of the literature on the psychology of emotions makes clear that the essentialist conception of emotions has contributed little in the way of understanding emotional life, of making sense of everyday narratives of sadness, joy, anger, pride, shame, and so on. An implication of the essentialist view is that conceptualizing emotions in substantival terms invites speculations and claims as to the number of basic emotions. This ancient search (which continues to the present) reflects the ontological premise that emotions are quasi-objects, sometimes with cranial location, sometimes with visceral location. This ontological premise flows in part from the tendency to take events experienced as happenings and doings and transfiguring them to substantives, thus providing boundaries around events now reconstructed as thing-like entities.

It is traditional among the practitioners of the human sciences to treat "emotion" as a fundamental category of behavior. Growing out of the ancient tripartite division of the soul, the uncritical acceptance of emotion as a fundamental category has influenced generations of scholars to establish lists of emotions. Aristotle identified fifteen, Descartes six, McDougal offered a list of seven. More recently, Plutchik identified eight primary emotions, Tomkins nine. That authorities cannot agree on the number of basic emotions suggests that they are operating from an outmoded ontology. In every list, ancient or modern, the authors have preferred to label emotions with nouns. The use of the nominative form reflects the older psychologies' passion for reification, taking complex human actions denoted by verb forms and transforming them into literal entities denoted by nouns, with an implication of thingness.

Over the past 20 years, I have been conducting an informal study, the results of which support the distinction between "emotion" and "emotional life" and incidentally provide a kind of warrant for a narrative interpretation. I have asked almost 100 adults in casual conversation to define "emotion." After he or she is satisfied with the definition, I ask the informant for an example of emotion. With few exceptions, the informants provided definitions that would qualify as instances of psychophysiological symbolism (Averill, 1974). Many definitions included "feelings." Metaphoric references to bodily states such as "butterflies in the stomach," and "lump in the throat" were common. The subsequent exemplifications, however, made no mention of bodily states and were presented as stories with multiple actors, told with a beginning, a middle, and an ending. In all cases, the stories hinged on the protagonist (usually the self) relating "emotion" to some moral issue and its resolution. Without being told to do so, the informants translated the instruction "give me an example of emotion" to "tell me a story about emotional life."

In the past two or three decades, with the rise of interest in dramaturgical and narrative psychology, the complexities of emotional life have been better understood through casting the principal actors as participants in ongoing narratives. Underlying is the ontological premise that we live in story-shaped worlds. In various papers and chapters, I have tried to advance the argument that the terms traditionally assigned to emotions such as love, pride, shame, joy, etc., are more felicitously construed as the names of narrative plots.

Another story of my identity as a practitioner of narrative psychology emerges from my involvement in understanding the false memory syndrome and the related conception of multiple personality. Beginning in the 1970s, a rash of cases labeled multiple personality appeared. Prior to this period, the literature reported an occasional case, perhaps one or two per year. After the publication of *Sybil* in 1973, thousands of people, mostly women, were diagnosed as having multiple personality disorder by a relatively small number of clinicians. With the diagnosis came the identification of the etiology of the disorder. Practitioners who advocated the use of this diagnosis operated from a narrative in which multiple personality (and other diagnoses) was the outcome of repressed childhood memories of physical or sexual abuse. That the patients could not report memories of such abuse was taken as a sign of repression or dissociation which reinforced the credibility of the diagnosis. These practitioners employed various procedures to induce the patients to imagine instances of abuse. Under the Aesculapian authority of the healers, and the need to complete a self-narrative to account for his or her unhappiness, the induced imaginings provided the basis for a story. The instances of this occurrence that came to light revealed that the patient and the healer assigned unequivocal credibility to the generated stories. Many patients were encouraged to confront the parent or other adult who was declared the victimizer in the abuse narrative. In a number of cases, the alleged victimizer was subject to being sued in courts of law. Some of the falsely accused parents enlisted the aid of a number of prestigious scientists to form the False Memory Syndrome Foundation, the purpose of which was to help families that had been broken up by false accusations. Martin Orne was a leader in this movement and he invited me to become a member of the board of directors.

I wrote several papers to rebut the claim that "repression" and "dissociation" were unconscious processes not under the control of the person (1995a, 1995b, 1997a, 1997b). Rather, these conceptions were narrative devices introduced to give an aura of scientific credibility to the diagnosis. The construction "believed-in imaginings," borrowed from my earlier explanations of hypnosis phenomena, was pivotal in providing credible arguments that could be used to counter the harmful effects of therapy based on fictional concepts. In 1996, Joseph deRivera and I, concerned with the necessity of publicizing scientific rebuttals of the claims of "recovered memory" advocates, organized a conference on believed-in imaginings. The product of this conference was a set of papers and commentary by the editors that not only demonstrated the error in the claims of "recovered memory" therapists but provided insights about the narrative construction of reality (deRivera and Sarbin, 1998).

The role of narratives in the poetics of identity

The previous pages offer abbreviated narratives that reveal my identity at different times and places in the trajectory of a career. Space limitations made it necessary to omit some narratives that supported related but different identities. These narrative sketches give form to the development and maintenance of my identities at various periods. Conventional psychologists have tried, with little success, to trace the source of identity to factors, traits, motives, and similar categories. Conceptually, these categories have only a proximal relation to identity formation, they are perceived as internal to the actor in space and time. Narratives, on the other hand, are distal – the time frame of an influencing narrative may be the recent past or may go back into cultural history.

The poetics of *who I am* follows from remembered stories in which I am but one actor in a multi-personed cast of characters. The remembered stories feature dialogues between myself and colleagues and students, not to mention psychologists holding views contrary to my own. As I mentioned above, my dialogues with Professor Kantor set the stage for later dialogues, the rememberings of which mark my identities.

I have told some of the stories that have formed my identities. At this juncture, I am constrained to add brief vignettes to prepare the way for the implied claim that identity formation is a dialogical undertaking. My understanding of hypnosis phenomena, for example, was influenced by frequent and instructive dialogues with Martin Orne, Nick Spanos, John Chaves, Ted Barber, James Council, and Jack Hilgard, all academics, all competent researchers. At different times, doctoral research conducted under my sponsorship by William Coe, Daniel Goldstine, Milton Andersen, and Donald Lim provided many occasions for dialogues that centered on the hypothesis that hypnotic performances were enactments of a social role. Later, Coe and I collaborated in publishing a book, *Hypnosis: A Social Psychological Analysis of Influence Communication* (1972). Dialogues in seminars with Berkeley graduate students were fruitful sources of my constructions about the self: I note especially Nathan Adler, Ravenna Mathews Helson, and Norman Greenfield, the latter who, among other things, coined the label "epistemogenesis" for my theory of self-development (1950). Dialogues with Robert Elliott and Nathan Adler, a decade apart, helped shape my observations about the death–rebirth metaphor in identity change. Frequent exchanges with Larry Nucci were instrumental in developing a theory of conduct reorganization.

The dialogical nature of identity formation is clearly demonstrated in my rememberings of the collaborative preparation of papers in the 1960s and 1970s with Joseph Juhasz on imagining, hallucination, and the futility of the medical model of madness, a collaboration that has continued for almost 40 years (1972). I elaborated on our dialogues about imagining as muted role taking in a chapter published in 1970. In the work on clinical inference and prediction, the dialogue began with E.G. Williamson at Minnesota, a dialogue that continued during the early years at Berkeley with Ronald Taft, later supplemented by frequent interchanges with Daniel Bailey. Since 1949, when we shared an office in Berkeley, Harrison Gough and I have had a continuing dialogue about personality assessment. During my post-doctoral fellowship period my inchoate ideas about role taking were sharpened in dialogues with J.L. Moreno, who had initiated the use of drama as a therapeutic tool and who encouraged me to write my first systematic article on role taking (1943b). It was in dialogue with Vernon Allen that role conceptions were refined and tested, and later described in the second edition of the *Handbook of Social Psychology* (1968). Over a period of 45 years, dialogues with Karl Scheibe and Rolf Kroger influenced many of my constructions. They were collaborators with me during the 1960s in the elaboration of a theory of social identity that provided a conceptual background for a number of issues. Scheibe and I later elaborated the theory which became the centerpiece of an edited book: *Studies in Social Identity* (1983). My contributions to the psychology of metaphor began in dialogues with Ki-Taek Chun preparatory to his doctoral research. Our dialogues eventuated in a paper identifying the nature of the metaphor-to-myth transformation (Chun and Sarbin, 1970). Further development of my constructions of metaphor was in response to an "assignment" by Vernon Allen and Karl Scheibe who had volunteered to collect and edit some of my writings (1982). Dialogues with Kenneth Craik made it possible for me to consider place as a stage for one's identify enactments (Sarbin, in press). Dialogues with Martin Orne about disruptions of families created by false memories were instrumental in my devoting a couple of years to studying and writing about psychological and forensic issues connected with the use of false memories by therapists. Dialogues on social constructionism with my Santa Cruz colleague, John Kitsuse, initiated an edited book that advanced the social constructionist perspective (1994). In this latter instance, the dialogues between Professor Kitsuse and myself were publicly exchanged in small seminars with students from a variety of disciplines.

Dialogues with James Mancuso about the failure of the medical model to provide useful understandings of deviant conduct led us individually and jointly to write critical papers and the book on schizophrenia mentioned before. Mancuso and I had many dialogues with Stephen Pepper, the author of the often reissued book, *World Hypotheses* (1942) that influenced us to promote contextualism as a more productive worldview than mechanism, the dominant worldview. Together with Steven and Linda Hayes we organized a conference on the varieties of scientific contextualism in which I presented the results of my dialogues with Pepper and Mancuso and others on contextualism (1993b). A few years later, dialogues with George McKechnie resulted in our publishing a paper (1986) advocating contextualism as a productive epistemology for a theory of personality. Stimulating discussions with Henry Nash Smith, distinguished professor of American literature, and with Marvin Rosenberg, a Shakespeare specialist, facilitated my belletristic forays. I remarked before how the dialogues with Erving Goffman contributed to my further development of the dramaturgical perspective.

During my fellowships at Wesleyan University's Center for the Humanities, multiple dialogues with historian Hayden White, author and historian Paul Horgan, and philosophers Phillip Hallie and Stephen Crites were instrumental in my becoming a narrative psychologist. Since 1986, dialogues with my co-worker, Ralph Carney, helped me clarify my thinking on narrative, emotional life, and the issue of gay men and lesbians in the military. Over the past few years, dialogues with Frank Barrett opened new horizons during our preparing a historico-linguistic essay on the concept of honor. Penetrating insights into the narrative quality of emotional life have emerged from frequent stimulating dialogues over the past decade with Gerald Ginsburg. In the 1990s, Ernest Keen and I collaborated on a paper (1997) resulting from dialogues about emotions as emplotted narratives. A spirited dialogue with Robert Pellegrini on the storied nature of human action led to other dialogues the ultimate result of which was our co-editing a book containing autobiographical father-and-son narratives (2002). My dialogues with Michael Chandler and Cynthia Lightfoot were richly rewarding in my attempts to relate identity development to cultural factors (2004a). One outcome of these exchanges was a chapter on the role of imagining in narrative construction and comprehension (2004b).

I made the claim earlier that identities are supported by remembered narratives in which the actor has played a part. The cataloging of my dialogue partners in the previous paragraphs offered brief synopses of remembered narratives over a 70-year period. Some, but not all, of the dialogues eventuated in publications. My purpose in listing the dialogue partners was not only to acknowledge their participation in my life but also to illustrate that self-narratives are not solipsistic undertakings. Our self-stories are inevitably co-authored, most often unwittingly composed during dialogical interchanges. Whenever we have an "I," a "you" (thou) is necessarily a part of the social context and ultimately enters into the formation of identities. Past theoretical formulations based on the implications of entrenched Cartesian beliefs formed a hermetic seal between the "I" and the "you" thereby producing a one-sided monological view of self.

The dialogical self, a construction abundantly described by Hermans and Kempen (1993), is the most felicitous way of denoting the social context-dependent nature of reflexive constructions signified by first-person pronouns. Contrary to the implications of a monological view of self, one's identity is fashioned in the narrative construction and reconstruction of narratives emerging from dialogues.

Coda: Persistence and change in answers to "Who am I?"

In my contribution to the Lee book mentioned earlier (1993a), issues of identity were discussed in response to the editor's advice to the authors to note what insights emerged in the course of writing their autobiographies. To bring this chapter to completion, I abstract and update what I learned about some of the sources of my identities as the author of an autobiography.

I have provided a narrative of aspects of my career that reveal changing identities over time. These identities reflect the postures that I adopted in working out various theories of action. This narrative, together with the stories I told in my earlier autobiography, awakened me to the observation that my career reflects the adoption of an oppositional, nonconforming posture. In almost every case, I advanced a theoretical position that challenged the dominant discourse. As an example, my incursions into role theory embraced the work of sociologists who focused on the *actions* of people rather than what took place in their postulated minds. Another example is my conceptualization of hypnotic phenomena as role taking rather than the traditional view of hypnosis as a mental state. Still another example is my work on imagining as attenuated role enactments rather than the conventional "pictures in the mind." These are examples of efforts that were nonconforming to traditional and long accepted models. This oppositional approach appears to be a feature that has persisted through various identity transformations.

My self-analysis reveals at least two reasons for the development of a nonconforming identity. I am reasonably sure that one of the origins was my absorption of an iconoclastic rhetoric from my mentor, J.R. Kantor. He promulgated "interbehaviorism," a psychological system that was contrary to the ahistorical approach of Watsonian behaviorists at the time when behaviorism was in full swing. An important part of his life work was the justification of his rejection of the implications of Cartesian mythology that had been incorporated into psychology, implications that persisted even during the heyday of behaviorism. My close reading of Gilbert Ryle's *The Concept of Mind* (1949) reinforced what I had learned from Kantor about the misleading effects of mentalistic psychologies.

A second reason is the recognition of the historical sources of this oppositional feature of my identity. During my undergraduate education, I was motivated to do well. It was not until I was a graduate student that I set my goal to establish a reputation as a productive scholar. My reconstruction of the development of this goal begins with two memorable events.

From today's perspective, it is almost incredible that anti-Semitism in academia was a fact of life. The prejudice was of the gentlemanly variety – no baiting or bashing, only exclusionary practices. The extent of the practices are fully documented in a recent book edited by Andrew Winston (2004).

As an undergraduate, I was unaware of the practices that supported the prejudice. But shortly after I entered the doctoral program, I learned that the university was not a shelter from racial and ethnic discrimination. Like most minority group members, I experienced instances of discrimination that might be called annoyances. Two poignant events stand out in my reconstruction. The first was a conference with my faculty advisor who had called me to his office during my second quarter in the doctoral program (1938). He asked me about my goals and I told him that I hoped to teach in a university. He wanted me to know that it would be virtually impossible to place me in an academic job because I was Jewish, even though it was the department's policy to find academic jobs for all its doctoral students. He went on to assure me that, personally, he was not prejudiced, but universities and colleges recruited mainly gentile, white males, especially since jobs were scarce in the midst of the Great Depression. He wanted me to face the facts, and not to labor under any illusions about becoming an academic. He urged me to consider other options.

A second event that smacked of anti-Semitism was my not being invited to join the graduate student fraternity in psychology. The fraternity had no residence. The members met once a month to hear a speaker, usually a faculty member, report on research or theoretical developments. Only 2 of the 25 or more graduate students were not invited to membership: both were Jewish. Classroom relations with fellow graduate students were cordial. Several of us studied together to prepare for qualifying examinations. Two or three showed great promise and later became well established in their respective specialties, but most were pedestrian students. In seminars, none ever challenged a professor or even a fellow student. They conformed to the prevailing ideology.

I am offering the hypothesis that my oppositional behavior, my taking positions on the margins, was a way of demonstrating that the traditional frameworks – with which I identified those who excluded me – were unproductive and not useful for the psychology of human action. It may appear irrational to equate conventional views – the targets of my counterclaims – to the professors and graduate students who excluded me from membership in an academic society. At the time it did not occur to me to engage in political action, to tell about the injustice produced by stereotypes. My analysis of my reaction to the discriminatory practice is that I would deal with this insult to my identity by becoming visible as a productive scholar, thereby demonstrating that the professors and graduate students were simply wrong in excluding me. Underlying my resolve was the subtext of an ancient story exemplified by the biblical account of David and Goliath: a champion rises to do battle with what appears to be an invincible antagonist.

The foregoing account, I believe, gets to the heart of the editors' query about the "whoness" of Ted Sarbin. I have located the energy for my story in the exclusionary events that happened many years ago. Their motivating power has certainly diminished with time. The painful insult associated with being the victim of exclusionary practices is now but a dim memory. However, I continue to publish critical essays that reflect the weakness of mechanistic and mentalistic psychologies. In these essays I advocate drama and narrative as apt metaphors for a contextualist, constructionist psychology.

It is reasonable to seek an explanation for this continuity in the light of the fact that I have received a number of prestigious awards attesting to my having earned a reputation as a professor and a scholar. To account for my persistence in working at the margins of the discipline, a first step would be to take Gordon Allport's "functional autonomy of motives" (1937) and transform it to the "functional autonomy of identity." The latter construction would show, through narratives, that it is possible for some aspects of identity to persist in the face of conditions that might call for changes in the topics of discourse.

Note

1   Because of space limitations, I have not written about my identities as a criminologist and as a psychotherapist. Suffice it to say that as a faculty member of the School of Criminology, University of California Berkeley, I conducted research on the degradation of identity, on the myth of the criminal type, on new approaches to criminal justice, and, in collaboration with Mordechai Rotenberg, a study of prison social types (Rotenberg and Sarbin, 1971). After retiring from the university, because of my credentials as a psychologist and criminologist, in 1979, I was invited to participate in a seminar on military deception at the Navy Postgraduate School. From 1986 to the present, I have been employed in a government research center dealing with policies and practices to

reduce the loss of government secrets through espionage and the violation of security rules. In the years 1944 to 1949, I had an independent practice as a clinical psychologist in which I employed role conceptions and the psychology of imagining as therapeutic tools. During my tenure at Berkeley, and subsequently, I continued clinical work on a part-time basis in which I focused on "narrative repair." Experiences in the role of therapist were invaluable in the formation of my identity as a noncomforming clinical psychologist, discussed in the text.

References

Allen, V.L. and Scheibe, K.E. (eds) (1982) *The Social Context of Conduct: Psychological Writings of Theodore R. Sarbin*. New York: Praeger.

Allport, G. (1937) *Personality*. New York: Henry Holt and Co.

Averill, J.R. (1974) "An analysis of psychophysiological symbolism and its influence on theories of emotion." *Journal for the Theory of Social Behavior 4*, 147–190.

Bruner, J. (1986) *Actual Minds, Possible Worlds*. Cambridge, MA: Harvard University Press.

Cameron, N. (1943) "The development of paranoic thinking." *Psychological Review 50*, 219–233.

Chun, K.T. and Sarbin, T.R. (1970) "An empirical study of metaphor to myth transformation." *Philosophical Psychologist 4*, 16–20.

deRivera, J. and Sarbin, T.R. (eds) (1998) *Believed-in Imaginings: The Narrative Construction of Reality*. Washington, DC: American Psychological Association.

Friedlander, J.W. and Sarbin, T.R. (1938) "The depth of hypnosis." *Journal of Abnormal and Social Psychology 33*, 453–475.

Heidbreder, E. (1933) *Seven Psychologies*. New York: Century.

Hermans, H.J.M. and Kempen, H. (1993) *The Dialogical Self*. San Diego: Academic Press.

Kermode, F. (1967) *The Sense of an Ending*. Oxford: Oxford University Press.

Levin, H. (1970) "The Quixotic principle." In M.W. Bloomfield (ed) *Harvard English Studies I. The Interpretation of Narrative: Theory and Practice*. Cambridge, MA: Harvard University Press.

Lewis, J.H. and Sarbin, T.R. (1943) "Studies in psychosomatics: The influence of hypnotic stimulation on gastric hunger contractions." *Psychosomatic Medicine 5*, 125–131.

Meehl, P. (1954) *Clinical Versus Statistical Prediction*. Minneapolis: University of Minnesota Press.

Pellegrini, R.J. and Sarbin, T.R. (eds) (2002) *Between Fathers and Sons: Critical Incident Narratives in Men's Lives*. Binghamton, NY: Hawarth Press.

Pepper, S. (1942) *World Hypotheses*. Berkeley: University of California Press.

Rotenberg, M. and Sarbin, T.R. (1971) "Impact of differentially significant others on role-involvement." *Journal of Abnormal Psychology 77*, 97–107.

Ryle, G. (1949) *The Concept of Mind*. London: Hutchinson's University Library.

Sarbin, T.R. (1941) "Clinical psychology: Art or science?" *Psychometrica 6*, 391–401.

Sarbin, T.R. (1943a) "A contribution to the actuarial and individual methods of prediction." *American Journal of Sociology 48*, 593–602.

Sarbin, T.R. (1943b) "The concept of role-taking." *Sociometry 6*, 273–284.

Sarbin, T.R. (1944) "The logic of prediction in psychology." *Psychological Review 51*, 210–228.

Sarbin, T.R. (1950) "Contributions to role-taking theory I: Hypnotic Behaviour." *Psychological Review 57*, 255–270.

Sarbin, T.R. (1954) "Role theory." In G. Lindzey (ed) *Handbook of Social Psychology*. Cambridge: Addison Wesley Press.

Sarbin, T.R. (1972) "Imagining as muted role-taking: A historico-linguistic analysis." In P. Sheehan (ed) *The Function and Nature of Imagery*. New York: Academic Press.

Sarbin, T.R. (1982) "The Quixotic principle: A belletristic approach to the psychology of imagining." In V.L. Allen and K.E. Scheibe (eds) *The Social Context of Conduct: Psychological Writings of Theodore Sarbin*. New York: Praeger.

Sarbin, T.R. (ed) (1986) *Narrative Psychology: The Storied Nature of Human Conduct*. New York: Praeger.

Sarbin, T.R. (1989) "Emotions as situated actions." In L. Cirillo, B. Kaplan and S. Wapner (eds) *Emotions and Ideal Human Development*. Hillsdale, NJ: Lawrence Erlbaum Associates.

Sarbin, T.R. (1993a) "Steps to the narratory principle: an autobiographical essay." In D.J. Lee (ed) *Life and Story: Autobiographies for a Narrative Psychology*. Westport, CT: Praeger/Greenwood.

Sarbin, T.R. (1993b) "The narrative as a root metaphor for contextualism." In S. Hayes, L. Hayes, H. Reese and T.R. Sarbin (eds) *Varieties of Scientific Contextualism*. Reno, NV: Context Press.

Sarbin, T.R. (1995a) "On the belief that one body may be host to two or more personalities." *International Journal of Clinical and Experimental Hypnosis 43*, 163–183.

Sarbin, T.R. (1995b) "A narrative approach to 'repressed memories'." *Journal of Narrative and Personal History 5*, 51–69.

Sarbin, T.R. (1997a) "The power of believed-in imaginings." *Psychological Inquiry 8*, 322–325.

Sarbin, T.R. (1997b) "Multiple personality disorder: Fact or artifact?" *Current Opinion in Psychiatry 10*, 136–140.

Sarbin, T.R. (2004a) "A preface to the epistemology of identity." In C.J. Lightfoot, C. Lalonde and M. Chandler (eds) *Changing Conceptions of Psychological Life*. Mahwah, NJ: Erlbaum.

Sarbin, T.R (2004b) "The role of imagination in narrative construction." In C. Diaute and C. Lightfoot (eds) *Narrative Analysis: Studying the Development of Individuals in Society*. Thousand Oaks, CA: Sage Publishers.

Sarbin, T.R. (in press) "If the walls could speak: Places as stages for human drama." *Journal of Constructivist Psychology*.

Sarbin, T.R. and Allen, V.L. (1968) "Role theory." In G. Lindzey and E. Aronson (eds) *Handbook of Social Psychology, Second Edition*. Boston, MA: Addison Wesley Press.

Sarbin, T.R. and Coe, W.C. (1972) *Hypnosis: A Social Psychological Analysis of Influence Communication*. New York: Rinehart and Winston.

Sarbin, T.R. and Keen, E. (1997) "Sanity and madness: Conventional and unconventional narratives of emotional life." In W.F. Flack Jr. and J. Laird (eds) *Emotions in Psychopathology: Theory and Research*. New York: Oxford University Press.

Sarbin, T.R. and Kitsuse, J.I. (eds) (1994) *Constructing the Social*. London: Sage.

Sarbin, T.R. and Mancuso, J.C. (1980) *Schizophrenia: Medical Diagnosis or Moral Verdict?* New York: Pergamon Press.

Sarbin, T.R. and McKechnie, G.E. (1986) "Prospects for a contextualist theory of personality." In R. Rosnow and M. Georgeoudi *Contextualism and Understanding in Behavior Science*. New York: Praeger.

Sarbin, T.R. and Scheibe, K.E. (eds) (1983) *Studies in Social Identity*. New York: Praeger.

Sarbin, T.R., Taft, R. and Bailey, D.E. (1960) *Clinical Inference and Cognitive Theory*. New York: Holt, Rinehart and Winston.

Winston, A.S. (ed) (2004) *Defining Difference: Race and Racism in the History of Psychology*. Washington, DC: American Psychological Association.

CHAPTER 2

Lessons from Relics about Self and Identity

Karl E. Scheibe

A black and white photograph of a little girl, perhaps three years old, is mounted on my office wall. She is standing in front of an ornately carved, upholstered chair. Her head is cocked to the left. Sunlight pours into the room and she is squinting slightly. She is wearing a short white dress, and her long blonde hair is adorned with a pretty bow. She has on white sandals and patterned anklets. Her legs are straight and a bit chunky. Her posture seems rather self-consciously posed. She is standing up tall, her arms are by her sides, her eyes are fixed on the camera and a hint of a smile is on her lips.

This little girl is Karl Scheibe. No, Karl Scheibe was this little girl. No, I was never a little girl. But the photograph is evidence that my parents must have thought it amusing to dress me up as a little girl and to take my picture. This practice was common when I was a child – suggesting that the masculine emerges out of the feminine in more ways than one. All men are born of women. But childhood is often constructed as a tender and feminine thing, out of which boys emerge into toughness and have their hair cut short. While I have absolutely no memory of dressing up as a girl or of having my picture taken, I must perforce own that the image is, in some sense, me. Somewhere in a trunk is a lock of golden hair in an envelope, labeled – "Carl's hair, June, 1940." I don't remember the haircut either. But the hair, like the photograph, I surely own as mine – an artifact in proof of qualities once possessed. My head is now mostly bald and my fringe of hair is mostly gray. What have I to do with these and other silent relics of the past?

These relics revive an old memory. My mother had two sons before me. The story goes that when the new baby was announced to be a boy, her spontaneous comment was, "Take him back." This was often told to me as a joke – and I took it as such. But I wonder if my knowledge of this hint of rejection, combined with my having been made up as a girl, at least once for display, did not work at some deep level of my being to dispose me to feelings of inferiority, at least in comparison to my nearest older brother, Paul, whose hair was blonder and curlier than mine. Paul always seemed to be Mom's favorite. But while I may have had feelings of inferiority, I always knew that such feelings were transitory, not indicative of anything but a problem of regard, which would be righted in time. Soon I was to become my Dad's "sidekick" – and I came to be secure in his positive regard. I am (or pretend to be) so secure that I choose to display a photograph of myself dressed up as a little girl, and thus reveal possible ambiguities about myself without embarrassment to disbelieving students.

Other relics adorn my office as well. There is a photograph of Ted Sarbin, my graduate student mentor and constant friend, another of Martin Orne, now deceased, a major influence in my early career as a psychologist. My family is displayed – my wife, Wendy, my sons, David and Daniel. Next is a photograph of me in academic regalia with a smiling, dark-skinned man, Edson Arantes do Nascimento, otherwise known as Pelé, the Brazilian soccer star. There is more, of course – much more. Here is a photograph I took of my father's natal village in Germany, taken from a mountain called the Meissner. Next to it is a photograph of Judd Hall, which houses the psychology department at Wesleyan. A student gave this to me a few years ago. There are my six grandchildren, and nearby a picture of a pair of classic MG cars I once owned. My son David and I are in the picture as well, posing in immaculate white coveralls after having finished complete restorations of both cars.

I reflect. Nothing is more boring than to be shown through an album of photographs of a stranger. It is like a visit to a museum, and such tours quickly lead to fatigue, producing a case of "museum legs." I recall looking at a display of Etruscan relics in the British Museum. Yes, the Etruscans once existed. But why on earth should I be thinking about them? And yet these relics in my office seem vital to me – reminders of who I am and who I have been. They form a presentable set of images, a set of points about which stories might be woven, testimonies to ways I have chosen to manage the impression I convey to others and the general image I strive to maintain for myself. I reflect again, sadly. In one year, I must vacate this office as I move into retirement after 42 years as an active faculty member at Wesleyan. I will strip the walls and tables of artifacts and relics, put them in boxes. Perhaps a few will find their way into my new and smaller office, as an emeritus professor. In truth, I am the primary consumer of my own story. I cannot expect others not to yawn or jangle their car keys. I hope I will have the courage to be ruthless in discarding relics, so as not to leave a burden for my progeny. But now I am spinning a story about my becoming a psychologist absorbed in the importance of narrative, so all of these dead relics have for the moment a living purpose, unlike the Etruscan figures in the British Museum.

Once I visited the Freud Museum at Maresfield Gardens in London. There I saw Freud's consulting room. I ventured to take a picture of it. It was a cold, rainy afternoon, and my son and I were the only visitors in the place, so the guard relaxed the normal rule against taking pictures. The picture I took of Freud's famous couch also shows a portion of Freud's large collection of ancient relics, mostly small figurines of bronze and stone and wood – artifacts from ancient civilizations, including the Etruscans.

I was reminded of a revealing story about Freud. As he was rushing to leave Vienna in 1938, aided by the financial support of Marie Bonaparte, he made sure to pack his treasure trove of relics to bring with him to London. But he neglected to bring his four elder sisters with him, and they were later to die at the hands of the Nazis. Freud's relics must have been important to him, a critical part of his portable story. There they are still, in the museum, mute testimony to the range of his intellectual curiosity, or less charitably, when one thinks of his abandoned sisters, they attest to his scale of values.

A partisan of Freud would not tell the story this way. Ernest Jones relates all the facts to which I have alluded in the previous paragraph. But he does not consider that Freud neglected his sisters. He notes that Freud did not have room for them in his London house and in any event he later sent them some money that they might have used to emigrate. Alas, it was too late, and Jones simply notes that the sisters were incinerated five years later, well after Freud's own death in 1939. The past is silent. We speak in the present to revivify the past.

That I should have chosen to remember and relate a less flattering version of these events says less about Freud than it does about me. For I have never had much sympathy for many of Freud's most basic principles – his rigid determinism, his claim of ultimate authority on matters of interpretation, his insistence on reducing all of human motivation to sex and aggression. At the same time, I have great respect for Freud's revolutionary impact on the development of psychotherapy. All of us who practice some version of the 'talking cure' are in his debt. A person who invents a new profession is, by definition, a genius – and by this criterion Freud certainly qualifies.

When I was an undergraduate, my physics professor made the claim that loyalty to Aristotle did as much to retard the development of scientific thinking as his genius did to advance that thinking from earlier and more primitive conceptions. The same could be said of Freud. Busts of Aristotle and of Freud abound in our world – relics that suggest at once genius as well as the freezing of intellectual progress. Freud had a revolutionary and altogether salutary effect on the development of psychological thought. But loyalty to Freud has been a virtual deadweight for psychology throughout most of the 20th century. Ernest Jones is a total loyalist to Freud. I am not. These twin claims might be seen as absolute and unconditional. But they are better seen as products of two distinct life stories. Jones's life brought him into frequent and intimate contact with Freud. My own life story has transpired in an entirely different realm; one that produced for me some claim to being a "narrative psychologist." I will leave Jones and Freud aside now, and proceed with a version of my own tale, guided by occasional reference to the relics and artifacts in my current surroundings.

My self and my identity

The invitation to contribute this chapter is an occasion to survey my contributions to the field of narrative psychology, or to psychology more generally. I started off, as most young psychologists do, publishing empirical studies – based on experiments, surveys, or direct observational work in mental hospitals. It took me awhile to recognize that I do not have the experimentalist's imagination. I was drawn instead to the more conceptual side of the enterprise. I had to conclude that I am not a social psychologist in the mold of Kurt Lewin, Solomon Asch, Stanley Milgram, or Leon Festinger – brilliant innovators in making social psychological problems amenable to empirical attack. Rather, I am more akin, however faintly, to William James, Charles Horton Cooley, George Herbert Mead, and Erving Goffman – none of whom did much by way of gathering fresh and systematic data, but all of whom were ingenious at recognizing and describing human experience in a way that gives new coherence to our understandings, particularly of the social nexus of our lives.

One of the advantages of having job security in an academic institution is the freedom that security confers to depart from the standards of one's discipline in search of fresh territory. Graduate students and assistant professors hew closely to the given boundaries. As I grew older, I found that my interests would take me not only to the works of James, Mead, Cooley, and Goffman, as

I have noted, but in addition to George Orwell, José Ortega y Gassett, and Ralph Waldo Emerson, or the poetry of Frost or Yeats or Wordsworth. I became and am now less dutiful and more selfish in my reading habits – insisting that a book repay me directly with new ideas and insights, and not just furnish my mind with stuff that I am supposed to know as a respectable professor of psychology.

Here again, artifacts are revealing. As I glance at the surface next to my writing table, I find a copy of *The Open Door: Thoughts on Acting and Theater*, by the director and theoretician of theater, Peter Brook. And there is *Beyond Belief*, by the theologian, Elaine Pagels, right on top of *Ultimate Fitness*, by the science writer, Gina Kolata. The poet David Whyte contributes to this happenstance collection with *Crossing the Unknown Sea: Work as a Pilgrimage of Identity*, right next to a paperback edition of Charles Darwin's *The Expression of Emotion in Man and Animals*. Two recent books about gambling at Indian casinos in Connecticut complete this odd collection. I probably have 700 books on the shelves and tables of my office, and most of them are conventional psychology monographs. But my interests and current mental life are more clearly represented by the books on my table, including, I now hasten to add, my two most recent books, *Self Studies* (1995), and *The Drama of Everyday Life* (2000).

If I think of contributions to understandings of narrative psychology, these two books, together with a precursor volume, *Mirrors, Masks, Lies, and Secrets*, (Scheibe, 1979) would be centerpieces for my claims. And if I were forced to choose one particular item out of all of these pages to cite as a centrally important idea for the current enterprise – of telling my own story as a narrative psychologist – then it would be the distinction I draw in Chapter 1 of *Self Studies* between the closely related concepts of self and identity.

In *Memories, Dreams, and Reflections* (1965), Carl Jung draws a distinction between the part of him that dreams, that has reflections, that reviews memories – and the part of him that engages in conversation and other interactions with people. He describes this first part of him as engaging in a process that is vertical – meditating about what is above him, below him, what his connection might be with the cosmos. This self is ageless. He regarded this part of him as the authentic home of his being, capable of feelings ranging from ecstasy to profound despair, but relatively insulated from commerce with the external world. He testifies that even as a boy he was aware of an ancient spirit within him. He would have us understand that when he first began to converse with others – other children, his parents, adults – he felt this as a compromise from his true being, a falsification. Following Jung, I say that this vertical dimension is a manifestation of *self* – conceived of not as an entity, but rather as an abstraction, knowable through its natural means of action – that of meditation. One might also think of self as a bundle of dispositions or preferences. In developing his theory of psychological types, Jung was attempting to develop a taxonomy of selves. Surely his attempt must be regarded as partial and incomplete, even though such dimensions as introversion–extroversion have stood the test of time and are regarded by modern personality psychologists as robust and useful. I am not concerned here with how selves ought finally to be described. But I wish to extend the claim made in *Self Studies* that a conception of the human Self is required on pragmatic and functional grounds. Human beings have the capacity for agency.

Selves are agents. I think of the agent as at once out of time and yet formed by the events in the passage of time. Identity is transient – a product of interactions with the social order. Both self and identity are in flux, or in the river of consciousness, as James would say. But the self floats along in the stream with relative constancy of form, while identity is a matter of continual relocation in relation to the markers along the banks of the river, the labels that are posted and recognized, the coordinates always requiring adjustment as one both navigates and is pushed and pulled by currents of air and water. I have never been as old as I am today. My chronological age is surely an identity marker, as are my ratified claims to being a father, a psychologist, a man, a US citizen, a speaker of Portuguese, and an athlete. On the other hand, my experienced maturity of vision about myself and my world cannot be outwardly displayed, but is inwardly known.

I am an agent. I enact this agency in the social order but also, in a meditative way – contemplating, as Jung did, my relation to the darkness before my birth, the darkness after my death, the light of the sky above me, the mystery of the earth below me. When I encountered Carl Jung's writings, I was still an undergraduate and Jung himself was still alive. Something in my inner compass resonated with Jung's musings about the collective unconscious, the notion of archetypes, and the idea that the task of self-integration takes place over the entire span of life. Shall I say that Jung's reasoning or marshalling of evidence to support his claim was superior to Freud's? I don't think so. In fact, my senior project on Jungian psychology almost came to grief because I was unable to produce arguments for my positivist-behaviorist professor that would support my claims for the value of Jung's approach. From my current perspective, I simply say that this was a vote of the self – a declaration of a felt affinity that had little or nothing to do with evidence or argument. It was as if I sensed that Jung's self matched my own in some ineffable way. My act of agency was to tune in to Jung. But in terms of identity, I certainly did not become, then or since, a Jungian.

I am more likely to be considered a Goffmanian, though I would never enter this claim for myself. My writings make use of the same language of drama that Goffman used as a scaffolding for his own work. Behind me on my bookshelf are the 11 books that Goffman composed in his brief but effervescent professional life – from 1958 until his death in 1982. Goffman has taught me much about how to observe and understand the interaction order. That he was a sociologist and had disdain for most of psychology is of no importance to me.

In front of me is a photograph of my mentor, Ted Sarbin, who was also my link to Goffman. He introduced me to Goffman in person when both were on the faculty of the University of California at Berkeley. But he also provided inspiration and example for how a psychologist might use the language of social roles in a way that illuminates not only the banal conventions of social life, but also as a way of understanding profound relationships among thought, language, feeling, emotion and conduct. Ted Sarbin is prodigious as a scholar – his publishing career spans over 60 years. His mind is restless – constantly thinking of new angles on old problems. I have witnessed his development over the past 45 years into *the* seminal figure in narrative psychology (see Sarbin, 1986). While he has never demanded fealty to his way of looking at things from me or any other of his students, I found myself drawn inexorably to a social constructionist position on social life, using contextualism as the root metaphor and conceptual foundation for my work and thinking.

Sarbin has a rare combination of personal geniality and raw intellectual force. As I write this, he is 93 years of age, and yet I know he is currently engaged in half a dozen writing projects. Shall I say that he is a role model? Oh, yes!

On a filing cabinet near my desk is a small trophy – about six inches in height. It is a representation of the comedy and tragedy masks, both rendered in gold (well, not *real* gold). The base contains the engraved legend "Role Theorist, 1973 – Karl E. Scheibe." I remember the occasion on which Sarbin gave me this award – the "Role Theorist of the Year." It was in Montreal at the annual convention of the American Psychological Association, in the summer of 1973. The first such award was presented to my colleague, Vernon Allen, at a gathering of Sarbin students in Berkeley at the end of the summer of 1965. Ted Sarbin, of course, is the inventor and patron of this honor. He alludes from time to time to a selection committee, but its identity is a closely guarded secret. As the spirit moves and as occasions arise, usually at APA meetings, Role Theorist of the Year awards are presented. Twenty-eight such awards have been presented.

On the one hand, all of this might seem frivolous – and to be sure, the exercise is carried out in the spirit of good fun. But underneath the frivolity are some serious lessons about narratives and human life. The creation of a new award might be just an act of whimsy. Once a thought occurred in the inner self of Ted Sarbin, out of mere nothing. But the thought germinated and was translated into a set of events that now constitute the basis for the telling of stories for many people.

The same might be said of the creation of a new human institution of any kind. Yonder on a table in my office is a brochure representing the Saybrook Counseling Center, of which I bear the lofty title of Executive Director. About 15 years ago, I and a partner conceived the idea of starting a private practice in psychology, and the Saybrook Counseling Center is the result of that initiative. In order to navigate my identity in this direction, I had to get licensed as a psychologist. I became a retread clinical psychologist, forced to take courses, assemble references, and take examinations more than 20 years after receiving my PhD. Later I bought out my partner, and hired six clinical associates in the practice, as well as an office manager and a receptionist. This year, thousands of hours will be spent in therapy sessions with hundreds of clients at this place in Old Saybrook, Connecticut. Like the Role Theorist of the Year, this institution started off as a mere idea in someone's mind. This idea had to be acted upon – made public and tangible with declarations, signs, combined with investments of money and time and composition. But there it is. Something is created out of nothing. An institution, whether it is an award or a business or a university or a nation or a family custom, quickly develops a history, a story that can be told. Human history is in part a product of design, of careful planning and execution. It is also in part a product of caprice – of chance and unpredictable events. The arbitrary becomes essential. Events, once formed out of mere possibility, come to be real and enduring.

The arbitrary becomes essential

I don't remember when this formulation first entered my head or first passed from my lips. I think it might have been during a choir rehearsal at the Congregational church I attend, in a moment of banter between songs with my friend and colleague, the then-minister of the church, Bill Roberts. Perhaps we were discussing music – how Mozart's *Ave Verum* seems eternal, the world unimaginable without it once you have sung it. Yet we must recognize that no one had heard this ethereal melody prior to its composition in the 18th century. Mozart's brief life provided, in my view, a cosmic opportunity for the music of the spheres to be channeled into human culture, evermore transformed by that contribution. The arbitrary becomes essential.

I look around my office for artifacts that suggest my relation and connection to religion and to music. To music, there are plenty of reminders – CDs by the score, a boom box for playing them, a concert program. My Self is musical, if nothing else. It seems that I always have a tune running in my head, and I often whistle, more or less unconsciously, in my office or in the corridor or field or public place. This is not a matter of identity display. In fact, when my sons were young, they were more or less mortified by my tendency to whistle – or to sing in public, sometimes in Portuguese – and they hastened to quiet me.

Recently I reviewed a book, *Individual Differences in Conscious Experience*, edited by Kunzendorf and Wallace (1999). In it, I learned of enormous differences among sentient human beings in how the world is experienced. Some are color blind, some are tone deaf. Some are super-tasters, some have profoundly clear eidetic images. Some mental chambers are haunted by other-worldly visions and voices, in a way that might suggest madness to the surrounding social order. These characteristic forms of commerce with the world are properties of individual selves. I say that my arbitrarily formed inner self merits the descriptor musical, among others. It is a quality I am at ease to display.

Inspection of my office, however, reveals little of my interest in religion. The book I have noted by Elaine Pagels is perhaps an exception. James's *Varieties of Religious Experience* is on my shelf, as is a Bible given to me by my father, who was a Baptist minister. But this is a small representation of something that is actually quite a strong feature of my self – my interest in matters religious and spiritual. I am forced to conclude that I am rather shy about displaying this aspect of who I am, for I have had some profoundly unsettling experiences around religious identity. Even as I approach this topic, I am aware of dangers – that some reader, familiar or strange, might think me improperly formed or informed. I think of a remark by the lawyer, Clarence Darrow, who gained fame in the Scopes monkey trial of the 1920s. To this effect: "I have suffered much from being misunderstood. But I would have suffered much more had I been truly understood." A major psychological principle then, must be placed near the center of the narrative enterprise, to wit: Fear often operates to create major distortions in the way the self is storied. The lack of religious artifacts and relics in my office (and my home) provides testimony to this principle.

In brief, the unsettling experiences were these. My eldest brother, Bob, was a hellion as a youth – a constant embarrassment to his minister father. He smoked and drank, and ran around with loose women – dropped out of school as soon as he was 16, and was constantly in trouble. But when he was 22, he suddenly got religion of the fundamentalist Christian variety. He quickly directed his energies to attempts to convert everyone he could reach, including his family, to the true faith. I was 15, and my older brother, who formerly had been for me an object of considerable fear and an example of how not to behave, was then wringing me out over defects in my faith. I felt trapped and desperate. It did not help that my nearest brother, Paul, appeared to capitulate entirely to Bob's forceful arguments – and both of them went off to train to be foreign missionaries as I entered my junior year of high school. Neither did it help that my minister father, whom I both loved and feared, and my beautiful mother, whom I both loved and distrusted, fought constantly and were finally divorced. What a mess!

I churned a lot in mighty seas of faith and doubt. I tried a stint in a mission training school in the summer before my entry into Trinity College. I studied the Bible avidly and I talked with my fellow trainees, who did not seem to me, in general, admirable human beings. Even so, when I landed at Trinity, I remember sticking a bold poster to my dorm room door, quoting the Apostle Paul: "I am not ashamed of the gospel of Christ, for it is the power of salvation for all that believeth." I shudder when I think of the utter stupidity of this act of displaying identity. Little did I know that a good percentage of my classmates at Trinity would be Jewish. I was prepared to challenge the Episcopalians, who were even more numerous, and of course the non-believers were many. But unlike the missionary trainees, I found among my Trinity College classmates many quite admirable human beings – intelligent, aware, curious, and fair-minded.

Once again, I felt trapped and rather helpless. I chose psychology as a major, a common refuge for those with unconfessable religious problems. My primary professor there was an atheist. He openly expressed his contempt for my naive faith. My religious identity was forced into retreat. While I inwardly retained my spiritual interests and preferences, I could no longer profess my faith in any but the most timid fashion. I tore down the sign on my door and wondered that I could ever have been so injudicious. I had a Jewish roommate who became a dear friend – and we did not discuss religion.

Most of the important influences in my formation as a psychologist were also Jewish – Ted Sarbin, Martin Orne, and Julian Rotter, with whom I worked for a year while he passed a sabbatical at Berkeley. Later, my best friend on the faculty at Wesleyan, the philosopher Philip Hallie, was at once a Jew and also one of the most challenging and congenial minds I have ever encountered.

What then of my Christian identity? Perhaps surprisingly, I retain it. My wife and I joined the local Congregational church more than 30 years ago, where the atmosphere is at once liberal and Christian. Our children were raised in the Protestant tradition, were duly baptized. Our six grandchildren are all christened. Occasionally, a Wesleyan student has been at a service at the church, and has expressed surprise at seeing me singing in the choir. I feel about this much as I feel about the picture of me dressed as a girl. That is, I feel secure enough about my inward self to risk some ambiguities in how I present my outward identity – as a skeptical and questioning scholar, and yet as a participating believer. But the lemma that has helped me enormously in bridging this divide is captured by the phrase, "The arbitrary becomes essential." I could have been born and raised a girl or a Jew, and if those arbitrary characteristics of self had been laid down, I would certainly now own them as essential to who I am.

Of course, some choose to navigate themselves into new channels in such a way as to reduce what must be an unbearable dissonance between self and identity. If I had been born a Nazi, I would certainly take pains to dissolve that essence and to become something less alien. I know Jews who have become Christian and Christians who have become Jews. I know men who cannot own the traditional identity of maleness in our culture, and women who cannot own the traditional female identity. Great navigational force and skill is required to bring about transformations that can reduce these dissonances between the inner formation of the self and the outer requirements of ratified identity. The external social world must provide the means of attaining these transformations. Today one can come out and be openly homosexual in our culture – even to marry one's partner in certain states. This allows an alignment between the inner requirements of self and the outward affordances of identity. Political and cultural changes that allow alignments of this sort are ultimately progressive. They are helpful in allowing the narratives of self and identity to unfold in a satisfactory way. I have been fortunate in merely being able to accept my arbitrary ascriptions without a sense of dissonance with the surrounding social order. I cannot preach to others about the superiority of who I happen to be – as a man, as a Christian, as an American, or even as a psychologist. I can only teach others to understand that their natural endowments of self might have been distributed in quite a different manner, and that tolerance and appreciation for others are the proper consequences of this humble recognition. The posture of a narrative psychologist, in my view, must be one that rests on no fixed foundation of truth. Rather, one must be able to appreciate that the story could have been vastly different, but for a small set of accidents along the course of life. Humility is endless; pride is only possible by recognizing the primacy of humility.

Brazil and other mysteries

The attentive reader will have noticed the appearance of several details that do not seem at all integrated or connected with the flow of my story. For example, I mentioned the lock of hair, labeled "Carl's hair, June, 1940." Carl? Not Karl? No, not Karl. My parents named me as they named me, and they themselves wrote my name out for enrollment in school with the more Anglicized C and not the Germanic K. I was born in 1937, in southern Illinois. My father was born in Germany, but gave up his Johann Heinrich for John Henry. It made a lot of sense, as World War II approached, to steer one's identity away from German and toward English. So I was Carl until the fourth grade. When I entered fifth grade in 1947, the war was over. Somehow, it seemed to me more masculine and altogether safe to change the spelling of my name to Karl. I had seen my brother's birth certificate with his name registered on it. I asked to see my own. To my surprise, I discovered that the certificate, duly impressed with date and footprint and names of parents, did not contain my name at all. Instead, the space marked "Name" was left blank. My mother explained that they didn't name me until some days after the birth, and had simply neglected to fill in that blank when they finally made up their minds. So I took the opportunity to write my own name on the birth certificate. But I wrote Karl Edward Scheibe, leaving Carl behind me forever. It was an easy move of navigation, for my parents did not object, and I rather imagined that my father approved. I think of this now as a simple vote of the self, a slight readjustment in the course of claimed identity. I believe names to be deeply significant. I don't believe my life would have been the same if I had been named Luther or Allen. How it might have been different is unknowable. A little nudge of course correction early on can bring miles of divergence years down the stream.

I have mentioned earlier a photograph on my wall showing me together with Pelé – himself in full academic regalia. Three years ago, he received an honorary degree from Wesleyan, on the occasion of his daughter's graduation. Since I speak Portuguese, I had the honor of being his host on campus, even though his English is good. My proficiency in Portuguese is the product of quite a lot of time spent in Brazil since 1967, the beginning of my first sabbatical. I went to Brazil because my oldest brother, Bob, had died there in the previous year when the small plane he was flying crashed. My father had departed for Brazil to join Bob in his missionary work. Dad resolved to stay in Brazil, in a small town in the remote interior of the state of Minas Gerais. My younger brother, Steve, resolved to go to Brazil to help Dad as best he could.

These circumstances seemed to me to require a substantial course correction for myself and for my young family. At age 29, I resolved to learn Portuguese, go to Brazil for my first earned sabbatical in 1967–68, and to provide such support as I might for my father and younger brother. Wendy agreed. We packed up our two small boys, aged six months and three years – and so went to Belo Horizonte, the capital of Minas Gerais. It was my intention to write a book during this year, as well as finish up the writing of a number of empirical reports based upon work I had done in the previous four years, collecting data on the impact of college students as volunteers in the state mental hospitals of Connecticut. As I look back upon this period, I think that the challenges were so vast as to require the abandonment of common sense. It is amazing to me to observe that we met the challenges. We did install ourselves in Belo Horizonte. We did provide support for my father and brother. We did learn Portuguese. I did write a book (*Beliefs and Values*, 1970) and a number of research reports. In April, 1968, I was invited to teach two courses, *in Portuguese*, at the federal university in Brasilia. We returned to the US in July 1968 – to a country in turmoil, after the assassinations of Martin Luther King and Robert Kennedy, the escalating war in Vietnam. Soon, we were watching the tumultuous Democratic National Convention in Chicago, and it seemed as if the identity coordinates of the country as a whole had come unglued. Somehow it seemed helpful, even reassuring, to look at all of this from the perspective of our year in Brazil, where we had achieved some major transformations in our own identities, in virtue of a year's total immersion in a distant culture.

I was to return to Brazil in 1972, under the safer and more respectable auspices of a Fulbright fellowship, to teach in an incipient graduate program in social psychology at the Catholic University of São Paulo. Once again, Wendy and I and the boys were installed for a year in Brazil – this time with Portuguese already well begun, if not mastered. My students at the university became friends, and over the course of years, professional colleagues.

My office walls contain many other reminders of Brazil. There is a photograph of Alberto Guerreiro Ramos, Brazilian sociologist and political scientist, lighting a cigar. Alberto occupied my Wesleyan office and our home as well during my 1972–73 Fulbright year. Next is a painting of Abdias do Nascimento, famous for his advancement of Afro-Brazilian art and culture. I helped bring Abdias to Wesleyan in 1969, and have learned much from him over the years. The largest painting in my office is a modernistic composition by Sergio Rabinowitz, a young artist from Salvador, whom Wendy recruited as a Wesleyan student back in the 1970s. One of the smallest artifacts is a wrapper from an Afro-Brazilian delicacy, purchased on a beach in Salvador, during a visit that Wendy and I made to Sergio and his family in 2000. It reads, *O melhor acarajé*, a reminder of a taste treat that is simply indescribable.

And on and on. In my imagination, I can hear the car keys jangling again. One point of introducing the Brazilian dimension of my life is that it provides yet another set of examples of the way in which the arbitrary becomes essential. But for my brother becoming a missionary, he would never have gone to Brazil. But for his dying there, I would never have resolved to go to Brazil myself. But for us going to Brazil, my younger brother, Steve, would not have met his Brazilian wife, Angela. But for my going to Brazil and learning the language, music, taste, and culture of that land, my intellectual and emotional life would have never taken the course it has. My most recent book, *The Drama of Everyday Life* (2000), is replete with examples of life in Brazil.

What of the Etruscans? Why refer to Etruscans in this essay on my development as a narrative psychologist? The answer is strange, but revealing about the way in which life stories can make the incoherent cohere. As I was thinking of writing this chapter, I settled upon the idea of using artifacts in my office as guides to the weaving of a story about my development as a narrative psychologist. At about this time, in early spring 2004, I was leafing through the most recent issue of *The American Scholar*. I noticed an article by my former Wesleyan colleague, Annie Dillard. Now reading Annie Dillard virtually guarantees me ample repayment. No matter what she is writing about, she gives off fresh thought in a clear voice. This article was about Etruscan artifacts. Here is the sense I got from it.

The Etruscans are known mostly for and by their bronze relics – little statues of the stylized human form – unstoried, unlettered, unnamed, created by unknown hands in a time that is only known by a range of years (ca.). They are to be found in glass cases in museums and antiquity collections throughout the world, though they were all dug up in what is now modern Italy. These silent relics still speak to us, though their voice is ours, not theirs. Dillard says:

"We forgot where we found them, we keep carrying them about, and we utterly lost their people" (2004, p.62).

I stand in relation to my photograph as a little girl as a modern Italian might stand in relation to an Etruscan bronze statue. An abyss of silence and darkness separates the traced or formed image from the past to a creature whose life pulses in the present. And yet there is an ethereal ribbon of connection, a relevance that is not just arbitrary and made up, but quite believable and real. When I visit Tuscany, I certainly think of those Etruscan statues – ineffable, solid and yet only vaguely storied, yet storied enough to provide value for contemplation. I expect that this is why Freud's collection of antiquities included Etruscan bronzes.

The essential becomes arbitrary

These statues provide a suggestion of how what once was essential can decay into nothingness. Without a story to back them up, objects are quite worthless. Etruscan statues still have enough story about them to make them objects worth having – at least for certain cognoscenti. But I think of another case. In the elegant living room of my in-laws, the Mixters, was a heavy bronze circular object, about six inches in diameter. One side is ornately carved, with representations of animal figures, and an obvious metal loop, to which some sort of ribbon or heavy string might have been attached. The object is perhaps one inch thick, and the other side is completely flat, though the surface is dull and unpolished. When I asked about the object, I was told that it was an ancient Chinese mirror, purchased by some Mixter in 1927. A typed document, dated 1927, was on the letterhead of a dealer in oriental art in Boston. It described the provenance of the object, including the probable date of its creation and its appraised value in 1927 dollars. Dr. and Mrs. Mixter are now deceased. All of their goods have passed to their children, and some to their grandchildren. My son now possesses the object in question, described in the accompanying document as a mirror. But the document is lost. Somewhere, somehow in all of the moving and shuffling of goods, the typed letter has disappeared. I observe, sadly, that the value of the object is thereby severely damaged. Yes, it is possible that an expert in Chinese relics will somehow be able to identify its nature, its provenance, and hence its value. But I do not think that my son is likely to take the trouble to seek out expert opinion. Let us imagine that he passes it on to one of his children, who might think it useful as a paperweight or doorstop. His child, in turn, might utterly discard the object as an old piece of clutter, without any sense of what it was, what it is. History, it turns out, is utterly dead outside of the range of human imagination. The essential becomes arbitrary. Cosmic anabolism is followed by cosmic catabolism. Depend upon it.

Objects once richly imbued with meaning and significance lose their essence with the passing of human imaginations trained upon them. Thus, all of these relics and artifacts in my office are at once precious and just so much junk. From dust we came and to dust we shall return. But in between, what glorious stories are to be told and shared.

The eternal return: A pixilating possibility

But there is no need to end on such a despondent note. Just as decay follows growth, so growth follows decay. As I was musing with a student about these mysteries of self and identity in a tutorial this past semester, an idea emerged between us that seems to me worth conveying. The idea, strange to tell, has to do with the prospect of eternal life – not a topic that psychologists are wont to touch, ever since William James got labeled as a credulous old fool for his musings in this direction.

But suppose that we are to take as established the distinction I have posed between self and identity. It is quite obvious that one's identity continues to exist in a palpable sense after one is dead. There is a tombstone engraved with the name of the deceased.[1] Mine shall carry the legend Karl Edward Scheibe, preserving for posterity the little vote of self that emerged as a minor course correction back in 1947. In my case, I shall leave also a couple of books bearing my name, as well as some reputation among those of my students who remain alive. There are, of course, worldly goods, houses and lands, and artifacts of various kinds, not a bad accumulation of mere stuff for a poor preacher's son, come from the dirt farms of the Midwest. My family and friends shall retain memory of me for a while, and with luck no accidents of discovery will emerge to sully my fair name and serviceable story. Surely my identity will not be much in a couple of hundred years. And eventually, of course, my identity, like the identities of virtually everyone else on the planet, will fade into the background noise. No essence will remain. No story. Nothing.

But what of the self? Earlier, I have proposed that the self dies when the body dies, even as identity continues unanimated. But what if one imagines a self that has no identity – an abstraction, to be sure, and utterly unsupported by a physical body or a narrative of any kind? Suppose we were to posit a law of conservation of selves – so that any self that comes to exist must continue to exist, even though it might have no identity at all, and hence no means of connecting itself, via story, to any previous time, nor of projecting itself, via purpose or plan, to any developing drama. If the self is timeless, it must also be without the means of binding time – and that means is memory. A self without memory might be said to exist, but its existence would be utterly without anxiety about its future, since without a sense of time, there is no future to worry about. I am only in the eternal present, a kind of existential nutshell that simply is what it is.

The reader who has followed me this far is now, perchance, full of exasperation and is already striding forth with car keys in hand. I have indulged my fancy in a way that is both playful and serious. I scarcely know what to think myself of what I have written, except that I enjoy making stories and welcome occasions for doing so.

Note

1   My gravesite is already purchased. And thus I know who my neighbors will be. Mom and Dad are already there – a bit of a joke on them, since they couldn't stay together in life. An anecdote about my mother's grave marker reveals something of the character of my inner self – a self that is prone to error, and yet compulsive. When my mother died, in 1993, I had a marker prepared with her full maiden name, the dates of her death and birth, and the place of her birth, which I initially had cut in stone as Salem, Washington. Alas, my brother, Paul, pointed out to me sometime later that the place of her birth was Quincy, Washington, not Salem. Apparently, I had mistaken the south shore Boston town name for a north shore Boston town name. In fact, there is no Salem, Washington. Discovering this mistake, what was I to do? I thought of just leaving it. But I could not bear the thought of my mistake being recorded as a truth in the narrative of her life, as perhaps it would never be, since very few people will give a care. In the event, I had the old stone dug up and destroyed and had a new one made up with the proper place name now engraved. It cost me upwards of $550. Perhaps the most value I will get for the money is this anecdote. Good grief!

References

Dillard, A. (2004) "Etruscans, losing their edge." *American Scholar 73*, 59–63.

Jung, C.G. (1965) *Memories, Dreams, Reflections*, trans. R. Winston and C. Winston, recorded and ed A. Jaffe. New York: Vintage/Random House.

Kunzendorf, R.G. and Wallace, B. (eds) (1999) *Individual Differences in Conscious Experience*. Amsterdam and Philadelphia: John Benjamin.

Sarbin, T.R. (ed) (1986) *Narrative Psychology: The Storied Nature of Human Conduct*. New York: Praeger.

Scheibe, K.E. (1970) *Beliefs and Values*. New York: Holt, Rinehart and Winston.

Scheibe, K.E. (1979) *Mirrors, Masks, Lies, and Secrets.* New York: Praeger.

Scheibe, K.E. (1995) *Self Studies: The Psychology of Self and Identity.* New York: Praeger.

Scheibe, K.E. (2000) *The Drama of Everyday Life.* Cambridge, MA: Harvard University Press.

CHAPTER 3

Objects, Meanings, and Connections in My Life and Career

David E. Leary

On the wall of my home-office in Richmond, Virginia, are pictures of St. Francis of Assisi, William Shakespeare, Johann Wolfgang von Goethe, and William James. This may seem an odd collection to others. To me, it seems natural and right. Though I didn't plan the collection – each picture having gone up at a separate time – I see now that these four objects represent central meanings and connections in my life. Apparently even a relatively reflective academic can be too busy living his life to spend much time ruminating on the relations that hold it together. Yet I find that these relations are all around me, expressed by objects waiting to be noticed.

On the mantel over my home-office fireplace are pictures of my family. They are the most immediate source of meaning and connection in my life. Without them, I wouldn't be exactly who I am, and I cannot imagine that the difference would be an improvement. If I say little more about my family in what follows, it is only because I have a particular purpose, with a different audience in mind. My wife Marge and my children Emily, Elizabeth, and Matthew know how much they mean to me. Others, knowing that I am sustained by a loving family, can infer much with reasonable accuracy. The same sort of thing may be said with regard to my other relatives, my friends, and my colleagues.

Also in my office are several pictures – a painting and a photograph – of Yosemite. The photograph shows my grandmother on her honeymoon in the early 1900s, standing before the glorious triple cascade of Yosemite Falls. It reminds me that some connections extend across generations. I too honeymooned in Yosemite. It is my favorite place on earth. For me, its well-known objects – Yosemite Falls, El Capitan, Happy Isles, and many others – exude meanings that can only be called spiritual. They point beyond themselves, connecting me to past experiences of awe and wonder and promising me the possibility of future retreat, reflection, and renewal. Without such experiences and possibilities – and without a continuing connection to nature in general, however infrequently I am able to indulge in it – I would be *less* me than I want to be.

My office is naturally full of books, files, papers, and all the other tools of my vocation. It is hard to imagine who I would be without this vocation – the vocation of the "scholar teacher." It is *this* me, who answers to both "scholar" and "teacher" – and, at certain points in the past, to "academic administrator" – that I have been asked to consider in relation to the rest of my life. In thinking about this invitation, I have found it useful to reflect on the meanings that I now connect with those pictures of St. Francis, Shakespeare, Goethe, and James.

St. Francis of Assisi

The fact that I was once named after St. Francis of Assisi – that for a while my name was Francis, or Frank – is something that bears discussion. This temporary name change came about in 1965 when I was inducted into the Franciscan Order at the beginning of novitiate at Mission San Miguel in central California. By then I had been in the Franciscan Seminary for six years, beginning with high school located just behind Mission Santa Barbara, and then extending through the first two years of college at Mission San Luis Rey. I was working my way, year by year, towards priesthood in the Catholic Church. Though I never reached ordination, I remained a Franciscan friar ("brother") for more than two years after my year of novitiate. During those years, I completed college and undertook theological studies at the Franciscan School of Theology in the Graduate Theological Union in Berkeley, California. What all of this reflects – that I was born into a loving and devout Catholic family, that I took religion very seriously, and that I responded to a religious calling – says much about who I am and about my continuing frame of mind, even though I have long since stopped "believing" in the traditional religious sense. Since the early 1970s – primarily as the result of long-term personal development, but secondarily because of my negative reaction to the American Catholic bishops saying, in essence, that the Vietnam War was not an appropriate topic for the Church's moral consideration – I have not gone to church or engaged in any other religious observances, except on rare occasions, generally related to weddings and funerals. Nevertheless, I continue to think of myself as being "spiritual" insofar as questions of meaning and the pursuit of good remain central to my sense of who I am.

This illustrates, I suppose, that anyone raised in an environment that is permeated with a deep belief that everything ultimately makes sense, that order exists in the universe despite apparent chaos, and that whatever is mysterious or troubling can be turned to account, if only by God, is likely to go through the rest of life in search of meaning, even if he or she has come to believe that meaning must be made as much as found. This search, which I have "always" felt to be intimately connected to a person's identity and hence to a person's commitments and orientation, comes even more "naturally," I also suppose, to someone raised within a system of reference that defines what is good to do on Sunday morning and what is bad to do on Friday night.

If One Answer was no longer sufficient to my commitments and orientation, other answers had to be sought. If those answers no longer reflected Divine Knowledge or Will, they had at least to fit within some alternative frame of reference, however idiosyncratic in origin and finite in reach. The amazing thing, in retrospect, is how relatively easy it was for me to shift from a belief in absolutes to the construction of contingent understandings. I am convinced that this more or less smooth transition was facilitated by my preceding study of the Bible and theology from an honest, scholarly, historical perspective. This study not only demystified the notion of God, but it also underscored the role of human agents in representing the supernatural as well as the natural. (My reading of religious mystics during these years – and especially my realization of the role of metaphor in their attempts to describe their ineffable experiences – is relevant here, though it will be discussed later.)

I was also deeply impressed by the spirit of openness displayed by the Vatican Council and the courageous advancements associated with the Ecumenical Movement. At the same time, the Civil Rights Movement and the War Against Poverty did much to help me understand those who came from backgrounds different from mine. My specifically *Franciscan* orientation facilitated a growing respect for, and desire to comprehend, other points of view. Not only love of others, but service to others was and remains a hallmark of the Franciscan way. Even before my year of novitiate, I had devoted a summer to working with the poor on the east side of San José, California; spent time in

Mexico assisting a priest who ministered to the physical as well as religious needs of destitute people; and – inspired by the example of Cesar Chavez – worked with *braceros* in the picking fields and orchards of Santa Clara County. In each case, I learned valuable lessons about the resilience and positive spirit that often typify those who endure dire poverty and discrimination. I also recall another powerful experience, listening one evening to Saul Alinsky organizing a group of citizens to improve conditions for the underprivileged in Pasadena, California. I was seeing life from new perspectives at the same time that I was learning to understand biblical stories and God Himself (or Herself!) from different perspectives. Although I was concerned about the possibility of losing my faith, I sensed that I was somehow *expanding* my faith, getting not less but more in touch with "reality," now seen – like the Bible – as subject to variant interpretations.

Around the same time, while still in college, I came into association with Carl Rogers and the Encounter Group Movement that was just then gathering momentum. Rogers had recently moved to La Jolla, not far from where I then lived (at Mission San Luis Rey). He and his associates were reaching out to religious communities as possible conduits of his insights regarding the optimal functioning of the human self and the positive impact that less guarded experiences – and better communication – could have in the enhancement of individual lives and the development of a better world. For all the simplistic tenets, group pressure, silly aphorisms, and occasional catastrophes associated with the Encounter Group Movement and with the many forms of "sensitivity training" that were then being espoused, Rogers and all that he stood for made a huge difference in my life, not least in convincing me that I could pursue what still mattered to me by switching my goal from the priesthood to counseling or clinical psychology. Being a psychologist (as I intended when I left the seminary at the end of 1968) may seem a very secular calling in relation to the priesthood, but in fact it was not so far removed from the religious roots, concerns, and experiences of my earlier life. It was only later that I learned that Rogers himself had once been in a seminary and that his distinctive psychological orientation grew out of experiences, in 1922, at a World Student Christian Federation's Conference in Peking, China.

By the time I left the seminary, I was in deep sympathy with the Humanistic Psychology Movement, had seen and heard both Abraham Maslow and Rollo May, had witnessed the infamous Fritz Perls swaying on a porch at Esalen, and had decided to earn a master's degree in psychology at San José State University (then still San José State College) to make up for my lack of undergraduate courses in psychology. (I had taken only a few courses in psychology, during consecutive summers at San Diego State and the University of California at Santa Barbara.) What I didn't fully appreciate at the time was the extent to which the education I had received and the educational community I had experienced in my nine and a half years in the seminary (reaching back to the beginning of high school) would prove so relevant to who I became, what I would value, and all that I've done in my later career. For in my seminary-college I had not only majored in philosophy, but had also completed the near-equivalent of second and third majors in history and English. Moreover, since our seminary faculty and student body were small and lived together, faculty and students were in frequent contact and developed a strong sense of community. (No, I was never aware nor was I ever a victim of inappropriate "close contact" during my seminary years.) We students not only prayed and studied together, we also played and worked together. Since then I have understood the power of community as a context for identity, trust, support, and strength of character.

Our faculty were both scholarly and dedicated to their responsibilities and to us. I also had a superb set of classmates, including Joseph Chinnici, who subsequently received his doctorate in history from Oxford, became (and remains) a leading historian of the Catholic Church in the United States, and served for almost a decade as the provincial of the Franciscans in the western United States, and Thomas Coates, who earned his PhD in psychology from Stanford University and is now a leading researcher and practitioner of behavioral medicine, specializing in the prevention of HIV and AIDS. Other classmates have been similarly successful in architecture, city planning, communications, community action, legal affairs, and the like. Though few were eventually ordained – such were the times – I suspect that each of them would say that his life was changed, entirely or mostly for the better, by his experiences in the seminary.

If my seminary years confirmed my interest in service to others, nurtured my inclination to search for meaning, provided a marvelous educational background, and exposed me to the power of community, it also reinforced the lessons my parents had taught me regarding the importance of following the dictates of conscience. Soon after leaving the seminary, I had to consider what to do about my opposition to the Vietnam War. I decided that my opposition compelled me to be a conscientious objector. I was approved for that status, but was never called to serve in that capacity. (My lottery number was among the last to be selected.)

As I look back, I realize that it was remarkable and fortunate to be associated with many of the fundamental challenges that were transforming both

Church and society: the Vatican Council and all it signaled regarding changes in the Catholic Church, the Anti-War and Pro-Peace Movements, the Civil Rights and Anti-Poverty Movements, and the Encounter Group and Humanistic Psychology Movements. Although I haven't previously mentioned it, my life was also energized by my peripheral but nonetheless exciting relation to the revolution that was going on in the realm of music. Though I was no more than a bit player, I helped to usher folk and folk rock music into church settings and enjoyed opportunities to sing with a group of friends in other venues. As a last hurrah – a few years after I left the seminary – we performed in Europe for a month, even singing war protest songs before American troops stationed in Germany. (They were appreciative.) The only major current of the time in which I did not participate was the drug revolution, though I was affected by it as various friends and acquaintances experimented with mind-altering substances.

Reflecting on all of this more than 30 years later, I find that there is much to say in support of the many analogies that have been posed over the millennia regarding the relationship between the macrocosm and microcosm: What was happening in the world at large was clearly reflected in my own little sphere and in my own individual self. The times they were a changin', and so was I.

William Shakespeare

When I put Shakespeare's picture on my home-office wall some years ago, I did so out of respect for him – particularly for what he contributed to world culture – but I realize now, in retrospect, that his picture can also be seen as having more particular significance. If Shakespeare is the apotheosis of literature in general, his picture bears witness to the overall importance of literature in my life and career.

When I was fairly young I loved to read. In grade school and high school I read all that I could, and in college I had a charismatic teacher, Ben McCormick, who inspired me to appreciate the insights and beauty of literature. By the end of my college years, as mentioned, I had earned the virtual equivalent of a degree in literature, and to this day, I look forward to those moments when I can *lose myself* in literature – whether poetry, drama, or novels – so that the vicarious experiences conveyed by literature can enrich the quotidian understandings and the very life that literature helps me to escape. Go figure. What, after all, do I really care about the 19th-century British navy? Yet in reading Patrick O'Brian's wonderful Aubrey-Maturin novels I've learned not only about life in the 19th century, but also about the operations of human character, both in myself and in others. Literature isn't simply about learning what you could have picked up in a history book or a psychology article; it's about experiencing things in ways that cannot be reduced to conventional formulations. Literature may be composed of words, but those words convey meanings and connections that transcend referential stipulations. All experience exceeds immediate and full comprehension, but literary experience does it – or at least can do it – in particularly concentrated and powerful ways.

None of this was in the forefront of my mind when I started studying psychology at San José State in the fall of 1969, yet as I look back it seems reasonable to connect my early unease with certain aspects of psychology to the sensitivities that had been fostered through my engagement with literature and with my experiential understanding of the processes involved in its production and interpretation. (My study of biblical literature and of the hermeneutic tradition was relevant here as well.) Before long, I had concluded that contemporary psychology was doing a poor job of characterizing the creative and expressive powers of the human mind. It was offering a reductive vision of the mind, which made the actuality of literature and the understandings that come from it all but incomprehensible. The computer-driven analogs of then emerging cognitive psychology served only to illustrate the foresightedness of Jonathan Swift's satirical treatment of naive theories of the mechanical generation of concepts and texts. The picture of the mind that was offered by psychology was pale and thin compared to the richness and complexity of the human imagination, as I had experienced it as a lover and student of literature.

Largely for this reason, I did my master's thesis on the human imagination. This thesis changed the course of my life and career. Most importantly, the call for "subjects" for this study attracted the woman who eventually became my wife – the former Marjorie Bates. Marge responded to my advertisement because she found the topic of interest. (She scored among the highest on several indices of imaginative capability.) Marge and I were married a little more than a year later in June 1972. After more than three decades of marriage, I have no reason to regret the topic of my thesis. Such happiness and success as I have had are due in large part to the support and encouragement that she has given to me. Beyond that, Marge was the unwitting reason – in Aristotelian terms, the "efficient cause" – of my shift from counseling or clinical psychology to the history and philosophy of psychology. Before I discuss that shift, I want to make one other comment about the motivation of my master's thesis.

While I was at San José State, the war in Vietnam – and public debate about it – had been heating up, as had similar events and controversies regarding civil rights and other issues pertaining to human welfare and social justice. It was a very confusing time in which being a "good guy" or a "bad guy" – or, more importantly, being "right" or "wrong" – was a matter of perception, which shifted frequently. (I recall, for instance, having to walk through a gauntlet of angrily chanting student protesters in order to get to class one day – thus seeming to be a supporter of the war – when in fact, on the previous day, I had myself sung at a major anti-war rally. Boycotting classes simply wasn't *my* way of showing concern about the war, though I understood and accepted that it was *their* way.) My interest in the imagination, however much it was based on sensitivities fostered by literature, was also based on my concerns about "Where do we go from here? How will we be able to move beyond the outrage and animosity generated by the war and by other ongoing social conflicts?" In this context, I was inspired by William F. Lynch's insightful little book on *Images of Hope: Imagination as Healer of the Hopeless* (1965). Thus, my research, as far removed as it must have seemed from the realities of current events, was motivated in part by them. I mention this too as background for my then growing incredulity about then current views of science as "value free." Not only did I doubt that science was ever completely value free, but I also felt strongly that it *shouldn't* be. The best protection against undue bias is not pretense of unattainable neutrality, but rather an upfront admission of what values and concerns have motivated a particular study (why was the topic chosen? what long-term consequence was hoped for? and so on). My experience at this time prepared me to be open to the newer, more historically based philosophy of science that I would encounter during and after my time at the University of Chicago.

Now, what about my change of interest from applied psychology to the history and philosophy of psychology? Because Marge was wrapping up her education at San José State at the time of our marriage, we needed to stay in the area for another year or two before I could head off, as then expected, to a doctoral program in counseling or clinical psychology. Fortuitously, as we considered our short-term options, I received a call from the Franciscan School of Theology, asking if (master's degree in hand) I would be interested in serving as a Visiting Assistant Professor of Psychology and Religion and teaching courses on psychology and religion as well as on personality. Had Marge already completed her studies at San José State, I would have said no to this invitation and in all probability would have gone on to a satisfying career as a counseling or clinical psychologist. (I was already doing some counseling on the side, had received positive feedback, and had found this work to be very gratifying.) Since Marge wasn't finished with her degree, I said yes and embarked on the teaching aspect of my career.

As has often happened since that time, it was students who then set me straight. Because of my background in philosophy and history as well as literature, I naturally – unthinkingly, really – organized my courses to provide the requisite philosophical and historical contexts for thoughtful consideration of the nature and functioning of personality as well as the relations between religion and psychology. The students pointed out how unusual my approach was and told me that they found it both enlightening and useful. Thus, during that year, besides coming to realize that I enjoyed teaching, which would not have been a significant part of a career in counseling or clinical psychology, I became aware of the need for at least some persons associated with psychology to elucidate the discipline's historical and philosophical foundations; I learned that I enjoyed the kind of research involved in doing so; and I discovered that – through no foresight of my own – I was reasonably prepared to do so. I should also admit that, as much as I enjoyed counseling and took satisfaction in helping others, I had a gnawing concern about the long-term effects of a career in this area: Could I stay fresh and effective after dealing with some of the same problems over and over?

Hence, I started thinking about applying to graduate programs in the history of science, with the idea of focusing on the history of psychology and giving attention, as appropriate, to philosophical issues. I took a broad view of the matter, however, seeing the history of psychology as a subset of the larger story of how humans have understood themselves and their world. The implicit questions I asked as I thought about this topic – which I defined as "the history of consciousness" – were: "Under what conditions did people stop turning as much to custom, myth, religion, philosophy, or even literature in order to understand themselves?" and "When and why did they begin asking psychologists to help them decide who they were, how to live, and what their futures held?" My later research on the connections between religion and psychology, philosophy and psychology, and most recently literature and psychology has reflected these initial questions as well as my multidisciplinary educational background. My research on metaphorical thinking also stems ultimately from those original questions about the history of consciousness, even though the connections have not always been obvious.

Marge and I ended up going to the University of Chicago, for which I will always be grateful. When we arrived there in August, 1974, we were welcomed into an extraordinary intellectual community, and we formed lasting relationships with teachers like George Stocking, the well-known historian of anthropology, and Stephen Toulmin, the noted philosopher. I was fortunate to work with Leonard Krieger and Keith Baker in history and with Sal Maddi and Norman Bradburn in psychology, and I had Robert Richards (now a full professor with multiple appointments at the University of Chicago) as a fellow student who shared my interest in the history of psychology and related fields. One of my fondest memories of Chicago is of a seminar on the history of psychology that was planned and directed by Bob and me, for which we received graduate credit. The other "students" in the seminar were the three faculty members who had approved this unusual arrangement. I suspect that this could have happened only at Chicago. Enjoying colleagues and opportunities like these, while also having access to a world-class library, was more than I could have asked.

I was profiting so much from my studies that I was almost disappointed to learn, midway through my second year, that there was a faculty opening in the History and Theory of Psychology Graduate Program in the Department of Psychology at the University of New Hampshire. The position was so perfect and the job market so tight that I applied for and then accepted the position, when it was offered, with the proviso that I be allowed to start a semester later than advertised. The reason for this condition was simple: I had not yet proposed, much less defended, my dissertation. During my interview I had never claimed to have started my dissertation; my future colleagues had simply assumed that the research I presented was from my dissertation. (In fact, I had expected the seminar project that I presented to evolve into the first chapter of my dissertation.) In the event, it *became* my dissertation, and since most (other) dissertation proposals are far too grandiose, I was once again fortunate that "reality" changed my plans in a way that served me well. After eight months of intense work, I was told that my dissertation, which focused on the historical influence of Immanuel Kant on the development of scientific psychology, had been completed in record time and had been accorded special honors. Soon thereafter, in early January, 1977, Marge and I were traversing a very snowy and icy landscape, as we drove to New Hampshire in the aftermath of the huge blizzard of 1976.

Johann Wolfgang von Goethe

I have admired Goethe for many years. He was not only a great writer, he was a scholar, a scientist, and a statesman, and in each arena he contributed something of value. Even in old age, he refused to stand on past laurels; he always *lived forward*. He moved beyond past triumphs and even changed fields of endeavor when he felt that life demanded it. I'd like to think that my own life and career have reflected, to some small degree, the same willingness and ability to handle multiple responsibilities, to assume new challenges, and to move on when the time comes. I have tried to contribute as much as possible as teacher, scholar, colleague, and administrator. Although these various roles have been intricately related, time spent on any one of them has necessarily meant time not spent on others. Like every other academic, I have had to set priorities and make choices.

My first priority has always been teaching, which is to say, my primary concerns have revolved around my students, their learning, and their development. That doesn't mean that I haven't enjoyed research, deeply, for its own sake. Far from it. But I have always felt that one of the important reasons for engaging in research is that it helps assure that I deserve the privilege of teaching and that I have the best possible things to say, both in the classroom and through presentations and publications. My endeavors as colleague and administrator have similarly revolved around my fundamental desire to contribute to the learning and development of others. Indeed, the first challenge I assumed upon arriving at the University of New Hampshire was to create and offer meaningful courses. At the undergraduate level, besides several courses in the history of psychology, I was asked to teach Introduction to Psychology, the Psychology of Personality, Abnormal Psychology, and several other topics. I also participated in the development of interdisciplinary courses and programs, including an undergraduate Humanities Program, offering courses that typically drew upon psychology, history, philosophy, and literature, and sometimes theology, in order to address fundamental issues faced by the self and society. At the graduate level, where students could earn a PhD in psychology with a specialty in the history and theory of psychology, I taught an open-ended series of seminars ranging from historiography and the philosophy of psychology to different problem areas in the history of psychology.

Having to develop and teach undergraduate and graduate courses, sometimes very broad in coverage and sometimes very narrow, advanced my own education. The same thing can be said about the master's and doctoral committees on which I served, both inside and outside the Department of Psychology. And I was blessed from the beginning with my own graduate students, from whom I learned much and whose teaching and research were frequently inspiring. Few satisfactions in academic life have matched the pleasure of having former graduate students produce courses or research that I would have loved to call my own.

By the time I left UNH in 1989, my academic title – Professor of Psychology, History, and the Humanities – reflected the variety of my teaching interests and commitments over the preceding 12 years. Most of my teaching, however, was in psychology, and it went well enough that no one seemed to care (or even remember) that my PhD was in history, with a specialty in the history and philosophy of psychology, rather than in psychology proper. From the time I arrived at UNH, I have considered myself a psychologist who happens to use historical and philosophical methodologies in order to assess critically the nature, history, prospects, and means of understanding of the human self (psychology being one of those means). These ultimate concerns have been clearer in the teaching that I've done since my return to regular faculty status at the University of Richmond – in courses on Selfhood in particular, but also in courses on Religion and Psychology, Psychology in American Society and Culture, and Exploring Human Experience. But it was hopefully apparent, also, to perceptive students in my courses at UNH. In any case, although I see myself as a psychologist interested ultimately in how the human self comprehends and makes its way through the world and through a life that is framed by historical contingencies, I have been fortunate to be seen, also, as an historian and philosopher. This has created multiple audiences for my research and provided occasions for useful feedback. Membership in various communities of scholars has sustained me as it has sustained so many others.

In the early years of my career I published several articles and a couple of chapters based upon my dissertation, but I was anxious to move on to other projects. Once again good fortune struck. In the fall of 1977, as chair of my department's Colloquium Committee, I arranged for Sigmund Koch, an eminent psychologist who was also a distinguished philosopher, historian, and critic of the discipline, to come to UNH. He and I hit it off particularly well, and this led to his subsequent request that I serve with him as co-organizer of a scholarly program that would provide a retrospective assessment of scientific psychology on the occasion of its 1979 centennial (as dated from the founding of Wilhelm Wundt's laboratory in Leipzig, Germany). Fortunately, I accepted. It was a lot of work for a young assistant professor to take on, but the 60-hour program that resulted, offered as part of the 1979 annual convention of the American Psychological Association, was eventually revised and published as *A Century of Psychology as Science* (Koch and Leary, [1985] 1992). This 42-chapter book not only received the Association of American Publishers

Award for "the most outstanding scholarly and professional book in 1985 on the social and behavioral sciences," it was reissued by the APA in 1992, with a new Afterword and Postscript, as one of a small number of specially designated "centennial publications" commemorating APA's 100th anniversary. It remains an important historical marker of the discipline's history.

I mention this program and book partly because they helped to establish my reputation as an historian of psychology, but also because they illustrate a powerful lesson that I try to pass on to my students: Fulfill your primary responsibilities as best you can, but also stay vigilant for unexpected opportunities. Seize those opportunities when they arise, and make the most of them. Fortune seems to favor those who are prepared for it, wittingly or not.

My work with Koch, plus my own independent research, resulted in an invitation to be a fellow at the Center for Advanced Study in the Behavioral Sciences in Stanford, California. Accepting this invitation allowed Marge and me to spend a wonderful sabbatical year near our extended families and old friends. We arrived in California in July, 1982, with two children in tow; a third child was on his way when we headed back to New Hampshire in August, 1983. During that year I learned a great deal from the other fellows and moved from somewhat casual to serious research on the role of metaphor and rhetoric in psychology. I also organized a very successful fellows seminar on the nature and function of metaphor, and I began soliciting research by others, which eventually led to an edited volume on *Metaphors in the History of Psychology* (1990).

All of this organizational and editorial work, like the work I had been doing at UNH as co-director of the History and Theory of Psychology Program, demonstrated my ability and inclination to assume leadership roles, both as a scholar and teacher. My experiences in almost every one of these roles had been personally gratifying, especially to the extent that they ended up stimulating the learning of others. Hence, it was a natural step for me to become chairperson of the Department of Psychology several years after I returned to UNH – the year before I became a full professor in 1988. As I had done in committees with colleagues and in other administrative roles, I tried as department chairperson to do all I could to make a positive difference. I was successful enough in facilitating the teaching and research of my colleagues, and in overseeing the enhancement of curricula and facilities, that my attention was drawn in the spring of 1989 to an advertisement for the deanship at the University of Richmond. Being a dean had not been an objective while I served as chairperson, just as being a chairperson had not been an objective while serving as a faculty member, but it followed, almost logically, from the enjoyment and satisfaction of doing what I could do, at each previous stage, to improve the quality of life and work within the environment that constituted my academic home.

Many faculty do not understand why a more or less successful colleague would agree, much less want, to be a chairperson or dean. However, as a faculty member, I could only teach so many students and could only do so much research. But as a chairperson or dean I could facilitate the teaching and research of 17 – or 200 – other colleagues, and through them have an impact, however indirect, upon the satisfaction, productivity, learning, and growth of many more individuals. Even now, happy as I am to be fully re-engaged in teaching and research, this rationale makes good sense to me. I take pride in having done all that I could, as dean, to enhance a particular academic institution during a period of significant change, and I am particularly happy to have fostered a sense of community – of common endeavor and achievement – among more or less like-minded and like-committed individuals.

Besides serving as Dean of Arts and Sciences at the University of Richmond for 13 years, from 1989 to 2002, I have contributed leadership to various professional organizations (e.g., as president of APA's division of the History of Psychology, as president of its division of Theoretical and Philosophical Psychology, and as chairperson of the American Conference of Academic Deans). But since the fall of 2002, following a sabbatical in my final year as dean, I have enjoyed the opportunity to approach both teaching and research from fresh perspectives. As a University Professor at the University of Richmond, I have designed and taught new courses, several of which are co-listed by multiple departments, and I have initiated an exciting new line of research. Entering the final decade of my career, I can think of nothing I would rather do than enjoy the rights, privileges, and responsibilities of a faculty member.

William James

If St. Francis epitomizes the influence of religion in my life, and Shakespeare suggests the relevance of literature to my career, and Goethe symbolizes the multiple commitments reflected in my professional activities, then William James expresses the tone and trajectory of my intellectual life. I have yet to encounter another historical figure who so completely represents the intellectual virtues and methodological values that I espouse: James was earnest, honest, and open-minded; he sought the truth without needing to believe – or pretending to believe – that he would ever completely possess it.

He respected the experiences of every human being and criticized those who were blind to the dignity and worth of other individuals. And when it came to his own academic work, he was not only among the first pioneers of the "new psychology" that evolved into the psychology of today, but he also helped to initiate a philosophical orientation that maintains its vitality and relevance right up to our own time, both within the discipline of philosophy and across a range of other disciplines, psychology included. Finally, with regard to the basic concerns of this chapter, James wrote insightfully about the intimate relations between person and perspective, between temperament and cognition, between – in effect – life and career; and his treatment of the human self still commands attention, more than 100 years after its classic expression in *The Principles of Psychology* ([1890] 1981).

I feel no embarrassment in noting that more than one-third of my publications have dealt with James in one way or another and that more than ten per cent have focused primarily on him and his work. I am proud to be associated with James in this way and to affirm my allegiance to what he stood for, including his openness to the value of religion despite the fact that he himself was not a "believer" and could not claim to have had a religious experience. Indeed, my current research – on the impact of literature on James's life and work – draws upon and in many ways culminates much of my previous scholarly work, including my research on the role of metaphor and rhetoric in the history of psychology. (In light of the way I have organized this chapter, it might be interesting for me to note that among the things I've been studying is the influence of Shakespeare and Goethe on James and his work. It turns out that their influence was substantial. As for my other organizational figure, James read a number of works about St. Francis and considered him to be a primary example of religious healthy-mindedness. So these four figures are connected after all – and not just in my mind and on my office wall.)

Though I admire much of what James wrote, I hasten to add that my own views on the self emerged, as James himself would have wished, from my own experiences as well as from observations of the apparent experiences and actions of others, reinforced by a wide range of reading and rumination. From early on, as noted above, I wanted to understand the self. When I first encountered James's thought (as when I previously encountered Carl Rogers's experience-based views on the self), I had a strong feeling of having found someone who had a genius for expressing *my* incipient insights. I was particularly struck by James's ability to discuss complex matters in a straightforward yet subtle and supple manner, using fresh metaphors and apt examples to give form to things unknown (as Shakespeare described the creative process).

James's use of metaphor was particularly attractive to me. I felt drawn to it and to him, based partly (no doubt) on my own previous realization that metaphor is our means of first and last resort. Earlier I mentioned my reading of the writings of religious mystics. What had struck me was the number of times mystics said, in essence, that "my experience is ineffable, it exceeds anything that I can possibly say, it is beyond all words, *but if I must say something about it...*," and then went on to speak of their experiences, necessarily, in metaphorical terms. The best they could do was to say their experiences were *like* this and *like* that. They had to compare their unique experiences to experiences that people shared in common. Even back then, I had a sense that mystical experience could be seen as a metaphor for *all* experience. Every experience, if attended to closely enough, is one of a kind; but if we wish to convey its essence to others, we have to express it through words, images, or some other form of representation with which they are familiar.

What attracted me to James was the fact that his thought stays so close to the descriptive, empirical level, without ascending, too precipitously and arrogantly, into an abstract and formalized theory that claims both too much and too little. Instead of refined and polished theory, James's thought typically conveys a compelling theoretical perspective – an angle of vision that highlights certain aspects of whatever he is describing and that often continues to influence one's understanding long after its provenance has been forgotten. In an age in which the scholarly work of too many academics could be subsumed under the slogan "Have Theory, Will Travel," I have been deeply impressed by James's more modest, but ultimately (to me) more truthful approach. As I was learning independently through my study of the philosophy of science, the distance between fact and theory has often been excessive. And even when a constitutive relationship exists, theory has too often been wagging the facts rather than facts constraining theory.

As one of my teachers, Stephen Toulmin, has put it: One should strive to be "reasonable" even if one doesn't believe that Reason is the one and only means of making sense of experience, and one can be "truthful" even if one is not persuaded that Truth can be attained once and for all. James was a proponent of this tempered approach, and he was an exemplar of an admirable combination of traits: He always strove to reach beyond what was known and thought, yet he never assumed that the point from which he reached at any given time would be the point from which he or others would reach on another occasion. James realized that today's best angle of vision might not be tomorrow's. The stream of experience may be similar from one time to another, but it will also be different. And the same can be said of the self, which after all may be understood as the point of relative sameness within our ongoing experience.

"Relative sameness" suggests a significant shift, for me as for many others, from an earlier, more or less static view of the self (as an abstracted, universalized, resolutely identical "I" that functioned essentially as a secular surrogate for the religious "soul") to a much more organic view of the self as developing over time – a view that provides a much better representation of my own experiences as an historically situated and changing "me."

Although James had long since given a finely nuanced phenomenology of the historically embedded self, the psychological literature was not yet "back up to date" when I first started teaching courses on the psychology of personality. With the passage of time, however, a pertinent literature – based increasingly on empirical research as well as conceptual insights drawn from philosophy, anthropology, literary and cultural studies – has emerged. In my recent offerings of a course on Selfhood, I have used a wide range of readings, including George Lakoff and Mark Johnson's *Metaphors We Live By* (1980) and Dan McAdams's *The Stories We Live By* (1993). I want my students to understand how we come to terms with our experience through metaphor and how we understand ourselves through stories. I offer them a picture of the self that is more like a movie than a snapshot, a self that is dynamic and changing, yet has detectable structure and continuity, as I've tried to convey regarding my own self in this chapter. Along with others, I've found that this structure and continuity are described more readily through the metaphor and practice of narrative than through the more traditional metaphor of portraiture. Unlike a static portrait, the self – at least as I experience it and James and others have described it – is open-ended and subject to revision, as later experience casts new light on former experience.

James was among the first to be aware that individuals can and do have multiple stories to tell about themselves. Given the constraints to which we are subject, both as embodied individuals and linguistic storytellers, most of the self-narratives that people tell are variants or subplots of their more or less coherent master plot. In some cases, these stories are so different that the tellers may be said to have multiple selves, sometimes including "hidden selves," as James called them. James was open to all sorts of possibilities, even of a sort so radical that John Dewey spoke later of "the vanishing self" in James's psychology. However, on my own experiential grounds, I have categorized James's thoughts in this regard as peripheral to my considerations on the self (as indeed they were to his own). In fact, on the basis of particularly powerful experiences, I have drawn a line short of the kind of ultra-constructionist views that make the self *only* a fiction created by time and circumstance. The struggle to express my experience has at times been quite tangible, involving a clear sense of a gap between experience and expression. That is, I am sometimes aware that the best words I can find are inadequate to a full mapping of the exact contours of my experience. At those moments, I have no doubt that it is language – the particular word, metaphor, or story I am using – that falls short, is not quite right, and that my experience is a reality more basic than language, as shown by the fact that it resists the pull of inadequate words. How else am I to explain, for instance, the insistent conviction that: "That isn't exactly what I want to say," or "That doesn't capture how I think or feel," or "That isn't precisely what I mean"? Experience, in other words, rather than language or any other representational system, is the rock bottom upon which I base my view of the self and my knowledge of the world. We are not simply products of some kind of linguistic or paralinguistic game that we play with others, or that "culture" plays through us, as some theorists have suggested.

Who am "I"? I am a person who is trying to do his best to live in a way that enhances my existence and that of others, and who strives to make sense of my experience of life, world, and self, often in relation to other objects in my environment, to the persons and things that give me meaning, and to the varied connections that I have established and that have helped to establish me. As I come full circle now in my reflections on the objects, meanings, and connections in my life and career, I am reminded again of the important relation between the individual and the community, which I have noted several times in this chapter. Community is important to the individual, not because the self is determined by community, but because the self's experiences and expressions are significantly enhanced or limited by the kind of community in which it exists. And this enhancement or limitation works in both directions. As James once wrote: "The community stagnates without the impulse of the individual." And as he hastened to add: "The impulse dies away without the sympathy of the community." I am fortunate to have my own interests and inclinations encouraged and rewarded by my family, friends, and scholarly communities of which I have been a member.

Conclusion

As I think back on what I have written and note aspects of my life that barely appear in this chapter, or do not appear at all, I realize that in my home-office, too, is a plaque commemorating my selection as the Best Little League Player in Burbank, California, in 1957; a photograph showing me standing at the beach, surfboard under arm, in 1968; a guitar offering silent testimony to my short but exciting career as a semi-professional musician in the late 1960s and early 1970s; a child-made ceramic sign pronouncing me "Dad" in very bright colors, from the mid-1980s; cards from my wife containing messages that sustained my efforts when my energy lagged; and a stack of annual calendars containing hundreds and hundreds of notations about dinners, movies, trips, and other engagements that have invigorated the course of my life and career. If I were to walk into other rooms of my home, additional objects would call out meanings and connections that have not been articulated in this narrative sketch. But I'm not about to complain that my life has been richer than I have been able to express in these few pages.

References

James, W. [1890] (1983) *The Principles of Psychology*, ed F. Burkhardt, 2 vols. Cambridge, MA: Harvard University Press. (Original work published 1890.)

Koch, S. and Leary, D.E. (eds) [1985] (1992) *A Century of Psychology as Science*, 2nd ed, rev. Washington, DC: American Psychological Association. (Original work published 1985.)

Lakoff, G. and Johnson, M. (1980) *Metaphors We Live By*. Chicago: University of Chicago Press.

Leary, D.E. (ed) (1990) *Metaphors in the History of Psychology*. New York: Cambridge University Press.

Lynch, W.F. (1965) *Images of Hope: Imagination as Healer of the Hopeless*. Baltimore, MD: Helicon.

McAdams, D.P. (1993) *The Stories We Live By: Personal Myths and the Makings of the Self*. New York: Guilford.

CHAPTER 4

From Poppies to Ferns: The Discursive Production of a Life

Gerald Monk

Introduction

I demonstrate more than a touch of pompousness by agreeing to write a chapter about myself. It is an indulgent undertaking to write about one's evolving social self (or selves, which I will explain later). In New Zealand, there is a metaphorical phenomenon called "The Tall Poppy Syndrome": the act of standing out and drawing attention to yourself. The stem of a tall poppy is very exposed and easily broken and cut to size. In New Zealand, even feigned self-deprecation is better than the proposition of standing as a taller poppy in a field of shorter poppies. Safety and survival come from not placing oneself higher than others. Thus, writing about oneself has numerous risks from the place that I come from. To some extent, the problem with the privileged "I" comes from New Zealand's roots in certain egalitarian practices. The Maoris have another metaphor that promotes a self-effacing, non-attention-getting demeanor: "The kumara (sweet potato) does not speak of its own sweetness." Emphasis is on valuing, defining and acknowledging the group's voice rather than placing value on the individual voice.

You as audience

As I reflect on writing this chapter, I consciously pay attention to you the audience. What do you want out of these pages that makes this undertaking worthwhile for you? I am mindful of shaping this text around you, my imagined audience. The point here is that this text is produced and reproduced within the context of an audience – both real and imagined. Suppose I imagine you to be an academic. If so, I pay attention to realms of scholarly thought, dressed in a genre that is fitting for the task. Captured by these assumptions – erroneous or not – I mold these narratives into a style and composition that I fantasize is pleasing to my audience and editors. Alternatively, if I think you want to be entertained and not overloaded with turgid reflection, these machinations direct the kind of text I lay before you. This is much more complicated than my arranging and rearranging of text. It is you, the reader, with implicit meanings and varying perspectives brought to this text which consigns this process to a degree of ambiguity and indeterminancy. J. Bruner (1986) mused that the relative indeterminancy of any text allows for a spectrum of possibilities that will be formulated. This text initiates a range of performances of meaning rather than the text itself formulating meaning.

"From where" rather than "I am"

I come from Aotearoa (the Land of the Long White Cloud). This is significant to me. I am drawn to the alternative story about the nation within which I was born. Aotearoa was discovered around 800CE by the legendary Polynesian explorer, Kupe, who journeyed from Hawaiki Nui, Hawaiki Roa, Hawaiki Pamamao. Aotearoa was inhabited by Maori for 1000 years before Europeans set foot in the country. I didn't learn this in elementary school. I learned instead that the real name for the country was New Zealand, which was discovered by the Dutch Explorer, Abel Tasman, in 1642. Multiple narratives describe this nation and their inhabitants just as multiple narratives give an account of who I am. The contexts within which I speak, perform, and live will shape the stories that become privileged and are enacted in the foreground.

I pay attention to where I come from, a tradition that I value in Maori culture. Maori, in Aotearoa, typically ask "Where are you from?" and "Who are your people?" before you are asked "What do you do?" I identify with the indigenous people from Aotearoa/New Zealand more when I am not in the country than when I am living there. When in New Zealand, I am Pakeha, the Other (from an indigenous perspective). When I am in the United States, I am the Other as the New Zealander or Kiwi. A Euro-American context affords me the option of embracing a Maori association not afforded me in the country in which I was born.

Whenever I open my mouth in the United States, I am immediately reminded that I am from somewhere else: "Oh, where are you from?" "That's an unusual accent." "You're not from here. Are you Australian?" The *where*, the *when*, with *whom* become central to the narrative constructions that tumble into and out of my life. I will elaborate later on what I see as the value of considering the relationship between self-identities and the contexts from which they arise.

Despite the discomfort created by egalitarian and communal influences that were somewhat prominent in shaping me as I grew up in Aotearoa/New Zealand, I embrace them right now. They throw me in the direction of the social and the cultural. They provide a context from which I can introduce a text that is co-constructed. This reflex to move to the social and the cultural comes from a number of years of attempting to escape from the pervasive cultural legacy of liberal-humanism that was instilled in me in my early training.

The prominence of liberal humanism

I am particularly proud of my first experience of a tertiary education, where I trained as a teacher in the early 1970s. I gained my bachelor's degree at Massey University, majoring in geography at a historically agricultural institution, in Palmerston North, New Zealand. While I was captured by many distracting events of early adulthood, I can also identify the pedagogies in my training that were dominated by liberal-humanistic principles in education and psychology. While I was exposed to the works of critical theorists and neo-Marxists, such as Adorno, Alinsky, Gramsci, Freire, and Horkheimer, the assumptions underpinning liberal humanism were infused into all aspects of the curriculum. In the field of psychology, liberal-humanist discourse privileges the quest for self-actualization, independence, autonomy and mastery. The conception of the humanist self in psychology is eloquently described by Geertz (1979) as a "bounded, unique, more or less integrated motivational and cognitive universe, a dynamic center of awareness, emotion and judgment, and action, organized into a distinctive whole and set contrastively against other such wholes" (p.229).

This singular unique self becomes the central core of any inquiry constructed on the notion that humans are rational, unitary beings who are fundamentally separate from the historical and social world (Davies, 1993). Development and advancement are primarily hinged upon an individual's choosing. This focus is favored over the recognition of external influences born within the socio-cultural and socio-historical milieu which impact upon human volition and action. It was with this mindset that I entered the University of Otago, completing my training there in 1985 as an educational psychologist. This training was dominated by the theory and application of cognitive-behavioral psychology with its very clear origins in the empirical traditions of modernism. Despite the significant thrust of an empirically driven, scientist-practitioner orientation (Hayes, Barlow, and Nelson-Gray, 1999), I was immersed in my field experiences with supervisors working from humanist foundations.

Old discourses hang around

Even after many years, I feel I must address how liberal humanism continues to act as a discursive net that gets cast over me in all kinds of professional and personal ways. I resist and challenge this entrapment every step along the way. Humanistic discourses are so pervasive and captivating that they do, without my even being aware of them, occupy cultural spaces in my day-to-day interactions in ways that I preferred they did not.

The discourses of humanism continue to circulate in my day-to-day interactions, attempting to frame how my life is understood, evaluated and reflected upon. Such discourses emphasize the individual attributes of self-determination and material success that have dominated the cultural landscape through which the Western self is understood. The emphasis on the unitary nature of human functioning draws a tight boundary around the nature of the self and its possibilities. Such an emphasis also creates a context that invites thinking patterns that become dependent on measures such as goodness, badness and appropriateness.

Personality and humanism

In the West, we are taught that we all have different personalities based upon certain internal predispositions which become actualized when young and then these characteristics or dispositions provide us with a unified, stable sense of who we are throughout our lives. We tend to accept that personality structure stays with us until there is a physiological breakdown of our bodies, such as a stroke or something similar. Since personality has such a central place in understanding ourselves, it is hard to believe that the concept of personality is only a modern-day psychological invention. Of course, personality can only be inferred. However, when we act in certain ways, we can hold our personality responsible. One would expect to find that all cultures embrace the notion that we have a personality. Many cultural communities around the globe, even at the beginning of the turn of the 21st century, have an alternative view to the notion of a pre-fixed psychological structure that shapes the way people behave. Some indigenous cultures and religious communities in the West account for their actions through the clash of good and evil spirits or demons. We, however, come to accept global descriptions of people and their personalities. We see qualities such as competitiveness, greed, caring and love as descriptors of a kind of person rather than the type of action engaged in.

The Western construction of personality can be viewed as pessimistic. Some developmental theorists have proposed that once a person has reached a certain age, his/her personality is set. This viewpoint inadvertently leads to blaming others for whatever predicament they find themselves in, since, as individuals living in their own cognitive universe, they are completely responsible for their circumstances. As a humanist psychologist in the early days, it was easy for me to blame others for their failure to respond to my creative interventions. While I teach the importance of considering the socio-cultural, socio-political and socio-historical influences in shaping human distress, I continue to be surprised how I keep slipping into individualistic, negative and totalizing descriptions to depict students, peers, clients, and others who I struggle with or are challenged by so as to somehow feel personally less ineffective or inadequate. The prominence and dominance of Western culture tugs at me even while I want to diminish its potency in shaping how I live my life and how I understand myself to be.

A regime of truth

The monolithic conception of the humanist self (with cultural representations matching majority white and male culture) plays a dominant role in Western schools of thought and is accepted as a fundamental truth on which psychology is founded. Foucault gives an account of how these dominating discourses shape what we hold as truth, writing:

> Each society has its regime of truth, its general politics of truth: that is, the types of discourse which it accepts and makes function as true; the mechanisms and instances which enable one to distinguish true and false statements; the means by which each is sanctioned; the techniques and procedures accorded value in the acquisition of truth; the status of those who are charged with saying what counts as true. (Foucault, 1989, p.131)

I lay this material before you because regimes of truth are so captivating of what is accepted and acceptable. Like critical theorist Giroux (1992), I reject the humanist assumption that the individual is both the source of all human interaction and the most important unit of social analysis. I say this while recognizing that every move I make toward rejecting humanist assumptions is done through the discursive lens through which Western life, including my own, gets scrutinized. That I am using "I" is an illustration of the potency of Western thought that assumes the "I" is a unique, stable, coherent, independent meaning maker and purveyor of life. I have witnessed and experienced the limitations and implicit arrogance that accompanies liberal humanism in therapeutic practice and with my dealings with people in my community. I was coached through my early professional career by my clients who didn't share the Eurocentric world that I struggled against.

White, able, heterosexual and male

It is a small leap from liberal humanism to Eurocentrism. Eurocentrism embodies an individualistic analysis. Its standard of normalcy is based upon middle-class, white, heterosexual, able-bodied men – a description that not surprisingly matches my own heritage. My male gender and white skin pigment and other obvious phenotypical characteristics match the identities of bodies that are favored in many social contexts; there are powerful cultural forces inviting me to maintain the privileges of the status quo. I acknowledge the enormous effort required to create a preferred sense of self in the face of the bombardment of individualism and self-aggrandizement within the cultural and political media of Western life.

Processes that redescribe

It is a struggle to avoid the embrace of a Eurocentric position and the autonomous voice that stands in stark contrast to the collective voices of communality. Yet, what is helpful is to recall and be reminded of those galvanizing, searing moments where what I assumed to be the truth of a position, the truth about the nature of life, about who I am, was shaken so violently that I could never reoccupy that earlier imagination. Such disorienting moments take place when I have assumed that my audience, fellow colleagues, students, clients, and family share the same assumptions about the nature of the problem and the nature of the solution. These moments are often conflictual and painful and embolden me to explore alternative possibilities about how I want to conduct my personal and professional life. A memorable example occurred early in my practice as a psychologist when I returned to my own town to work as an educational psychologist. I made suggestions to a Maori elder about how "we" could introduce a wrap-around sexual abuse team to address the sexual abuse occurring in my local community. I was anticipating at least an affirming response, recognition of my expertise and acknowledgement of the valuable contributions I was making. Instead I was told in no uncertain terms that my European ideas had little relevance to addressing the needs of *whanau* (family) and *hapu* (subtribe) where the *mana* (integrity and status) was trampled on by sexual violation. It was a painful lesson to recognize the ignorance and arrogance I exhibited towards esteemed community members who inhabited a different cultural world than my own.

The postmodern umbrella

I would like to explore an alternative meaning-making framework that has dominated my professional life for the last 15 years – social constructionism and narrative practice. This orientation arose from the postmodern turn in the sciences and social sciences over the last 30 years. My introduction to postmodernism came in the early 1990s when I returned to theoretical study at the University of Waikato, New Zealand (where I also taught and gained my PhD) after working for six years as a psychologist and a mediator working for the Family Court with couples filing for divorce, custody and visitation.

Postmodernism embodies the politics of resistance towards the knowledge and truth that grew out of the Enlightenment of Europe in the mid-18th century. Postmodernism questions the idea that human behavior can best be understood in terms of meta-narratives of modern science and their promise of ongoing social progress. Seidman (1994) summarizes Western culture and the modernist assumptions that accompany it as that which assumes the individual as the creative force of society and history, that the West is superior to all other cultures, and that science is synonymous with truth and necessarily leads to social progress.

Postmodernism has tended to challenge all boundary fixing and the hidden ways in which people subordinate, exclude, and marginalize others (Bernstein, 1983). Advocates for a postmodernist approach, such as Jencks (1992), suggested that this means an end to a single worldview, a resistance to single explanations, a respect for difference, and a celebration of the regional, local, and particular. For Yeatman (1994), postmodernism called into question the fundamental premise of the project of modernity – that societal progressive development involved "the progressive mastery of society over nature" (p.8). While the postmodernist position has been characterized as the total acceptance of ephemerality, fragmentation, discontinuity, and the chaotic (Harvey, 1989), liberal-humanist and modernist perspectives tend to see chaos and fragmentation as problems to be overcome.

Postmodern theorizing addresses the problems that were apparent with my earlier struggles with liberal-humanist theory. As an evolving professional, I wanted a theoretical orientation that enabled my professional work to address the complexities inherent in the patterns of social injustice, particularly as these injustices are expressed unevenly across gender and ethnic lines. I desired an approach which could accommodate people's multiple and simultaneous positionings in complex, changing, and often contradictory patterns of power relations. This has been particularly important to me as the development of positive relations between Maori and Pakeha in New Zealand has been severely hampered by the perpetuation of narrow, rigid, polarizing descriptions about what Maori or Pakeha identity must be. Postmodern theorizing has emerged from a skepticism concerning the possibility or desirability of totalizing narratives which reveal essential truths about enormously disparate groups (Lyotard, 1984).

Many social science researchers reject the monolithic categories upon which liberal humanism and modernism have been constructed. Postmodern literature holds that discourses that propose a single definable reality are impositions that dismiss or distort the diversity and indeterminacy of human life. Any description of a movement or some form of change is a consequence of the coming together of a unique set of circumstances at a particular place and time. Descriptions of human behavior emerging from postmodern literature are generally concerned with local and specific occurrences rather than global descriptions based on context-free laws (Hoshmand and Polkinghorne, 1992). The modernist position tended to emphasize the primacy of the rational mind over body and emotion and its capacity to take up one non-contradictory position. Postmodern theorizing emphasizes the significance of the multipositioned subject, as opposed to the unitary notions of the self.

Self and identity

I find it preferable to view the person in terms of complex relational processes manifesting themselves on the site of the individual body. The term "relational selves" is useful in describing the complexity of human identity. Harré (1991) suggested that the self or the "I" has been used as a "device by which unified narratives and coherent commitments are created" (p.58). The "I" is not seen as an entity, although it can be portrayed as a singular point from which to view the world. The "I" occupies a multiplicity of discursive positions from which to speak. For Hermans and Kempen (1995), the "I" is regarded as a product of history which has evolved from institutions and traditions. From this standpoint, the self as a speaking voice is not an individual voice at all, but a collective voice carrying the collective stories people tell one another.

Other writers have spoken about multiple selves. Escoffier (1991) referred to overlapping identities, that is, the self is simultaneously connected to a number of different identity discourses and resides within overlapping identities. Shotter (1990) stated that "although the postmodern self may be something of a mosaic, no self is completely an island. In postmodern everyday life, as well as in postmodern science, one occupies a multiplicity of standpoints" (p.19). Similarly, Pedersen (1990) estimated that we all have over one thousand different roles or cultures to which we could belong on any occasion. These overlapping roles resemble a myriad of identities.

Context and identity

As I write, I am positioning myself within a field of particular historically produced discourses. My identity is a product of my culturally mediated interpretations arising within dominant, systemic and continuous social systems or social orders. It is also a co-construction woven together in a series of historical, contextual and dialogical maneuvers within a community's social fabric (McNamee and Gergen, 1999). From a postmodern perspective, our identity is the product of our own interpretation and reconstruction of history as mediated through the cultural contexts to which we have access.

Who we are depends upon the circumstances we are placed in and the discourses available in the setting we find ourselves. As I stated earlier, in the United States I am a foreigner, somebody that has come from some other place. When I am participating in a large Maori *hui* (gathering using Maori protocol) in Aotearoa/New Zealand, I am positioned as Pakeha. I am white skinned, conversant in English, and likely to be seen by some people as a member of an oppressive colonizing culture. I am most likely to be positioned as possessing a particular ethnic history associated with colonization by my looks and my language style. In these settings, I feel uncertain, somewhat deferential and near the bottom of the social orderings. As a professor in a US university environment lecturing in front of a group of students, I am aware of myself as professional academic rather than as Pakeha. In this setting, I am positioned as privileged, somebody with influence, in contrast to my lowly status on the *Marae* (traditional Maori meeting place). In contexts other than the one I have described above, I become aware of quite different identifying features of my self or selves. When I have been in a setting where the majority of the group is gay, I am aware of my heterosexuality in a manner that would never usually feature for me given the dominant cultural influences of heterosexism that normalize my sexuality. In a context where the power relations in dominant majority culture are inverted, my sexuality takes on prominence. The argument that selves are impermeable and fixed, such as sexual orientation, is debatable as they may also be subjected to change across location and time.

The construction of the other

Since all knowledge is situated, postmodern ideas emphasize the cultural boundedness of any voice. This approach offers a way to expose how dominant cultural practices systematically marginalize those located in a subdominant context. By showing how these processes are produced discursively, a postmodern approach can provide tools to deconstruct homogenizing categories which allow differences to be named. I acknowledge how new discursive orders, such as those produced by fundamentalist grand narratives, have the potential to produce their own forms of dominance. These new discursive orders can "Other" individuals who might be crudely categorized as being oppressors or colonizers. My position here is that there is no moral high ground from which any group can assert its freedom from committing acts of moral terrorism when grand narrative rhetoric is invoked.

Evolution of social constructionism

It is the movement of social constructionism and the narrative metaphor developed under the umbrella of postmodernism that has had the most direct influence on my teaching, mediation, therapy and way of living in the world over recent years. These are far from new ideas in sociology, which originated in the symbolic interactionist movement led by G.H. Mead's work in the early 1930s. Symbolic interactionism is the view that we construct our own and each other's identities through our everyday encounters with each other in social interaction. Berger and Luckmann's (1966) work built upon this earlier work and asserted that all social life is created and sustained by social phenomena. They suggested that human understandings are constructed through historical social practices, even though there is a tendency for people to explain their understandings through a world that is pre-given and fixed (Burr, 1995; Davies, 1993). Kenneth J. Gergen introduced Berger and Luckmann's social constructionist work into the field of social psychology in the early 1970s when he argued that all knowledge, including psychological knowledge, is historically and culturally specific. He suggested that psychology should extend its enquiries beyond the individual to the social, economic and political realms of life.

It is from the theoretical work of Berger, Luckmann and Gergen that my teaching, mediation practice and counseling and psychotherapy have been shaped. Social constructionism invites a critical stance towards all taken-for-granted ways of understanding. I cannot have direct access to understanding the nature of the world. Our observation of what exists is what we perceive to exist. Understanding and what I observe is filtered through a historical, social and cultural lens. I appreciate the fact that because my knowing and understanding are so culturally defined, I cannot, for example, assume that my way of understanding is necessarily better than yours or others. Therefore what I regard as truth is a product not of objective observation but merely knowledge produced from social processes (Burr, 1995; Fairclough, 1992; Parker, 1992; Sampson, 1993). This is a very familiar concept in the social sciences but I continue to be surprised about the implications this has for therapeutic engagement with clients. Unlike the liberal-humanist discourse that invites certainty about the nature of the world and selfhood, constructionist discourses invite me to take a tentative position when sharing ideas and information with clients and the students I work with. Through this theoretical lens, I will expose the assumptions on which I am basing my ideas and interventions.

Temporary essentialism

I view professional knowledge as provisional, temporary, limited and tentative. I hold professional knowledge lightly and through encounters with my clients and students I am prepared to revise certain therapeutic efforts and perhaps in some instances change previously held assumptions. The role of language also becomes pivotal in the production of our concepts and categories reproduced by everyone who shares a culture and a language.

Language as social construction

Language is significantly more important in shaping human life than traditional psychology has assumed. Language is more than expressing ourselves. This notion is very different to traditional psychology which looks for explanations and understandings inside of persons shaped by attitudes, motivations, cognitions and affective states. When people talk about their personality, they tend to assume that the dimensions of the self pre-date and exist separately and independently from the words used to describe it. It is assumed that people use language as a representational function where they give expression to things that already exist in themselves (Burr, 1995; Davies, 1993; Lather, 1992). Language is not a bundle of labels which we can choose from to describe our internal states. Language is a way of structuring our experience of ourselves in the world and producing meanings and concepts that in a sense makes us up. Language speaks us into existence.

A narrative metaphor

I will now invoke a text or narrative analogy to demonstrate how social constructionist ideas actively give expression and meaning to our lives, and discuss the centrality of how language serves a narrative function. From a narrative psychology orientation, human communities organize language into narratives that serve to make sense of our lives and the identities that we exhibit in the world (Neimeyer, 2000; Randall, 1995; White and Epston, 1990). Historically, in Western, communal and indigenous cultures, it is commonplace to observe that human beings give expression to their lives, or even live their lives, through stories. Narratives are cultural products communicated in families, in schools, in religious institutions, through all forms of modern-day media, and recited, to describe our "nature," our value and worthwhileness. Narratives construct the social as they get told by someone(s) to some other(s) (Cushman, 1995; Rosaldo, 1993, Winslade, 2003). They are shared experiences which help people define themselves as groups who share particular allegiances to a set of stories (E. Bruner, 1986; Gergen and Kaye, 1992; Sarbin, 1986; White, 1989; White and Epston, 1990).

Stories make us up

The narrative metaphor establishes for us a semblance of stability and coherence, not fixed essences. People seem to arrange their experience of events in sequence across time in such a way as to arrive at this coherent account of themselves and the world. Specific experiences of events of the past and present and of those that are predicted to occur in the future are connected in a lineal sequence to order our daily lives and the interpretations of further experiences (White and Epston, 1990).

There are literally hundreds of narratives that are composed by us, for us, and more typically through the multiple dialogical encounters we have with others throughout our lives. Here are a few descriptions as examples of the diverse narratives that make up my life. I am a Kiwi, a New Zealander, a professor, a Pakeha, an old, bald, white guy, a grandfather, a student, a husband, a surfer, a traveler, a writer, a mediator, a therapist, and more. Under each of these descriptions lie multiple narrative titles that are accompanied by elaborate narrative structures. My life gets organized around these narrative meanings which contribute to varying degrees of coherence and incoherence, stability and chaos, confusion and clarity, doubt and uncertainty, hope and possibility.

Narrative therapy

White and Epston (1989) describe the narrative metaphor in these terms when they write: "The stories that we employ determine our examination of the world, the questions we ask about events, and the realities we construct. Stories determine the very distinctions we pull from the world" (p.19). Narrative therapy has developed a following and a literature that has explained and developed White and Epston's original work (e.g., Freedman and Combs, 1996; Monk *et al.*, 1997; Morgan, 2000; Winslade and Monk, 1999, 2000; Zimmerman and Dickerson, 1996). Through narratives, our experiences are organized in circumscribed ways to reduce the degree of confusion and complexity going on in our lives. While narratives help us to draw particular distinctions about what meanings we make about a particular experience, they also constrain possibilities about what we see because of the influence of the storyline. It is the primary or dominant narratives that establish what is to count as important. Yet, if we are constrained by a storyline about meaning and the nature of what is, the narrative perspective also allows for the possibility of disrupting the storyline to engage with other possibilities.

Edward Bruner (1986) suggests that there are lived experiences that are not fully encompassed by the dominant narrative structure. When lived experiences are amorphous, the experiences are not storyable. There is a lack of performative and narrative resources or vocabulary to produce alternative narrative structures that can compete or vie with dominant narratives. Using the narrative metaphor, the therapeutic task is to engage with clients in a co-authoring relationship where lived experiences are identified and storied using a range of conversational moves (Epston and White, 1992; White, 1989, 1995; White and Epston, 1990). The purpose is to assist the client to develop new performative structures that can break through redundant, destructive or unhelpful storylines. Building alternative narrative structures constitutes new and as yet unperformed stories in the community. Edward Bruner (1986) described the process as "the performance of an expression that we re-experience, relive, recreate, re-tell, re-construct, and re-fashion our culture. The performance does not release a pre-existing meaning that lies dormant in the text…rather the performance itself is constitutive" (p.11).

One of the most influential cultural processes shaping our lived experiences are the ones that occur in our family of origin. I often tell the story about how I got involved in the field of psychology and mediation. It starts when I was 4 years old when my father would call me "big ears." "How are you 'big ears'?" he would say in an endearing way. He would even introduce me to family and friends as "big ears." This name was a shorthand description of my behavior when I would consistently interrupt my parents who were having a discussion about some topic I knew little or nothing about. I would say "Who's such and such?" or "What's such and such?" I remember feeling somewhat proud of the name, particularly as my ears in physical appearance were pretty small. This story gathered momentum when in high school I would go to parties and dances and would be found in the corner of the room sometimes talking but more typically listening to some interesting story from a friend or a new acquaintance. I experienced myself as a very curious individual who was fascinated by the experiences of others. I liked how it felt when people would confide in me. I don't know to this day whether it was the attention my father playfully gave me when I would ask questions and was curious about what was going on around me that was significant in shaping my professional choices. I do know that this is a dominant narrative about my life and in many respects I live by it. It is not surprising that I am attracted to a narrative orientation that emphasizes the importance of curious questioning.

As a narrative practitioner, I am very interested in the interface between the production of the dominant narratives in a family or community and how these narratives shape the personal and private stories of those clients seeking ways to become disentangled from a conflictual story. Narratives circulate in any community about particular identities affiliated with diverse ethnicities, sexual orientations, class membership, ability/disability, religious adherence, rural/urban, educated/uneducated, wealth and poverty. These narratives, and the various histories associated with them, are influential in shaping the personal stories that make up people's lives. In the community that I was raised in, there were well-developed prejudicial stories that relate to the superiority of some identities over other identities along the following superiority/inferiority dualisms: Pakeha over Maori; heterosexuality over homosexuality; ability over disability; urban over rural; upper and middle class over lower class; Christianity over other religious traditions; educated over the uneducated, and so on.

These narratives, purporting the superiority of one group over another, circulated within families, in religious institutions, in schools, and through the mass media in the community in which I was raised. It is necessary to consider how these dominant narratives circulating in a community open up possibilities for some individuals while systematically constraining the possibilities for others.

Discourses of the dominant and alternative kind

I find the concept of discourses to be very helpful resources in understanding how people act upon the world and with one another. Discourses are shaped and constrained by the wider social structure on the one hand, and socially constitute the social structure on the other (Gee, 1999). They are the domain in which what is regarded as normal, acceptable, right, and truthful, and what is possible is constructed. They serve as clusters of meanings, recurrent assertions and understandings or interrelated sets of statements that circulate among a community (Luke, 1995). Discourses are the basis from which performative actions are made and are expressed in a variety of forms, including nonverbal communication, visual symbols, and written or spoken words. In fact, discourses shape how we think, behave, talk, and respond to each other and our experience of life (Burman and Parker, 1993; Fairclough, 1992).

From a therapeutic standpoint, it is helpful to draw the distinction between dominant and alternative discourses. Dominant discourse systematically produces certain knowledges and practices that become privileged in a community. Alternative discourse is that which is not widely represented in mainstream cultural practice, but often acts in stark contrast to dominating cultural assumptions. These alternate discourses challenge the more dominant discourses and are often representative of marginalized cultural ideas circulating within a context or community.

Marginalized groups in any population are typically disadvantaged by some dominant discourse because they legitimize dominant culture and demean alternative cultural practices. However, we are not passive in the face of the negative effects of dominant discourses. They do not operate on us as some kind of mechanistic input which produces predictable outcomes on us. When people are seeking help from therapists, psychologists and mediators, they tend to be caught by competing and contrasting discursive patterns that may produce a variety of crises.

Positioning theory

As discourses are never individually produced, it makes sense to speak of our ability to make choices as constituted largely from the outside in. Choices arise from the multiple discourses at work in any therapeutic or everyday interaction. Davies and Harré (1990) suggest that as we move from conversation to conversation we are offered a panorama of different positions that create multiple experiences from which we can make decisions or choices in life. Some discursive positions can place significant constraints on people's choices. Within a dialogue, when a speaker expresses a viewpoint, the speaker both establishes a stance within a discourse and also calls the person being addressed into subject position within the structure invoked by the offer (Winslade, 2003). In this way, a relationship is established and a perspective on the world is invoked, even momentarily. Two different positions may offer the participants in the conversation different degrees of entitlement. One speaker may assume a position of deference, inviting the other person into a position of superior knowledge and expertise, shaping the subsequent moves in the conversation. This process in the constructionist metaphor is termed position calling (Drewery, 2002; Winslade, 2003). Positioning goes beyond mere words to a broader realm where socio-political actions shape what one is doing to another. This back and forth process results in the politics of meaning making. Speaking is not just reporting on what is being thought, but becomes an action in the social world. As we engage in conversation with another, we act upon ourselves and others within our social context (Shotter, 1993; Winslade, 2003). The implications of this analysis of change have significant influences on the nature of identity. Linehan and McCarthy (2000) suggest that this perspective offers "a dynamic agentive model of identity construction where a person creates a possible identity for themselves in a particular context through their active positioning in relation to or perhaps in opposition to elements in their discursive cultural context" (p.449).

For Mouffe (1992), personal identity accrues through participation in multiple discursive contexts but remains fragmentary, contradictory and unfinalized. Identities are inscribed by discourse and people experience enormous variation in the extent to which they are either constrained or encouraged by the discursive context. Through a social constructionist lens, it makes no sense to speak of somebody as powerless and having no ability to act in any total sense. This provides an opening to talk about the role, nature, and expression of power in human relationships.

Power as a capillary phenomenon

From a constructionist perspective, power is conceived of quite differently from the view of power as being possessed by one group and not another in a commodity sense. Power operates through and within discourses. Power is not a property but operates relationally. Power shifts in a context-dependent fashion rather than being inherent within categories of people. Power cuts across individuals' lives in a variety of ways that can entail privilege and oppression for the same person in different respects. This does not preclude the notion that power can be systematically applied with a degree of consistency so as to be more oppressing to some individuals in more contexts than other individuals in those same contexts. However, as Foucault (1989) suggests, "as soon as there is a power relation, there is the possibility of resistance. We are never trapped by power: we can always modify its grip in determinate conditions and according to precise strategy" (p.153).

Young (1990) proposes that to understand the meaning and operation of power in modern society, we must look beyond the model of power as sovereignty, the dialectic relation of ruler and subject, and instead analyze the exercises of power played out in the fields of education, medicine, corporations, and institutions of all kinds. Foucault's contributions to the analysis of power acknowledge its capillary action. The image of capillary power is that it is everywhere and pervades the entire social body. All social life then comes to be a network of power relations which can be viewed, not at the level of large scale social structures, but rather at very local and individual levels. This analysis of power as a capillary action allows us to examine, in day-to-day therapeutic interactions, how power is managed.

Social constructionism, biology and mental health

While I have to admit to personal and professional fervor about the social constructionist metaphor, I do not want to be guilty of presenting this perspective as a new dogma. Any theoretical construction has the potential simultaneously to offer a significant contribution to one area of inquiry while in another limit what can be achieved. I want to acknowledge a territory which the social constructionist metaphor does not engage – the interface between human biology and the social world (K. Tomm, personal communication, November 26, 1996). Many social constructionist theorists and practitioners keep the interrelationships between biological and social processes at arm's length. A large number of mental health commentators suggest a strong link between biological and psychological functioning. For example, the amount of sleep people have, the quality of nutrition, dietary intake, and neurological activity are important to consider when examining human functioning. Of course, there is a range of mental health difficulties that people experience which are addressed by important developments in psychopharmacology. Social constructionist and narrative practitioners are not all opposed to the use of pharmacological interventions in peoples lives, as long as the clients are treated in a way that acknowledges the impact of the socio-cultural influences in their lives.

Narrative therapists have been concerned with the totalizing pathological descriptions given by the mental health community to people struggling with serious mental health challenges: schizophrenia, bipolar patterns, obsessive-compulsive patterns, problems with anxiety, and major depressive episodes. Often people's mental health issues influence their lives in ways such that therapists and other practitioners can lose sight of the resourcefulness and strength deployed in their struggle with mental health issues. However, the interface between the constructionist metaphor and biology is crying out for exploration and investigation. Postmodern researchers Parker *et al.* (1996) suggest that the emphasis on language should not mean that biology does not have a central part to play in the way we speak and behave. There is considerable value in seeing a bridging between a social constructionist metaphor and biological functioning, while recognizing that socially constructed knowledge plays an intimate role in the constructs produced to "understand" the body.

Where to from here

When using the narrative metaphor in my work in counseling, I am very interested in addressing the power relations in the problem-saturated conflict stories with which people present. The most powerful therapeutic tool that arises from the narrative and constructionist work to address the power dynamics of disputes and problem issues is deconstruction. The objective of working with deconstruction is to disrupt the usual privilege given to dominant knowledges and in so doing not only understand, but also subvert, the ways in which systems constitute everyday social practices (Derrida, 1976). White (1992) described deconstruction as subverting:

> taken-for-granted realities and practices; those so-called "truths" that are split off from the conditions and the context of their production, those disembodied ways of speaking that hide their biases and prejudices, and those familiar practices of self and of relationship that are subjugating of person's lives. (p.121)

Deconstruction is a method of exposing how discourses expressed within stories inadvertently shut down or deny the legitimacy of alternative discourses being expressed within people's preferred narratives. Thus, conversations in narrative practice aim to deconstruct the constitutive effects of these dominant stories, discourses or cultural practices and open space in the narrative construction of people's lives for a re-authoring process to take place. Ultimately, the application of deconstruction in narrative practice examines the contextual staging of knowledge and exposes the constitutive properties of our use of language. The co-authoring of alternative stories in such a manner as to overshadow the potency of problem-saturated and conflict narratives facilitates the production of a client's voice in the therapeutic process.

Inviting people to find their voice in the face of considerable discursive constraints is what continues to drive my theoretical work and its practical application. To facilitate others having a voice and a genuine sense of agency for those who have been historically denied one is a difficult therapeutic task. It is much easier to understand the discursive constraints on freedom to act than it is to identify the discursive supports for agentic acts. The ability to have a voice on one's own behalf will always be incomplete since we only speak in the discourses available to us. As a result, our volition and action is to some extent out of our control.

Mikhail Bahktin (1986) provides insights into the nature of what it means to have a voice or the ability to express oneself. He describes how speech is double voiced in the sense in which it contains more than words of our own. Our speech is populated with words which are the echoes of many other voices. He states: "Each word contains voices that are sometimes infinitely distant, unnamed, almost impersonal, almost undetectable, and voices resounding nearby and simultaneously" (p.124). Since our actions are so populated with the accompanying voices from sources that we may or may not identify or know about, they will influence how we engage with life. In fact, our day-to-day contributions in life, our successes, and failures, may not be ours to lay claim to. Shotter (1993) went so far as to say that our mental lives are not wholly under our control, but rather are constantly shaped by content external to ourselves. Deconstructive moves in a narrative conversation address the textual staging of any act and how, through language, individuals are constituted.

While the goal of deconstructive conversation is not to seek specific answers or resolve specific problems, it does set up procedures to continuously demystify the realities we create and provide corrective moments to safeguard against our dogmatism, fundamentalism, rigidity and certainty. In this way, deconstructive conversation can promote the possibility that while we acknowledge certain harmful discursive patterns being perpetuated in our lives, we can ensure that these patterns do not eclipse the rising of voices that support us acting on our own terms. As an educator, therapist and mediator, I support a world where human beings have a voice to express their preferred identities without being dominated by the practices of others. I want to promote respectful engagement with others, and in so doing want to take a moral position where I can review and critique my stance and prepare to change it in response to this engagement.

In conclusion, I acknowledge that we can never accomplish things by ourselves. It is not possible to create something from individual achievement separate from the collective production of human endeavor. One can never be a tall poppy standing separate from the toil and labor of those who have come before. Perhaps progress and advancement really only emerge from the recognition of the continuity and interconnectivity of life. There is a Maori proverb that says: "*Hinga atu he tete kura, ara mai he tete kura*" (One fern frond falls as another unfurls). As one idea, one leader, one movement dies, there are always others that will grow and develop and ultimately take their place.

References

Bakhtin, M. (1986) *Speech Genres and Other Late Essays*, trans. V. McGee. Austin, TX: University of Texas Press.

Berger, P.L. and Luckmann, T. (1966) *The Social Construction of Reality: A Treatise in the Sociology of Knowledge*. London: Penguin.

Bernstein, R. (1983) *Beyond Objectivism, and Relativism: Science, Hermeneutics, and Praxis*. Philadelphia: University of Pennsylvania Press.

Bruner, E. (1986) "Ethnography as narrative." In V. Turner and E. Bruner (eds) *The Anthropology of Experience*. Chicago: University of Illinois Press.

Bruner, J. (1986) *Actual Minds, Possible Worlds*. Cambridge, MA: Harvard University Press.

Burman, E. and Parker, I. (1993) *Discourse Analytic Research: Repertoires and Readings of Texts in Action*. London: Routledge.

Burr, V. (1995) *An Introduction to Social Constructionism*. London: Routledge.

Cushman, P. (1995) *Constructing the Self, Constructing America: A Cultural History of Psychotherapy*. Reading, MA: Addison-Wesley.

Davies, B. (1993) *Shards of Glass: Children Reading and Writing Beyond Gendered Identities*. St. Leonards, NSW: Allen and Unwin.

Davies, B. and Harré, R. (1990) "Positioning: The discursive production of selves." *Journal for the Theory of Social Behaviour 20*, 1, 43–63.

Derrida, J. (1976) *Of Grammatology*, trans. C. Spivac. Baltimore, MD: Johns Hopkins University Press.

Drewery, W. (2002) "Everyday speech and the production of colonised selves." Unpublished paper.

Epston, D. and White, M. (1992) *Experience, Contradiction, Narrative and Imagination*. Adelaide: Dulwich Centre Publications.

Escoffier, J. (1991) "The limits of multiculturalism." *Socialist Review 21*, 3–4, 61–73.

Fairclough, N. (1992) *Discourse and Social Change*. Cambridge, England: Polity Press.

Foucault, M. (1989) *Foucault Live: Interviews, 1966–84*, ed S. Lotringer, trans. J. Johnston. New York: Semiotext.

Freedman, J. and Combs, G. (1996) *Narrative Therapy: The Social Construction of Preferred Realities*. New York: Norton.

Gee, J.P. (1999) *An Introduction to Discourse Analysis: Theory and Method*. London: Routledge.

Geertz, C. (1979) "From the native's point of view: On the nature of anthropological understanding." In P. Rabinow and W.M. Sullivan (eds) *Interpretive Social Science*. Berkeley, CA: University of California Press.

Gergen, K. and Kaye, J. (1992) "Beyond narrative in the negotiation of therapeutic meaning." In S. McNamee and K. Gergen (eds) *Therapy as Social Construction*. London: Sage.

Giroux, H.A. (1992) "Resisting difference: Cultural studies and the discourse of critical pedagogy." In L. Grossberg, C. Nelson and P. Treichler (eds) *Cultural Studies*. New York: Routledge.

Harré, R. (1991) "The discursive production of selves." *Theory and Psychology 1*, 1, 51–63.

Harvey, D. (1989) *The Condition of Postmodernity*. Oxford: Blackwell.

Hayes, S.C., Barlow, D.H. and Nelson-Gray, R.O. (1999) *The Scientist Practitioner: Research and Accountability in the Age of Managed Care*, 2nd edn. New York: Allyn and Bacon.

Hermans, J.M. and Kempen, H.J. (1995) "Body, mind and culture: The dialogical nature of mediated action." *Culture and Psychology 1*, 103–114.

Hoshmand, L.T. and Polkinghorne, D.E. (1992) "Redefining the science-practice relationship in professional training." *American Psychologist 47*, 1, 55–66.

Jencks, C. (1992) *The Postmodern Reader*. London: Academy Editors.

Lather, P. (1992) "Post-critical pedagogues: A feminist reading." In J. Gore and C. Luke (eds) *Feminisms and Critical Pedagogy*. New York: Routledge.

Linehan, C. and McCarthy, J. (2000) "Positioning in practice: Understanding participation in the social world." *Journal for the Theory of Social Behaviour 30*, 4, 435–453.

Luke, A. (1995) "Text and discourse in education: An introduction to critical discourse analysis." In M. Apple (ed) *Review of Research in Education*. Itasca, IL: F.E. Peacock.

Lyotard, J.F. (1984) *The Post-modern Condition: A Report on Knowledge*, trans G. Bennington and B. Massumi. Minneapolis, MN: University of Minnesota Press.

McNamee, S. and Gergen, K. (1999) *Relational Responsibility: Resources for Sustainable Dialogue*. Thousand Oaks, CA: Sage.

Monk, G., Winslade, J., Crocket, K. and Epston, D. (1997) *Narrative Therapy in Practice: The Archaeology of Hope*. San Francisco: Jossey Bass.

Morgan, A. (2000) *What is Narrative Therapy? An Easy to Read Introduction*. Adelaide: Dulwich Centre Publications.

Mouffe, C. (1992) "Feminism, citizenship and radical democratic politics." In J. Butler and J.W. Scott (eds) *Feminists Theorize the Political*. New York: Routledge.

Neimeyer, R. (2000) "Narrative disruptions in the construction of the self." In R. Neimeyer and J. Raskin (eds) *Constructions of Disorder: Meaning-making Frameworks for Psychotherapy*. Washington, DC: American Psychological Association.

Parker, I. (1992) *Discourse Dynamics: Critical Analyses for Social and Individual Psychology*. London: Routledge.

Parker, I., Georgaca, E., Harper, D., McLaughlin, T. and Stowell-Smith, M. (1996) *Deconstructing Psychopathology*. London: Sage.

Pedersen, P.B. (1990) "Inter-racial collaboration among counseling psychologists." In J.G. Ponterotto (Chair) *The White-American Researcher in Multicultural Counseling: Significance and Challenges*. Symposium conducted at the annual convention of the American Psychological Association, Boston, MA, August.

Randall, W. (1995) *The Stories We Are: An Essay on Self-creation*. Toronto: University of Toronto Press.

Rosaldo, R. (1993) *Culture and Truth: The Remaking of Social Analysis*. Boston: Beacon Press.

Sampson, E. (1993) "Identity politics." *American Psychologist 49*, 5, 412–416.

Sarbin, T. (ed) (1986) *Narrative Psychology: The Storied Nature of Human Conduct*. New York: Praeger.

Seidman, S. (1994) "Queering sociology, sociologizing queer theory." *Sociological Theory 12*, 2, 17–26.

Shotter, J. (1990) "Getting in touch: The metamethodology of a postmodern science of mental life." *The Humanistic Psychologist 18*, 7–22.

Shotter, J. (1993) *Conversational Realities: Constructing Life Through Language*. London: Sage.

White, M. (1989) *Selected Papers*. Adelaide: Dulwich Centre Publications.

White, M. (1992) "Deconstruction and therapy." In D. Epston and M. White (eds) *Experience, Contradiction, Narrative, and Imagination*. Adelaide: Dulwich Centre Publications.

White, M. (1995) *Re-authoring Lives*. Adelaide: Dulwich Centre Publications.

White, M. and Epston, D. (1989) *Literate Means to Therapeutic Ends*. Adelaide: Dulwich Centre Publications.

White, M. and Epston, D. (1990) *Narrative Means to Therapeutic Ends*. New York: Norton.

Winslade, J. (2003) "Discursive positioning in theory and practice: A case for narrative mediation." Unpublished doctoral dissertation, University of Waikato, Hamilton, New Zealand.

Winslade, J. and Monk, G. (1999) *Narrative Counseling in Schools: Powerful and Brief*. Thousand Oaks, CA: Corwin Press.

Winslade, J. and Monk, G. (2000) *Narrative Mediation: A New Approach to Conflict Resolution*. San Francisco: Jossey Bass.

Yeatman, A. (1994) *Post-modern Revisionings of the Political*. New York: Routledge.

Young, I.M. (1990) *Justice and the Politics of Difference*. Princeton, NJ: Princeton University Press.

Zimmerman, J. and Dickerson, V. (1996) *If Problems Talked: Narrative Therapy in Action*. New York: Guilford Press.

CHAPTER 5

Performing a Life (Story)

Lois Holzman

I grew up in a silent house. No one talked much in my family. My mother and father didn't gossip about their co-workers or the neighbors, recite the little successes and failures of their day, give voice to their dreams, or ask my sister, my brother and me, "How was school today?" Ours wasn't a tense silence of things unsaid, of anger or love repressed. It was just how we were together.

My mother had seven sisters and brothers and, until my teens, the families would get together a lot. In these gatherings, we all held our own in constant chatter. When visiting my friends for play or a sleepover, I was no more or less talkative than anyone else. I *was* fascinated, though, that they and their mothers and fathers and sisters and brothers talked so much to each other.

Since we didn't talk much, my family didn't have many stories. Not even the coming to America of my Russian-Jewish immigrant grandparents, or how my parents met, or the story of my birth. So it's kind of funny to me that one of the few stories, repeated often, was that I didn't talk until I was three. Actually, it was hardly a story. It was merely a statement – not followed by "and she hasn't stopped talking since" or "and see how smart she is" or anything. It was up to the listener to fill in the next line.

I tell *this* story in that same spirit – leaving it to the reader to continue it, or not. I find it interesting to reflect on my family's relationship to language in light of my love of words and over 30-year inquiry into speaking and thinking, but I draw no connections – causal or otherwise. Both are, simply, who I am/am becoming.

I knew when I accepted George Yancy and Susan Hadley's invitation to participate in this volume that doing so would take me to new places philosophically, psychologically and linguistically. I was excited by the journey I would create in writing this chapter (and was flattered at being asked). I did wonder, though, if it was dishonest or at least disingenuous to agree to "narrate my identity" and engage in "self-construction" when I don't believe in either identity or self! George made it clear from our very first correspondence that he was aware of the paradoxical nature of his invitation to me; had he not, I suspect I would have declined.

So, here I am, having told one little story and then another. I am trying to embrace the paradox of my task through *creating stories* of the people and events and ideas that "shaped" me, rather than telling *my story*. There is no such thing as my story. This is our story.

Fred Newman, my dear friend, mentor and collaborator for nearly 30 years (you can call him a major influence on me, as long as you don't turn him into *an explanation*), recently read me an essay he was writing. In it, Fred says he wound up at Stanford University's PhD program in philosophy by accident. (That's part of the story he tells. And it's part of the one I'm telling too – the story of how I wound up devoting my life to changing the world.)

I wound up with a PhD in psychology more by default than accident. I think I wanted to be a writer as a child and teenager. I wasn't burning with things I wanted to say, but I very much liked the activity and accoutrements of writing. When my mother took me to work with her when I was little, I would gather cardboard, paper, scissors, staples and glue and construct books and newspapers and magazines. Occasionally, I would write something in them, but mostly I left them blank. Throughout school I was a serious and good student; I especially liked literature and writing, but I adored geometry and grammar (I kept this latter proclivity to myself, so as not to appear too weird). To me, constructing and deconstructing proofs and sentences was fun and creative.

Like most of my friends, I was bored with school by the time I was a junior in high school, but I had the support of my best friend who wanted to do more than complain. In the early spring, she and I figured out how to graduate without doing our senior year. We convinced the principal to let us go to summer school and take the required subjects and exams for graduation with a college-prep diploma. My friend knew she wanted to study art and had already picked out her school. I just wanted to leave high school. I went to a college night and picked up brochures. I drooled over images of artsy Bennington College, but knew it was financially out of the question and that if my family could afford anything it would be a state school. At the State University of New York table there was information about a small college in Binghamton that had recently become part of the state system. Harpur College was the place, the woman at the table told me, for kids who get into

Cornell but can't afford it. I liked that, and the fact that it had fewer than 2000 students and no fraternities or football team. I presented my parents with my plan to leave school and go to college pretty much as a fait accompli. At first shocked, they were soon won over to the reasonableness of what I was proposing. Perhaps they were relieved that I took care of this myself, for they knew nothing about how to find a college or apply to one; neither of them, nor my older sister or brother had gone to college and, sensing that I wanted to, they might have been anxious about how they could help.

I declared psychology as my major. I didn't know what psychologists did. I didn't associate psychology with therapy (of which I was completely ignorant) or helping people (which I hadn't ever been interested in). I must have gotten the notion that psychology had something to do with the mind and would be a pretty interesting intellectual pursuit. Or maybe it sounded glamorous. But my encounter with psychology at Harpur College was neither intellectually interesting (large lecture courses and multiple-choice exams on classical and operant conditioning) nor glamorous (my very own rat in a Skinner box). And so it was shortlived – but nonetheless vital in my becoming. It generated a healthy skepticism toward social science experimentation, a passionate dislike for what I now refer to as pseudoscience, and an emerging interest in methodological questions of how to study life-as-lived.

It also was the occasion for my first adult love affair. In that cavernous hall where Psych 101 lectures were held, students were seated alphabetically by last name. To the right of Holzman (me) was Hood (a junior transfer student), the person on my left long forgotten. We listened to the professor and studied together that semester. He loved the course, and came to love experimental psychology and me. At the end of my sophomore and his senior year we moved to Providence, RI where he began Brown's PhD program in psychology and I transferred to the local state college, majoring in English. (We married a year later when I was 20 and lived our lives together for 10 years.)

Almost immediately, I found myself with an identity – graduate student wife – and I didn't like it at all. Graduate student (and faculty) wives had *jobs*; they were social workers and nurses and teachers. But graduate students (and faculty) had passions and intellectual pursuits and *important work to do*; they were scientists and writers and discoverers. If I had to have an identity, that was the one I wanted!

As I write, I realize that I am creating myself as I write. I am creating stories of a me with a disposition toward postmodernism. I feel pleased with this discovery and process.

From as far back as I can remember there are a few things I never believed in – Santa Claus, god, an innate human nature and an inner life (obviously, these last two I didn't have terms for right away). It wasn't that I thought a lot about their existence – weighing the evidence on both sides and reaching a conclusion – or went through any kind of philosophical or soul-searching process. I simply didn't believe. Even though I now live my life in the continuous activity of philosophizing, neither doubt nor certainty plays a role in my thinking about such matters. When I was young and unschooled, accompanying my "non-doubting-non-certain" not believing was an inability to understand how others could believe in such things, and a kind of acceptance of that fact of difference rather than a desire to debate or convince anyone to change their mind. And today, while I love to explore with people how all sorts of things (including people's beliefs) came to be and am enriched by that activity, I still am no closer to understanding how it is that they believe (any more than I understand how it is that I believe). I've come to appreciate (believe?) that seeking such understanding is seeking an explanation by another name. I also think it's a misguided illusion born of our culture's cognitively biased understanding of understanding.

Sheila McNamee and Kenneth Gergen have spoken, and invited others to speak with them, on the subject of relational responsibility (McNamee, Gergen and Associates, 1999). At the beginning of their book, relational responsibility is put forth as a discursive reaction to the "deeply flawed" and "long-standing tradition" of placing individual blame. However, by the book's end the concept becomes more inclusive, largely due to their dialogic partners who suggest such terms as relational responsiveness, relational appreciation and relational resonance. Relational responsiveness (a contribution from John Shotter and Arlene Katz) is the one that speaks to me.

In terms of my life, from quite a young age I think I had some sense that who-and-how I was couldn't be separated from context. I was keenly aware of how different I was depending on where I was. It was in my late teens that I began to articulate this (to myself). Going from high school to college was a shock – and a catalyst for questioning: I went from "being" a smart kid to "being" pretty average. I found this fascinating! How could that be? Which was I, smart or average? How would I know? How would people decide? Was there such a thing as smartness? Was there a me independent of other people and places?

I couldn't see any evidence for it. Me-and-the-environment were partners, like it or not. Sometimes we were good partners and sometimes not so good partners. Putting a contemporary philosophical-psychological spin (of which

I had no inkling at the time) on my teenage musings, I was questioning isolated individualism, identity, a core self, essences, duality. And perhaps I was discovering relational responsiveness.

In terms of the development of my psychological perspective and practice, the issue of context, environment and relationality loomed large. From descriptive linguistics to sociolinguistics and developmental psycholinguistics, from Piagetian developmental theory to Vygotsky's socio-cultural activity theory, from an ecologically valid psychology to social therapy, from mentors Lois Bloom to Michael Cole to Fred Newman – I investigated self and other/person and environment. Today I am wary of the concept of "context" as subtextually implying a separateness from what is (presumably) "in" it, for I now see person-and-environment as historically and radically monistic.

In 1976 a new friend invited me to a series of lectures on "Marxism and Mental Illness." I liked this new friend of mine; he was unlike anyone I ever knew. He was "political." He did something he called community organizing. He walked through the subway cars of New York City selling a left newspaper. He stood on street corners and stopped people to talk about the current fiscal crisis and ask them to help support the building of an independent union for people who were on welfare or unemployed. He read Marx and Lenin and Mao and also many others I hadn't heard of (I had barely heard of those three). He wanted to know what I thought about what was going on in the city, the country and the world. He wanted me to meet the person who taught him, the man whom he followed, the guy who was giving these lectures. Of course I went.

Having had no experience with the left, never having read Marx and knowing virtually nothing about mental illness (despite having a PhD), I had no expectations walking into the impressive Ethical Culture Society building on Central Park West (really none, as I didn't know what ethical culture was either). The hundred or so folding chairs were nearly all filled, mostly with people in their twenties and thirties. Fred Newman took the microphone and began to speak. He was large and loud. He was eloquent and erudite and funny. He spoke like I imagined union men to talk one minute and like I knew intellectuals to talk the next. I listened to him speak about economics, capitalism, Freud, the ego, the working class, science, Marx, Quine, power and authority – all new to me – and the mind, language, Chomsky, Skinner, and Goffman – which I was familiar with. He described a new kind of radical therapy he was developing called social therapy. What kept me spellbound as much as trying to follow the very sophisticated content was how passionate Fred was as he gave expression to both his politics and his intellect. In the discussion period after the formal talk, I asked him questions about things I knew about. I was probably testing him, and if I had asked about something I knew nothing about I wouldn't have a way of judging his answers. Fred passed my test and I signed up for a six-week seminar with him entitled, "The Crisis in Science and Society." I was sure he was someone I could learn a lot from. I responded to his style; I liked how he thought (to the extent that I could tell, given that what he was talking about was so over my head); and I resonated with his general topic (how the world got into the mess it was in and how to change it).

That resonance didn't surprise me, despite never before having been in a conversation about it with anyone (including myself). I wouldn't have known that I wanted to change the world, that I was in agreement with Fred's and my new friend's political views, or that I would choose to become a political activist and participate in creating a revolutionary method. I wasn't searching. It wasn't, "Here's what I've been looking for!" It was "This makes sense; it seems like a way to live my life." From my current philosophical-psychological perspective, I'd say it was a Vygotskian *completion* of my thinking.

Lev Vygotsky is my closest dead friend. I've been talking to him for years. Early in my relationship with Fred, I would talk to him about Vygotsky, but in the early 1990s, the three of us got together. *Completion* played a big role in that. It's a long story.

Before I met Fred, I thought little about therapy – and even less *of* it. My disinterest wasn't born of experience (for I had none) but came from skepticism toward what I took to be its premise – that an explanation or interpretation for how you were feeling could change how you were feeling. On his part, Fred's study of philosophy of science and foundations of mathematics at Stanford had led him to reject therapy's premises and major conceptions – explanation, interpretation, the notion of an inner self that therapist and client needed to go deeply into, and other dualistic and otherwise problematic conceptions.

So it was a big surprise to him when, in the late 1960s, Fred went into therapy and found it incredibly helpful. As he tells the story, this experience raised a contradiction for him:

> It never occurred to me that some of the attitudes and beliefs I had about what I took to be some of the mythic and irrational qualities of therapy were inaccurate. But it didn't make sense that therapy should work; it didn't make sense that it should be so successful. So I had to deal with the fact that therapy is of incredible value to lots of people, and the question that kept occurring to me was, "How in the hell could this thing possibly work?" (Newman, 1999a)

As Fred initially developed it and as it has emerged over 30 years, social therapy is a method of helping people with whatever emotional pain they are experiencing without diagnosing their problem, analyzing their childhood, or interpreting their current life. Its effectiveness must have something to do with what people were doing together in therapy, he reasoned.

All during the 1980s, Fred and I talked about this. What was going on in social therapy? What were people doing together? How was it the case that they not only were feeling better but were, by their own admission and apparent to others, growing emotionally?

Social therapy clients work in groups whose explicit task is to create an environment in which they can get help – to "grow the group" – because in that activity everyone can develop emotionally. This emphasis on the group activity of creating environments in which people can give expression to their emotional life challenges the notion of an individuated, isolated and internal life.

It was Vygotsky who helped us see that social therapy was a unique kind of tool for emotional growth that had everything to do with the dialectical socialness of speaking. One statement of his, in particular, seemed remarkable:

> The search for method becomes one of the most important problems of the entire enterprise of understanding the uniquely human forms of psychological activity. In this case, the method is simultaneously prerequisite and product, the tool and the result of the study. (Vygotsky, 1978, p.65)

Here was an entirely new way of understanding method as something to be practiced, not thought up and then applied to "real life." From as far back as 1979, Fred and I coined the phrase "tool-and-result methodology" for Vygotsky's grasp of dialectics which, it seemed to us, described social therapy to a T (Holzman and Newman, 1979).

Vygotsky's understanding of how young children learn and develop was itself an application of his tool-and-result methodology. Young children and their caretakers create what Vygotsky calls zones of proximal development (ZPDs), developmental environments that support children to do what is beyond them, to perform who they are becoming (even as they are who they are). They play language games, speaking before they know how. Their creative imitation of the language spoken to and around them is fully accepted. They learn to speak by playing with language; they perform as speakers (who they are becoming). The process of creating the ZPD *is* the joint (ensemble) creation of their becoming language speakers.

Fred and I found this accounting of children developing as speakers of a language to be equally coherent as an accounting of social therapy. For, in social therapy, adults are supported by the therapists to do what is beyond them (create the group), to perform who they are becoming. The work/play in therapy is helping people to create new performances of themselves continuously as a way out of the rigidified roles, patterns and identities that cause so much emotional pain (and are called pathologies). In social therapy, people create new ways of speaking and listening to each other; they create meaning by playing with language.

By this time, we had added Fred's old friend Wittgenstein to our conversation. Fred had studied Wittgenstein's writings but he hadn't until now explored the influence of Wittgenstein's unique philosophical sensibility and methodology on social therapy. Nor had he examined the family resemblances between Wittgenstein's and Vygotsky's views of language and language learning. I read Wittgenstein's work for the first time, and together Fred and I explored the idea of Wittgenstein as therapist. We found that others had commented on this, including Gordon Baker, the prominent Wittgensteinian scholar (e.g., Baker, 1992). In 1993, while on a speaking tour, Fred and I visited Baker at Oxford to learn more of what he was thinking. We talked together about how Wittgenstein had developed a method to help free philosophers from the muddles they get into because the way that language is used and understood locks them into seeing things in a particular way.

We began to see social therapy as a method to help ordinary people get free from the constraints of language and from versions of philosophical pathologies that permeate everyday life. Making the focus of the group's activity be the creating of the group exposed ways of talking that perpetuate experiencing ourselves as individuated products, at the same time as it generated new ways of talking. Wittgenstein's conception of language games as a form of life helped us see that social therapy groups were makers of meaning, not simply users of language.

So far, so good. But something was still missing. What are people doing together when they are making meaning? What is going on when people are speaking? Re-enter Vygotsky.

While I was doing post-doctoral research at Michael Cole's lab at the Rockefeller University in the late 1970s, I met and became friends with Valerie Walkerdine. Now a well-known critical psychologist, Valerie was beginning her career then and had come to the Cole lab as a visiting scholar. We greatly respected each other's work and stayed in contact over the years. When Valerie, along with John Broughton and David Ingleby, became co-editors of the Routledge series, Critical Psychology, she invited Fred and me to contribute a book on Vygotsky. So we began a re-examination of his writings.

One day as I was re-reading Vygotsky's *Thinking and Speech* (entitled *Thought and Language* in earlier English versions), I came upon a few passages I hadn't really noticed before. In presenting his understanding of thinking and speaking, Vygotsky challenges the belief that we speak our developed thoughts. He challenges a transmittal, or expressionist, view of language. His alternative struck me as very odd, but it also felt "right." I was very excited – I had discovered something important and I had no idea what! I went to Fred and said, "Listen to this!"

> The structure of speech is not simply the mirror image of the structure of thought. It cannot, therefore, be placed on thought like clothes off a rack. Speech does not merely serve as the expression of developed thought. Thought is restructured as it is transformed into speech. It is not expressed but completed in the word. Therefore, precisely because of the contrasting directions of movement, the development of the internal and external aspects of speech form a true identity. (Vygotsky, 1987, p.251)

Vygotsky was seeing thinking and speaking as one dialectical process, one activity. Children can perform as speakers – and thereby learn to speak – because speaking-thinking is a completive social activity. This non-expressionist understanding of language was a particularly satisfying alternative to the two separate worlds view (the private one of thinking and the social one of speaking) that Fred and I had rejected. Even more, though, it helped us understand what is going on in therapy. Here is how Fred described this discovery some years later:

> One of the immediate implications that I drew from this extraordinary new picture was that if speaking is the completing of thinking, if what we have here is a continuous process of building, then this undermines the notion that the only allowable "completer" is the same person who's doing the thinking. For, if the process is completive, then it seemed to me that what we're looking at is language – and this goes back to Wittgenstein – as an activity of building. That is, what is happening when speaking or writing, when we are participating in a dialogue, discussion or conversation, is that we are not simply saying what's going on but are *creating* what's going on... And we understand each other by virtue of engaging in that shared creative activity. (Newman, 1999b, p.128)

As Fred and I continued to develop our method, articulate it theoretically and expand its practice, it became clearer to us that the human ability to create with language – to complete, and be completed by, others – is, for adults as well as for little children, a continuous process of creating who we are becoming, a tool-and-result of the activity of developing.

I love dogs. How they are with each other and with humans intrigues and amuses me endlessly. Maybe if I lived in the country or the suburbs I wouldn't see so much of this, but in a city with a million dogs I probably run into a hundred dogs a day. (I had a dog during my twenties and thirties – who was of course the best dog in the world – and there are now two canines in my life, collectively owned, so my dog interaction is higher than the average New Yorker's.) One thing my dog fascination does is reinforce my non-belief in essences. When I look at dogs, it's impossible to see any one thing that's common to all (think chihuahua, Newfoundland and Basset hound, for example). I see, instead, almost endless ways they are related. I think dogs display beautifully what Wittgenstein called family resemblances – "a complicated network of similarities overlapping and criss-crossing: sometimes overall similarities, sometimes similarities of detail" (Wittgenstein, 1953, para 66) – which overlap and criss-cross in the same way as "the various resemblances between members of a family: build, features, colour of eyes, gait, temperament, etc. etc." (Wittgenstein, 1953, para 67). Family resemblance was Wittgenstein's response to the insistence that he must tell "what the essence of a language-game, and hence of language, is" (Wittgenstein, 1953, para 65). Dogs are a delightful reminder to follow his advice and "look and see" what is common, in language and in life.

My first published academic paper should have mentioned Vygotsky, but it didn't. It was a research study entitled "Imitation in Language Development: If, When and Why" that appeared in *Cognitive Psychology* (Bloom, Lightbown and Hood, 1974). I had begun graduate school at Brown University's PhD program in linguistics, switched to Columbia's linguistics department upon moving back to New York, then switched to Columbia's psychology department, and finally wound up where I belonged, working with Lois Bloom in the developmental psychology program at Columbia's Teachers College. Patsy Lightbown and I (still Lois Hood) were Bloom's research assistants developing, with her, longitudinal, observational research methods of studying early language development. Our orientation was in process; while theoretically we were drawn to both Chomsky and Piaget, our sensibilities were socio-cultural and ethnographic. But even at this early stage of the Bloom lab research, context and meaning making were primary.

Among the issues of debate at the time was how important imitation was in early language learning, the subject of this particular article. Our data for this study came from participant observations of six children who were transitioning from single word utterances to syntax from roughly the time they were eighteen months to two years old. We found that some of them imitated and others did not, and all were developing normally, so it was clear that imitation was not necessary for them to become speakers (I still think that's an important finding). What interested us even more was the overall context of their imitative speech in the flow of the conversations they were having. For the children who imitated did not imitate anything and everything they heard, but only words and structures they appeared to be in the process of learning (that is, ones they had only recently begun to use non-imitatively). Had any of us done more than skim the 1962 edition of Vygotsky's *Thought and Language* at the time, we would have realized that what we were seeing was the process of creating the ZPD where learning leads development. For those children who imitated, doing so was one way they performed as speakers. Twenty years later, after Fred's and my epiphany about others completing for you, I returned to this research study with a new understanding of the role of imitation in language learning (Newman and Holzman, 1997, pp.110–113).

"An experimental psychologist turned maverick cross-disciplinary explorer of human cognition" – that's how I described Michael Cole in a recent semi-autobiographical essay (Holzman, 2003, p.39). Not bad, but it does not do him justice. Mike had created a unique scholar-community institution and marvelous ZPD in his Laboratory of Comparative Human Cognition at Rockefeller University. He was the first to make me aware of the link between politics and psychology – by his commitment to bringing women, minority and non-western scholars into his work, his concern with inequality and the ways that psychological theory perpetuated it, and his Vygotsky-like "search for method" for an ecologically valid cognitive psychology. I worked closely with Mike from 1976 until 1979 when he moved his lab out west to the University of California at San Diego. It was a time of serious adult play – with ideas, methods of study, data collection and tools of analysis. What was it about schooling and about everyday life that made it the case that street smart kids were school dumb? Could we find even one instance of an individual cognitive act outside of a classroom setting? Could we pinpoint racism in a classroom? Could we show how learning disability was socially constructed? Could we not only provide evidence that experimental, cognitive psychology was ecologically invalid, but would we also succeed in creating an ecologically valid alternative?

These were challenging and socially-politically important tasks (ones "raised by history," to use a Vygotskian phrase, quoted in Levitan, 1982). Our recommendations? That the unit of analysis needed to be the "person–environment interface" and not the "individual" and that the laboratory was not merely a place but a methodology, a misguided paradigm that systematically distorted what was going on when children were and were not learning.

"Hi, my name is Lois Holzman. I teach psychology. I'm out here today because I think it's so important to support young people doing something positive for their communities. That's what the All Stars Talent Show Network, a city wide anti-violence program, is. I'm talking to people like you and asking you to support the young people of the All Stars by giving a dollar or 5 dollars or 25 dollars."

This was the "R and D" for what became known in the activist community of which my work is a part as "the street performance." Like all the programs my colleagues and I created, the All Stars Talent Show Network was built by volunteers like me reaching out to ordinary people – for financial support, for participants, for audiences, for fellow builders. For years we had gone door to door in city apartment houses and suburban homes. Now the idea was to talk a little bit to a lot of people. We created a 45-second "rap" that could stop and engage passersby on NYC's busy street corners. Five or six of us set up a literature table as home base, fanned out a bit into the crowd, made eye contact with someone and delivered our personal versions of the rap. Those who were interested we would speak with in more depth at another time. (We invited people to give us their names and phone numbers so we could call them back, give them an update and ask them to contribute more. Many, many did.)

Of all the research I've done, this is the project of which I'm most proud. Today the All Stars (www.allstars.org) not only continues to reach tens of thousands of New York City kids, but through its expansion to cities up and down the east and west coasts, thousands more are participating. My involvement with this extraordinary youth development/supplemental education project is many faceted (some of them more psychological in the traditional sense), but to have contributed in this way is very special to me.

How was it that I and artists, actors, social workers, teachers, doctors and secretaries could do this? We could and did by performing as other than who we were. We created the "stage" upon which we could perform bold and friendly and outgoing and proud of what we were doing, rather than behaving shy and intimidated and embarrassed. And in doing so, we became bold and friendly and outgoing and proud.

This kind of grassroots fundraising is essential if you've decided to be independent from government, university and corporate funding (as all the projects I'm involved in are). But it's more than just a way to raise money. It's community organizing. It's relationship building. It's giving people the opportunity to do something small. It's allowing them to be touched and to be giving, if they choose. It's finding out what people think. It's discovering that they care. For about 20 years I regularly talked in this way to people on the street and at their doors, as a community organizer who happens to be a psychologist. It's an antidote to cynicism.

From 1979 to 1996, I was on the faculty of Empire State College teaching and mentoring students in human development, community and human services and educational studies. The non-traditional part of the State University of New York, Empire was the kind of school I would have gone to if it had existed at the time – its organizational structure and design actually supported learning. Students got to create their own programs of study and degrees with the assistance and expertise of the faculty. A degree could consist of different kinds of learning activities, including individualized courses with a faculty member, independent study, group studies, courses at neighboring universities, practica and internships, and credit for life experience. As long as students could demonstrate "college level learning" it didn't matter how they developed it. The whole set-up presumed that the students were learners. These students were mostly working-class adults: changing careers; out of prison or off drugs; finishing their degrees after raising children; managers, administrators and mental health workers being pressured to get a bachelor's degree; NYC police officers required to obtain an associate's degree; artists and musicians wanting to work with kids. The few forays I made into traditional colleges and universities to teach an occasional course taught me just how radical this was.

Empire was a dream for an academic like me. It was a place that provided primarily working-class undergraduates with the attention, support, respect and responsibility that elite PhD programs provided to their graduate students. I had been privileged to have that at Columbia University and I loved being able to give it to these students. Besides, you could teach pretty much what you wanted in ways that you wanted – and, most wonderful to me, there were no tests or grades.

My colleagues were primarily progressives (several of them leftists) who had left more traditional and prestigious institutions to create this experimental college. At first, I fit right in. I was a leftist, and a political activist – a builder of a new independent political movement challenging the entrenched two-party structure of US electoral politics. Little did I know that, for some of my colleagues, this was politically incorrect. Unbeknownst to me, an underground letter denouncing my political affiliations and containing false accusations about the work Fred and I were doing (including social therapy) was making the rounds of the faculty. This McCarthyite tactic was spearheaded by progressives loyal to the Democratic Party who were not happy about the possibility of an independent party to its left. The letter recommended that I be fired or stop the political work I was doing.

When I finally found out about this from a friend, I immediately went to tell the dean who, it turned out, already knew. Naively, I thought he and my closest colleagues would be as outraged as I was. They weren't. No big deal, they said. Just forget it. I didn't. Instead, I called a faculty meeting at which we could have open dialogue on freedom of speech and academic freedom. We had the meeting and I remained at the college for many more years.

Fast forward to August 2003. About a week before the American Psychological Association (APA) convention, I received an email from one of APA's top executives telling me that they would be providing security at my presentations. It seemed that the APA office had received some phone calls and emails demanding that I not be allowed to present because social therapy was dangerous and harmful, and that Fred Newman was a cult leader. (Since then, I have been "graduated" – by some who attack our work – from a cult follower to a cult leader.)

In between that early 1980s secret letter and the 2003 APA convention, there were many other attacks on my work, character and associates. I have always tried to learn from these offenses: what it is about institutional psychology and popular psychology that contributes to people believing, even for a moment, ridiculous charges they may hear; what my own vulnerabilities are; and how to find a way to build something positive from such ugliness. Most recently, in the face of charges that social therapists violate boundaries, Fred and I have opened up dialogue among psychologists on the need to re-examine the very concept of boundaries if new postmodern and relational psychologies are to exist. Such approaches, in which human life is understood as relational rather than individualistic, raise a new set of methodological issues and call out for a new way of thinking through ethical issues.

Psychotherapy's legitimate concern with the possibility that therapeutic relationships might become exploitative and violate an individual's rights has turned to a worry about boundary violations, attempts to define and regulate how therapists and clients interact, and critiques of such attempts. But all this rests on the assumption of the individual as the primary human unit. If your practice does not accept that assumption, then what is a boundary violation? (For example, a tenet of social therapeutic practice is that people need to be organized as a social unit in order to carry out the task of getting therapeutic help and developing emotionally.) It's important to keep in mind such differences in the logic and ethics of paradigm-shifting psychotherapeutic practices so that they are examined and questioned as what they are – self-conscious attempts to transform psychotherapy – rather than as distortions of standard paradigmatic practices.

Tall and thin, Vesna Ognjenovic looked wispy at first. She spoke, too, in a soft voice. I walked in a little late and sat in the back of the room where she was presenting her work on poetry and drawing workshops with children affected by war in what had been Yugoslavia. Then I noticed her strong hands, watched her expressive face and listened to what she was saying and I felt what a strong woman she was. Her strength – I was to learn over many coffees that day – was born of pain and sadness (of war and destruction) and love and passion (for the work and play of creating life). It was 1996, and we were in Geneva for the Second International Conference for Socio-Cultural Research: Vygotsky–Piaget. I went up to Vesna at the end of the session and said, "We have to talk!" She and her colleagues were focusing on the emotional development of these children, not on their psychic states. The children's collective engagement in creative activity (poetry and drawing), they believed, was growthful for them – and growth was the way to deal with trauma.

I'd say we fell in love those days in Geneva, so moved were we by each other's lives and work. Vesna kept shaking her head in disbelief that here I was, a Marxist from New York, who had a practice and a community that were giving expression to all that she believed about building a better world. She said it gave her hope. I was deeply touched by this – and by her story. I heard how when the war broke out, she had sat in a café for days despairing over the end of socialism, the end of Yugoslavia, the horrible war, the end of meaning. How she then left the university to do something (she wasn't sure what) for the tens of thousands of refugees (especially the children), the trickle (at first) of friends and students who joined her, the growth of their community (called Zdravo da Ste/Hi Neighbor), and how much there is to do. Vesna was a Vygotskian who saw the revolutionary Vygotsky. She was a kindred spirit.

Just about every year since then, I have gone to Serbia or Bosnia-Herzegovina to participate in Zravo da Ste's trainings and seminars or Vesna and her colleagues have come to New York to participate in the broad community of which the Institute is a part. Our separate work has been growing and expanding over these years. (Through its dozens of educational and cultural projects involving many thousands of children, teens and adults, Zdravo da Ste/Hi Neighbor is doing among the most radically humanistic educational, human development and community building work anywhere.) So has what we have been creating together – at first out of our similarities and then, once we gave voice to them, our differences (for starters, we relate very differently to country and land, to tradition, to ritual, to performance, to emotionality). I think we have learned from our being together how American and how Slavic we each are, how these differences play out in how we support people to exercise their creative power to develop and build community, and how to accept and be more playful with these cultural identities. I feel greatly enriched.

My colleagues sometimes introduce me as the institute's international ambassador because I travel all over the world meeting people like Vesna. (I don't really like being called that, although I've never told them so because I love the pride with which they say it.) Going to conferences, lecturing, leading workshops, visiting programs, talking long into the night with newly met colleagues – whether in Belgrade, London, Moscow, Johannesburg, Amsterdam, Stockholm or Caracas – I feel very close to the New York City "street performance." This international outreach is a community organizer's dream (an organizer who happens to be a psychologist, that is). It's an adventure in community building in a very tough community (academia). It's an adventure in performing in a highly rule-and-role governed environment. It's an adventure in relational responsiveness in which I am (mostly) very responsive. It's a privilege to be able to learn firsthand about hundreds of innovative projects being developed in villages, towns and cities and to build relationships with so many extraordinary ordinary people. And just like talking to people on street corners, it's an antidote to cynicism.

I now have a name for the organizing I do – performing the world. That's the title of two international conferences and a broader community that emerged around them. The 2001 conference, subtitled "Communication, Improvisation and Societal Practice," was convened by me, Ken Gergen, Mary Gergen, Sheila McNamee and Fred Newman. In 2003, "Performing the World 2: The Second International Conference Exploring the Potential of Performance for Personal, Organizational and Social-Cultural Change" was convened by me, Sheila McNamee, Fred Newman and Lois Shawver. For all of us, performance is an alternative to individualistic, behavioral and cognitive views of what it means to be a person. We invited colleagues whose work taps into the human capacity to perform (on stage and off) to participate and put out a call to reach others doing similar work. We weren't disappointed. Both events introduced us to hundreds of people whose work – in psychology, psychotherapy, education, health care, youth development, organizational and community development – displays, investigates and plays with performance. Coming to know these committed and adventurous women and men greatly enriches my life. I see them as leaders of the difficult task of creating a new psychology based in social growth and collective creativity, a new psychology of becoming. They, and their communities, are the postmodern revolutionaries.

The events of the past century have shown that people cannot produce lasting revolution with Revolution. If you want an explanation for why, as a developmental psychologist, I decided to become a revolutionary and why, as a revolutionary, I'm so deeply concerned with development, this would be a good one. But let's treat it like we should all explanations – as a post hoc story (and not a bad one either). The process of rejecting the ideology of developmental psychology (indeed, of all psychology) has helped me understand better the danger of all ideology and watch for signs of it in my own work and talk. So, who better to quote now than Karl Marx.

It's people who change the world, Marx said. Many take him to mean "the working class" or "the proletariat," a sensible reading to be sure, but an ideological one that ignores Marx's substantial humanism and concern with people (all people) developing. His language in the following quote from *The German Ideology* is 19th century, but his sentiment is consistent with my 21st-century sensibility:

> We have further shown that private property can be abolished only on condition of an all-round development of individuals, because the existing character of intercourse and productive forces is an all-round one, and only individuals that are developing in an all-round fashion can appropriate them, i.e., can turn them into free manifestations of their lives. (Marx and Engels, 1973, p.117)

Developmental activity, the participatory process in which people exercise their collective power to create new environments and new "all-round" learning and development, is postmodern revolutionary activity. That's as non-ideological as I can be.

My sister changed her name from Sandra to Natanya sometime in the 1960s. My brother reversed his first and middle names (the child Freddie became the young man David) about the same time. My parents seemed OK with it. I thought it was a little strange that they cared that much about what they were called. But I was glad they did it if it bothered them so much. Natanya died in October 2002, a few months after being diagnosed with pancreatic cancer. Some sisters are pals; others are competitive. Natanya and I were neither. We were intimate without being close. We shared similar values yet chose to create our lives very differently. We liked that we had different skills and strengths and passions and weaknesses. We profoundly respected each other's independent path. It felt "right" to us that we were of the same family. We didn't reminisce or tell family stories. We talked. It was just how we were together.

References

Baker, G.P. (1992) "Some remarks on 'language' and 'grammar'." *Gruzer Philosophische Studien* 42, 107–131.

Bloom, L. Lightbown, P. and Hood, L. (1974) "Imitation in language development: If, when and why." *Cognitive Psychology 6*, 380–420. Reprinted in L. Bloom *et al. Language Development from Two to Three.* New York: Cambridge University Press.

Holzman, L. (2003) "Creating the context: An introduction." In L. Holzman and R. Mendez (eds) *Psychological Investigations: A Clinician's Guide to Social Therapy.* New York: Brunner-Routledge.

Holzman, L. and Newman, F. (1979) *The Practice of Method: An Introduction to the Foundations of Social Therapy.* New York: NY Institute for Social Therapy and Research.

Levitan, K. (1982) *One is not Born a Personality: Profiles of Soviet Education Psychologists.* Moscow: Progress.

McNamee, S., Gergen, K.J. and Associates (1999) *Relational Responsibility: Resources for Sustainable Dialogue.* Thousand Oaks, CA: Sage.

Marx, K. and Engels, F. (1973) *The German Ideology.* New York: International.

Newman, F. (1999a) "Therapeutics as a way of life." Talk given in New York City.

Newman, F. (1999b) "A therapeutic deconstruction of the illusion of self." In L. Holzman (ed) *Performing Psychology: A Postmodern Culture of the Mind.* New York: Routledge.

Newman, F. and Holzman, L. (1997) *The End of Knowing: A New Developmental Way of Learning.* London: Routledge.

Vygotsky, L.S. (1978) *Mind in Society.* Cambridge, MA: Harvard.

Vygotsky, L.S. (1987) *The Collected Works of L.S. Vygotsky*, Vol. 1. New York: Plenum.

Wittgenstein, L. (1953) *Philosophical Investigations.* Oxford: Blackwell.

CHAPTER 6

A Psychologist without a Country
or
Living Two Lives in the Same Story

Dan P. McAdams

Let me confess: I live a double life, split between empiricism and hermeneutics. I do so publicly, with little shame but more than a little awkwardness. It is awkward to explain to my scientific colleagues that I no longer "run subjects in labs" because I am too busy trying to understand what human lives mean. And it is awkward to explain to my humanist colleagues why I still insist on using statistical procedures to test hypotheses about the stories people live by. I would like to say that I am not bothered by the awkwardness, that I am comfortable moving back and forth between intellectual homes, that I have managed to rise above it all because I know, deep in my heart, that I am doing the right thing. But that would be a lie. The truth is this: I would love to live as a full-fledged patriot for both countries, loyal to their respective creeds and constitutions. But my dual citizenship never seems to achieve the comfortable fit for which I long. Nonetheless, my double life is not without its rewards. And I have even managed to make a story out of it.

From the steel mills to the Ivy League

The story is, in certain ways, embarrassingly trite. Poor boy rises from humble origins and makes good. Think Ben Franklin, Horatio Alger. Gary, Indiana in the 1960s had not yet experienced the precipitous loss of jobs in the steel industry that would eventually lay waste to its economy. But for a boy with intellectual inclinations and literary interests, Gary was a cultural wasteland, or at least felt like one. I knew *one* other boy who read books outside of class, and he moved away in the seventh grade. I played baseball, did very well in school, attended the local Baptist church, hung around the house a lot and complained, incessantly, of being bored. Unlike most of his peers, my father was not gainfully employed in the steel mills. He chose to sell cars instead, and he was very good at it. But my mother saw little of the money once they divorced. She raised my two siblings and me on her earnings as a telephone operator. It was a good union job, and her wages kept us above the poverty line, but just barely.

Adults I knew growing up in Gary seemed to live what I have since heard called a *declension narrative*. They romanticized their youth, but they had little good to say about the adult years: Danny, enjoy yourself when you are young, because it is all down hill after that. They put in their time in the steel mills, cleaned house, mowed their lawns, raised their families, drank pretty hard. By the time they hit 25, they were reminiscing about the good old days. For me, the good days would have to be in the future, I imagined. From about eighth grade onwards, I expected that the good days would begin when I got to college.

I was right. I enrolled in Valparaiso University in the fall of 1972, having received an Indiana scholarship that paid my tuition for any in-state school I might attend. For my life story, leaving Gary and going to college (15 miles away) is *the* watershed event. I might as well have gone to live in Paris, or Oxford. I made lifelong friends in college. Within months of arriving at Valpo, I met the woman who would eventually become my wife. By the end of my freshman year, I was reading many of the authors who would shape my intellectual identity – Freud, Dostoyevsky, Kierkegaard, Sartre, and Buber, especially. These authors, among many others, are like characters in my life story. I imagine dialogues with them. A few years ago, I heard a scratchy BBC recording of Sigmund Freud, from the end of his life. He sounds so much better in my head.

My dual citizenship in the world of ideas is foreshadowed in my double major at Valparaiso University. I majored in Psychology and in the Humanities. But I resisted thinking hard about the distinction between the two during my undergraduate years. I developed an interest in psychology through courses I took in Christ College, which is the name of Valparaiso's honors program in humanities. It was in Christ College, not the Psychology Department, where I first encountered Freud. For one seminar taken during my freshman year, we read Plato's *Republic*, Aristotle's *De Anima*, Freud's *Civilization and its Discontents*, and Skinner's *Walden Two*. We discussed each author's understanding of the relationship between self and society. Of the four, Freud spoke most clearly to me, perhaps because of the beauty of his prose, translated so eloquently by James Strachey. The literary quality of Freud's works – the stories he told, the metaphors he used, the poetry of his arguments – this all appealed to me as much as did his ideas. (Indeed, Freud won the Goethe prize for literature toward the end of his career.) I am less Freudian now than I once was in my view of selves and society. But I still feel the thrill when I read his original words.

When I enrolled in Harvard's graduate program in Psychology and Social Relations in the fall of 1976, I foolishly believed that I would continue to spend time in seminars talking about Freud, self, and society. Instead, the first year of graduate school was mainly about research methodology, construct validity, measurement, statistics, and the arcane debates raging in the field of personality psychology at the time regarding the relative efficacy of personality traits and situational constraints in the prediction of human behavior over time and across situations.

But this was not as bad as it sounds. Inspired by my graduate mentors (David McClelland and George Goethals), I continued to read literature, philosophy, and social and personality theory, though I kept these books hidden in my backpack when I walked into the lab, and I threw myself into the world of research. I developed an objective coding system for analyzing short imaginative stories told by research subjects in response to ambiguous picture cues (a method called the Thematic Apperception Test, or TAT). I used the TAT to assess individual differences in a personality characteristic that I called *intimacy motivation* (McAdams, 1980).

The TAT was the brainchild of Henry A. Murray, a maverick Harvard psychologist who championed the scientific study of human lives in culture during a period (1930 to 1960) when American psychology was dominated by the behaviorists. I was too late to Harvard to know Murray in his prime, but I read assiduously his masterwork, *Explorations in Personality* (Murray, 1938), wherein he laid out an agenda for studying persons that seemed to me, in the late 1970s, to blend psychological science and the humanities. Murray argued for biographical methods in the study of lives. The stories people told about their lives might serve as raw data for scientific inquiry, he insisted. A similar message, but with a marked developmental slant, came from my reading of Erik Erikson, who worked with Murray for a short time in the 1930s. Erikson viewed the human life cycle in terms of eight psychosocial stages, ranging from the basic "trust vs. mistrust" dynamic in infancy to the last stage of "integrity vs. despair," to be faced in old age. The two stages I found most intriguing were the late-adolescent stage of *identity* (vs. role confusion) and the middle-adult stage of *generativity* (vs. stagnation). Identity raises the question of "Who am I?" (and relatedly "How do I fit into the adult world?"). Generativity asks, "How can I contribute something to that world and to future generations as a positive legacy of the self?"

Murray and Erikson helped to keep me connected to Freud. Whereas Murray coded autobiographical memories for motivational themes in a way not completely dissimilar to Freud's treatment of dreams, Erikson composed full-length psychobiographies of Martin Luther and Mahatma Gandhi that were informed by his own psychosocial reading of Freud. For me and for a number of other personality psychologists, Murray and Erikson are founding fathers in what we call the personological tradition in the social sciences. The *personological tradition* seeks to blend the tough and the tender in the study of persons, employing a wide range of scientific and interpretive methods to understand individual human lives in their full developmental and cultural contexts. Many of my closest colleagues today are members of a small group called the Society for Personology. Many of them also live double lives.

Scientific research

I love the humanities, but I believe in science. I will read Dostoyevsky over Darwin any day. (Who wouldn't?) But Darwin is potentially right (or wrong) about something in the world in a way that Dostoyevsky can never be. Ironically, this may give Dostoyevsky, or any great novelist, a certain edge over the individual scientist when it comes to long-term relevance. We still read and discuss Plato and Aristophanes, but the scientific contributions of ancient Greece are mainly historical curiosities today. Shakespeare has a kind of staying power that no scientist can ever, in good conscience, expect. In principle at least, science moves relentlessly forward, ruthlessly discarding theories once they outlive their usefulness and abandoning any hypothesis that turns out not to be supported by the data at hand. The more or less data-driven, open-ended, progressive, self-correcting, and socially consensual characteristics of the scientific enterprise are among those factors that give it a priority over other systems and approaches when it comes to explaining how the world works.

At Harvard, I learned how to *do* personality psychology in a scientific way. A key lesson for me was the need to develop reliable and valid measures of difficult to pin down constructs, like intimacy motivation. In my first academic position, at Loyola University of Chicago, I continued to collect data and test hypotheses regarding intimacy motivation. Eventually, I turned my attention to the construct of generativity, which Erikson defined as the adult's concern for and commitment to promoting the well-being of future generations. Again, I began with measurement, designing scales and thematic procedures for assessing individual differences in different aspects of generativity (McAdams and de St. Aubin, 1992). Some people (at certain points in their lives and in certain domains of functioning) are more generative than others. These individual differences, measured via the procedures developed by my research team, have been empirically linked to a wide range of important behavioral and social outcomes, ranging from parenting practices, voting and volunteer work to motivational conflict, mental health, and identity.

Intimacy motivation and generativity are two constructs that have proven useful in scientific studies of personality. They constitute two psychologically important and socially consequential dimensions with respect to which persons can be said to differ from each other. But people differ from each other in countless ways. How might personality psychologists ever account for all of these differences? Different personality theories – Freud, Jung, Adler, Murray, social learning theories, humanistic theories, trait theories – all make different claims as to what variables matter in accounting for human individuality. Traditionally, the field of personality psychology has suffered from a lack of consensus on what the full domain of human individuality might or should look like. I have obsessed over this problem since my graduate school days, for it goes directly to the definition of the very field of inquiry with which I identify as a scientist.

If personality psychology is the scientific study of the whole person, then what do we know when we know a person? The answer to this question, I believe, should define the scientific field of personality psychology. I have argued that the answer to the question is threefold, suggesting three different levels or discourses of personality (McAdams, 1995, 2001). A growing number of personality researchers are adopting my scheme. While I am flattered to have the impact, I am also frustrated by the tendency among my scientific colleagues to treat the three levels I have identified as if they were objective, concrete, absolute things. There is still a naive realism that runs through the science of personality psychology, as if constructs like "extroversion" and "ego strength" were tangible entities rather than useful constructions developed by a scientific community to make sense of what we see. Even when we identify those brain functions that give rise to individual differences in, say, openness to experience, the construct itself is defined in a social and cultural context. And we would never bother to examine the construct if its manifestations were not judged to be important for life in the culture wherein we live.

Level One in my organizational scheme is the discourse of *dispositional traits*, which are described as broad and relatively stable individual differences in basic styles of thought, feeling, and behavior. Factor analytic studies suggest that these basic differences cluster into five general areas – introversion/extroversion, neuroticism, conscientiousness, agreeableness, and openness to experience. Important advances in the field of personality psychology over the past 25 years now demonstrate that individual differences in basic personality traits are relatively stable over time, substantially heritable, and highly predictive of important cognitive, emotional, and behavioral trends aggregated across different situations.

Level Two brings in more developmentally and socially contingent and contextualized constructs of personality, such as goals and values, motives, stage-specific concerns, and domain specific skills and tendencies. I call these *characteristic adaptations*. They generally refer to what people want (and do not want) in life and how they strive to get what they want (and avoid what they do not want) in particular situations, at particular developmental periods, or with respect to particular social roles. Level Two is where we find intimacy motivation and generativity. Whereas dispositional traits like extroversion show substantial consistency over time, characteristic adaptations like generativity may wax and wane in importance as a function of changing circumstances and contexts.

Dispositional traits sketch an outline of human individuality. Characteristic adaptations fill in many of the details. In describing and seeking to explain what makes one person different from another, the personality psychologist should begin with reliable and valid data regarding where the person stands on a series of dispositional dimensions of human functioning and then move to the more contextualized and personologically rich detail to be found in characteristic adaptations. Still, no combination of traits, motives, values, and developmental concerns will give the scientist a full understanding of what that person's life *means*. The meanings of lives lie, I believe, in stories, in the reconstructed *history* and anticipated future that come to be narrated as a self-defining personal myth. This is the sense, I now believe, in which Murray was prescient in 1938 when he wrote that the "hi*story* of the organism is the organism" (p.40). In modern societies like ours, people's internalized and evolving life stories constitute their *narrative identities*. Narrative identity is the third level of human personality.

Narrative identity: Making lives into stories

In the summer of 1982, I taught a graduate seminar at Loyola on the topic of self and identity. Only seven students signed up for the class, most of them from the PhD program in Clinical Psychology. They enjoyed reading and talking about Heinz Kohut's self psychology and the writings of Freud and the British object relations theorists, for the clinical applications in these works were clear. But the class conversations lagged when we considered William James's classic chapter on the self, Erikson's writings on identity, Goffman's dramaturgical approach, contributions from cognitive social psychology, and more philosophical offerings. The students found a bit too academic my obsession with these questions: What is identity? What would identity look like *if you could see it?* James imagined the "I" as a *stream*; Goffman invoked the imagery of roles and *performance*; Seymour Epstein described the self as akin to a *theory*, complete with axioms, corollaries, and hypotheses to be tested in everyday thought and behavior. I wanted a better metaphor.

No suitable metaphor arose that summer, but the students and I did make some progress in our thinking about self and identity, or at least they humored me into thinking we had. To frame class discussions, I found especially useful James's distinction between the self-as-subject (the "I") and the self-as-object (the "me"). James's stream of consciousness and the psychoanalytic conception of the ego are more about the I than the me, we concluded. Jane Loevinger describes the ego as a master synthesizer of experience. It is an active, agential force, a center of subjectivity, a position or stance, albeit shifting, from which the world is seen. Even if we believe in multiple Is in the same "person," each I is more like a perceiver or constructor of experience than like that which is perceived or constructed. By contrast, the me refers to aspects of selfhood that are potentially perceived or constructed, as in the notion of a self-concept, an enacted role, and Erikson's concept of identity. The I emerges early in experience, perhaps by the end of the first year of life. Once it emerges, the I begins to construct a me – an image of itself, as it were. Children's self-concepts (their mes) become progressively more complex and differentiated over time. "I am Amanda," my daughter would say, when she was seven years old. "I am a girl." "I live in a white house." "I am best friends with Jennifer." "I love to ice skate." "I want to be an artist when I grow up." "Other people say I'm cute." Amanda is describing her "me."

From Erikson's point of view, however, Amanda at age seven does not really have an identity yet. Sure, she has a self-concept. She knows what she is. She can ascribe traits and characteristic adaptations to herself – Levels One and Two in my personality scheme. But *who* are you, Amanda? What does your life *mean*? What provides your life with *unity* and *purpose*? These questions make no sense to Amanda at age seven because the issues of who she is, what her life means, and what kinds of purpose may be discerned in it are not *problematic* for her. What's the problem? she screams. Quit bothering me with these stupid questions! For Erikson, identity kicks in when these questions become problematic, when they no longer seem so stupid. Today, Amanda is a college student. Lately, she has been wondering: Who am I? What does my life mean? The I encounters identity, in the Eriksonian sense, when the Me becomes a problem. This typically happens, Erikson maintained, in late adolescence and young adulthood.

Why does identity wait so long? Why isn't Amanda bothered by identity questions when she is seven years old? Erikson argued that puberty helps to usher in a new concern with selfhood. I am no longer a child, the teenager comes to realize. What am I now? And how is what I am now similar to and different from what I was before? Cognitive development also plays a crucial role in the birth of narrative identity. With the emergence of what Piaget called formal-operational thinking, adolescents begin to understand the self (me) and the world in highly abstract and hypothetico-deductive terms. They perceive inconsistencies in their thought and behavior as they move from one life situation to the next, and they seek to resolve these inconsistencies and construct a more coherent self. The self-as-object – the me – becomes something of an abstraction itself, Erikson maintained. It becomes an introspectively relevant problem to work on, or what Anthony Giddens calls a *self-reflexive project*. Futhermore, societal expectations and pressures weigh heavily in the adolescent years. Now is the time, adolescents are told, to think seriously about *who* you are. What do you want to do with your life? What do you really believe in? How will you make your way into the adult world? Now is the time for the I to begin to *arrange* the me into some kind of *configuration*, Erikson suggested, that may potentially provide life with some measure of unity and purpose. The configuration of the me – one's emerging identity in late adolescence and young adulthood – should make sense of who I am, who I was, and who I may be in the future. What kind of configuration might that be? If you could see it, what would it look like?

Some few months after I taught the class on self and identity I found the metaphor I was looking for. If you could see identity, I surmised, it would look like a *story*. A story incorporates a beginning, middle, and ending, working to organize a life into a reconstructed past, perceived present, and anticipated future. A story might provide a sensible explanation of how a hero moves through many different situations over time, plays many different roles, develops from one thing to another, and yet remains, in some fundamental, existential sense, the same hero over time and across situations and roles. A story typically contains multiple characters, to personify the different social mes that William James identified, and yet all the mes are integrated, in a sense, in that they exist within the same narrative frame. Beginning in late adolescence and young adulthood, I reasoned, people put their lives together into stories. They construct, internalize, and revise stories of the self. Like novelists, they work with the material they have been (implicitly) gathering for many years – key experiences that may stand out as critical scenes in the story, important interpersonal relationships, the values and norms of their society, and just about anything else that presents itself as something that could possibly work its way into a narrative to portray who I am. Identity is an internalized and evolving life narrative. Psychologically speaking, the narrative's primary function is to integrate a life, to provide an adult life with some degree of meaning, purpose, and unity.

As a person who studies life stories (and one occasionally prone to delusions of grandeur regarding his own narrative), I find it frustrating that I cannot recall clearly an epiphany scene in my own life wherein I suddenly came to believe that identity itself is like a life story. I also cannot sort out clearly what intellectual sources I drew upon to support my new claim. One book that strongly shaped my early views on the issue was Charme's (1984) *Meaning and Myth in the Study of Lives: A Sartrean Persepctive*. Charme described Sartre's notion that human lives are, in some ways, like "true novels," which work to create narrative order out of the chaos of personal experience. But given that Charme's book came out in 1984, I must have read it after I began thinking of identity as a life story. An obscure source that may have had a direct impact early on was Steele's (1982) psychobiography of Freud and Jung, wherein he argued that Freud's and Jung's theoretical differences were largely a result of the radically different stories they lived. Yet another even more obscure source, an eight-page chapter by Hankiss (1981), may also have primed me to think of identity as a story. Writing from a life-course, sociological perspective, Hankiss described different "ontologies of the self," in which individuals "mythologically re-arrange their life histories" (p.203) to create narrative explanations for how they believe they came to be. Yet another source was probably Tomkins's script theory of personality, introduced in Carlson (1981). But my initial reading of Carlson's precis coupled Tomkins's conception of life scripts with Goffman and other dramaturgical perspectives. Only later did I come to see Tomkins as something of a kindred spirit, for his notion of life script shared many commonalities with my own idea of a life story.

Energized by the metaphor of identity as a life story, I began doing life-story interviews with middle-aged adults in the fall of 1982. Initially, I described this venture as an exploration of "developmental mythologies." Taking a lead from an interview protocol devised by James Fowler for studying faith development, I asked the participants to think about their lives as if their lives were books, to divide their lives up into chapters, to describe key scenes – like high points, low points, and turning points – in their lives, and to imagine the future chapters of their stories. I also collected TAT data and other self-report psychological measures. Trying to link the interest in life stories to the research program I had begun in graduate school, I looked for themes in life-narrative interviews that might be empirically associated with more established psychological variables, like intimacy motivation. Perhaps not surprisingly, I found that adults whose TATs suggested high intimacy motivation tended to construct life stories that placed priority on warm and close interpersonal relationships. By contrast, individuals high in power motivation (also assessed on the TAT) tended to tell more agentic life narratives, emphasizing content themes of impact, victory, autonomy, and self-mastery. I also examined the complexity of the life narrative accounts by identifying the number of different plot archetypes the narrators seemed to employ. Individuals with higher levels of ego development (assessed on a sentence-completion test) tended to construct more complex life narratives, drawing upon a wider range of plot prototypes and identifying more conflict and more change in their life stories, compared to individuals scoring lower in ego development.

A year later, I began work on my first book, *Power, Intimacy, and the Life Story: Personological Inquiries into Identity* (McAdams, 1985). The book describes this early research linking life stories to personality variables, and it lays out a theory of identity as a life story. Beginning in late adolescence, I argued, people put their lives together into integrative narratives of the self. Accounts of these internalized stories can be "collected" in life-narrative interviews (and in open-ended questionnaires) and analyzed in objective, quantitative ways. Life stories incorporate many different content themes, but two main *thematic lines* appear to be agency/power and communion/intimacy. With respect to structure, life stories range from the simple to the complex, and these differences can also be measured and linked to other personality variables. Life stories contain key self-defining scenes or moments, which I called *nuclear episodes*. Narrators split themselves (the me) into different characters in the story, constructing multiple idealized personifications of the self, which I called *imagoes*. Imagoes themselves may be high in agency (e.g., "the warrior," "the sage"), high in communion ("the lover," "the caregiver"), high in both agency and communion ("the healer," "the peacemaker"), or low in both agency and communion ("the escapist," "the survivor"). The imagoes enact plots against a backdrop of personal beliefs and values, especially those drawn from religion, which I called the story's *ideological setting*. Looking to future chapters, narrators often spell out how they will have a positive impact on the world and leave an enduring legacy, what I called a *generativity script*.

When I wrote *Power, Intimacy, and the Life Story*, I believed I had found an effective way to synthesize my scientific and literary sensibilities. As a personality psychologist, I could examine the stories that people "have" about their lives. I could analyze and measure them as one might analyze and measure any psychological construct. Like a good personality psychologist, I could assess individual differences. Stories might be more complex and more variegated than, say, traits and motives, but they could still be pinned down long enough and with enough confidence so that the researcher could perform the necessary thematic dissection. In a sense, I was not unlike the naive realists I decried above, blithely assuming that psychological constructs – in this case, life stories – were *really* out there, or rather *in* there – that is, *in* people's heads. Today, I still insist that stories are indeed in there, in some sense. But it all seems much more complex today (and problematic) than I saw it in 1985.

Problematizing the story

In 1989, I moved to Northwestern University. I took a position in the Human Development and Social Policy (HDSP) program, located within the School of Education and Social Policy (SESP). HDSP brings together psychologists interested in human development with sociologists, economists, and policy experts. The HDSP program trains students to study and understand human development in the broad context of families, communities, and society, and it seeks to promote applied research that will inform public policy.

Shortly after I moved to Northwestern, I also began to work with students in the SESP Counseling Psychology PhD program. When the program in counseling shut down in the mid-1990s, I negotiated a move of half of my faculty line into Northwestern's Psychology Department, where I now work mainly with students in Clinical Psychology. As a result, today I am half time in HDSP and half time in Psychology – two dramatically different intellectual cultures. HDSP is wide ranging and interdisciplinary: Researchers employ methods ranging from econometrics to case-based ethnographies. In HDSP, I am one of a number of scholars interested in narratives and in qualitative methodologies in the social sciences. My background in empirical personality research, furthermore, gives me the odd reputation in HDSP of being one of the more hard-nosed scientists in the school. By contrast, Northwestern's Psychology Department is a very straight-laced, laboratory-based operation, wherein almost everybody (except me) runs experiments in laboratories. Even quantitative survey methods are regarded with some suspicion in this Psychology Department, and life stories, well, what are they? Yet my Psychology colleagues seem to respect me, mainly because my empirical research in personality gets published in mainline journals. I am their token humanist.

Had I remained the person I was in 1985, with the publication of *Power, Intimacy, and the Life Story*, my life in the Psychology Department at Northwestern would be much easier today. But had I frozen things at the level of my first book, I would never have landed the job in HDSP in the first place. By the time I got to Northwestern, my research was already moving in a more explicitly developmental direction, which was to become apparent in my second book on life stories, *The Stories We Live By* (McAdams, 1993). I had begun to talk more about a sociologically ascribed life *course* over and against a psychologically mandated life *cycle*, and I was already paying much closer attention than I did a few years earlier to social and cultural contexts in the construction of life narratives. I had also begun to see problems with the easy synthesis I had forged in my first book. Not only were life stories constructed through social interaction, as I acknowledged from the get-go, but they were also performed with respect to particular audiences, told with respect to certain discursive aims and traditions, and tailored for short-term strategic ends. Not only did stories integrate lives and provide some semblance of unity and purpose, as I argued in my first book, but they could also disrupt lives, express discontinuity and incoherence, contradict themselves and confuse their audiences, and fulfill a wide range of other functions – psychological, social, economic, political – that had little to do with Erikson's conception of identity. Stories could still be pinned down (momentarily) and analyzed, I continued to believe, but the researcher had to be much humbler and more careful than I seemed to be in my first book, wherein I described clear thematic patterns in stories, universal mythic archetypes, and fully articulated ideological settings simpatico with the plots and characters portrayed. Stories now seemed more dynamic, complex, fragmentary, contradictory, strategic, and socially constructed than they had only a few years before.

By the time I moved into HDSP, I had lost interest in the construct of intimacy motivation and was focusing much of my empirical attention on generativity. Given that I was a new father at the time, this shift seemed to make personal sense. It also made professional sense, for generativity linked readily to such policy-relevant ideas as parenting, volunteerism, and citizenship – issues to which my HDSP colleagues routinely turned their attention. As my students and I examined the manifestations and correlates of generativity among midlife adults in the research we conducted in the 1990s, we began to explore the life stories of adults who distinguished themselves in the realm of generativity.

In two ambitious studies, we administered our generativity measures to hundreds of adults, ranging in age from 35 to 65 years, and then called back for life-story interviews those adults scoring either especially high or especially low in generativity. Our first study focused mainly on professional white adults; the second incorporated African-American and white adults, working class and professional. After poring over the interview protocols for many years and coding them for a wide range of topics and ideas, we discovered a set of themes that consistently differentiated between the two groups. Central among these themes is the idea of *redemption* – which we define as the deliverance from suffering to an enhanced status or state. Put simply, highly generative adults tend to construct life-narrative accounts that contain a greater number of redemption episodes – scenes that begin with suffering but move to deliverance – than do adults scoring lower in generativity. In addition, highly generative adults are more likely than less generative adults to construct stories in which the protagonist (a) enjoys a special advantage early in life; (b) expresses sensitivity to the suffering of others or societal injustices as a child; (c) establishes a clear and strong belief system in adolescence that remains a source of unwavering conviction through the adult years; (d) experiences significant conflicts between desires for agency/power and desires for communion/intimacy; and (e) looks to achieve goals to benefit society in the future. Taken together, these themes depict a common life-narrative prototype embraced by many productive and caring midlife men and women in contemporary American society – what I call the *redemptive self*.

The redemptive self is a life-story prototype that serves well the generative efforts of midlife American adults, both black and white, both male and female. Their redemptive narratives suggest that these especially productive and caring men and women seek to give back to society in gratitude for the early blessings their stories tell them they obtained. In everyday life, generativity is tough and frustrating work. But if an adult constructs a narrative identity in which the protagonist's suffering in the short run often gives way to reward later on, he or she may be better able to sustain the conviction that seemingly thankless investments today will pay off for the future generation. Redemptive life stories support the kind of life strivings that a highly generative man or woman is likely to set forth.

But the redemptive self also says as much about American culture as it does about the highly generative American adults who tend to tell this kind of story about their lives. In my new book, *The Redemptive Self*, I argue that the life-story themes expressed by highly generative American adults recapture and couch in a psychological language especially cherished, as well as hotly contested, ideas in American cultural history – ideas that appear prominently in spiritual accounts of 17th-century Puritans, Benjamin Franklin's 18th-century autobiography, slave narratives and Horatio Alger stories from the 19th century, and the literatures of self-help and American entrepreneurship in the 20th century (McAdams, 2005). From the Puritans to Emerson to Oprah, the redemptive self has morphed into many different storied forms in the past 300 years as Americans have sought to narrate their lives through the redemptive discourses of atonement, emancipation, recovery, self-fulfillment, and upward social mobility. The stories speak of heroic individual protagonists – the *chosen people* – whose *manifest destiny* is to make a positive difference in a dangerous world, even when the world does not wish to be redeemed. The stories translate a deep script of American exceptionalism into the many contemporary discourses of success, recovery, development, and so on. It is as if especially generative American adults are, for better and for worse, the most ardent narrators of an oh-so American story.

In the past 20 years, social scientists of many different stripes have come to construe individual lives, social relationships, and cultural trends in terms of *narrative*. A major insight coming out of this wide-ranging literature is that life stories are *cultural texts*. Life stories reflect class and gender categories, political and economic forces, religious traditions, history, folklore, and the shifting complexities and uncertainties of contemporary postmodern life. Strongly influenced by many of these writings, I now look to life stories, like the redemptive self, to learn about the cultural world that the narrator inhabits. What kinds of stories can be told in that world? What are the privileged, master narratives? What counts as a *good* story in a given cultural context? What kinds of stories are marginalized? What kinds of stories cannot be told? Yet these cultural texts come to the listener through the voice and the consciousness (the I-ness) of an individual narrator, an agential self (the I) who appropriates what culture has to offer, selects and discards, modifies and personalizes in order to tell a story that aims, in some sense, to be true to lived experience. Life stories are not the neat individual constructions I imagined in

1985, but nor are they the hapless social constructions described by some postmodern theorists. Culture shapes narratives for sure, but narrators appropriate culture. Today I see life stories as *psychosocial constructions* – doubly authored by self and the social world.

In 1985, I knew that narrators tailor their storied accounts for particular audiences. But I saw this fact as a nuisance more than an opportunity. My training in personality psychology taught me to look for true scores on psychological constructs amidst measurement error. The fact that my research participants might tell me one thing and their parents another regarding the worst event that ever happened in their lives suggested a measurement error that I would need to work around. To minimize error, therefore, I developed a standardized interview, trained interviewers carefully, and developed objective content analysis systems for coding the narrative data once we had obtained them. I still believe that these methodological maneuvers are essential for doing the kind of hypothesis-testing studies I conduct with life stories. Had I not done things this way, I would never have discovered and validated the thematic categories that I now see as comprising the redemptive self.

Today, however, I tend to see the interviews we do in terms of a *co-construction* of narrative identity. A narrative account is performed before a particular kind of audience (the interviewer) in a particular kind of research setting. What results is not "the-one-and-only" life story a person "has" – the "true" story behind all the other performances – but it is not any old fleeting account either. Participants come to the setting with a wealth of images, metaphors, and accounts at their disposal – narrative resources that they *have*. They also have a great deal of implicit knowledge about the nature of interviews and research. They know that the interviewer wants something akin to the "truth" as they, the narrator, understands it. They know that the interviewer wants to know who they are, how they came to be, and where their life may be going in the future. They see their role as that of the subject of a biography. People have read or seen biographies on television. They are conversant in the norms of the genre – that they should tell about how things began in their lives, for example, that they should tell how things developed as well as remained the same, that they should identify heroes and villains, high points and turning points, that their lives should seem to be going somewhere. People have stories about these kinds of issues – stories that are different from the ones they might tell when trying, say, to woo a lover, or get a job, or pass the time waiting in line at the Wal-Mart. It is exactly these kinds of stories, performed in the presence of a sympathetic and curious biographer, that reflect a person's narrative identity. I believe the kinds of interviews my students and I do are well designed to bring to the performance the kinds of internalized stories that do explain for people how they came to be, stories that provide their lives with some semblance of unity and purpose. I believe that the storied accounts we hear do reflect an inner sense of narrative identity.

But I do not believe this as categorically as I did in 1985. I now see life narrative accounts as serving many different purposes. They provide identity for sure, but they are also told to entertain, instruct, enlighten, deceive, and disrupt. Many scholars have emphasized these other, non-identity functions in their writings on narrative. Accordingly, I have become fascinated with the many different hermeneutical strategies and epistemological stances expressed by the growing number of social scientists who engage in what Josselson and Lieblich (1993) call *the narrative study of lives*. The narrative study of lives takes me further and further away from my graduate school training in personality research. I now find stories themselves to be just as interesting as the people who tell them – probably more interesting, if truth be told. I enjoy immersing myself in the texts of people's life stories almost as much as I enjoyed pouring over the texts of Dostoyevsky and Kierkegaard in my freshman year at college. I say to myself, forget about the author for a minute: What does the text itself say to me? Forget about trying to figure out what kind of person wrote this text. Instead, ask this: What meanings may I glean from the story itself? And what meanings are being kept away from me? What does the story *not* say? Why doesn't the story say that? And on and on. When I first came to the idea that identity may be construed as a life story, I thought I had begun to solve the psychological problem of identity. But now I see that stories themselves are the problem for me – but a fascinating one.

This chapter narrates aspects of my own life story – aspects centered on the development of my *ideas* in psychology. I do believe that the story I have told shows a certain degree of *progress* in my thinking about the intellectual problems that began to emerge for me in my freshman year at college. Although my suffering has not been especially intense, I do believe that the story also expresses a modicum of redemption. At the same time, certain problems and conflicts have not been resolved. I am still split between the world of empirical psychology and the humanities. I still want to do scientific research on stories, even as I realize that stories will always resist my best efforts. I still lead something of a double life. But the fact that I can tell it to you in what I believe to be a coherent story tells me that a story can provide a life, even mine, with some degree of unity, purpose, and identity, even as it does so much more.

References

Carlson, R. (1981) "Studies in script theory: I. Adult analogs of a childhood nuclear scene." *Journal of Personality and Social Psychology 40*, 501–510.

Charme, S.T. (1984) *Meaning and Myth in the Study of Lives: A Satrean Perspective.* Philadelphia, PA: University of Pennsylvania Press.

Hankiss, A. (1981) "On the mythological re-arranging of one's life history." In D. Bertaux (ed) *Biography and Society.* Beverly Hills, CA: Sage.

Josselson, R. and Lieblich, A. (eds) (1993) *The Narrative Study of Lives*, Vol. 1. Thousand Oaks, CA: Sage.

McAdams, D.P. (1980) "A thematic coding system for the intimacy motive." *Journal of Research in Personality 14*, 413–432.

McAdams, D.P. (1985) *Power, Intimacy, and the Life Story: Personological Inquiries into Identity.* New York: Guilford Press.

McAdams, D.P. (1993) *The Stories We Live By: Personal Myths and the Making of the Self.* New York: William Morrow.

McAdams, D.P. (1995) "What do we know when we know a person?" *Journal of Personality 63*, 365–396.

McAdams, D.P. (2001) *The Person: An Integrated Introduction to Personality Psychology*, 3rd edn. New York: Wiley.

McAdams, D.P. (2005) *The Redemptive Self.* New York: Oxford University Press.

McAdams, D.P. and de St. Aubin, E. (1992) "A theory of generativity and its assessment through self-report, behavioral acts, and narrative themes in autobiography." *Journal of Personality and Social Psychology 62*, 1003–1015.

Murray, H.A. (1938) *Explorations in Personality.* New York: Oxford University Press.

Steele, R. (1982) *Freud and Jung: Conflicts of Interpretation.* London: Routledge and Kegan Paul.

CHAPTER 7

Life as a Symphony

Christopher M. Aanstoos

Overture

Where did we come from? Where are we going? And what's the point of the trip? Always intrigued by these big questions, as I grew older I came to see they were not merely my own. They are the hallmark of human existence: we are the being for whom the meaning of our being is a question. As Heidegger has shown, we are the occasion for Being to manifest itself through our capacity to attend to what it means to be. In responding to that call to own our capacity for manifesting Being emerges our consciousness, and our freedom. And our mortal responsibility, because unless we enact the meaningfulness of our existence, we spend our lives as if they were mindless accidents, manifesting nothing more than random collisions of protoplasm.

Psychology's contribution is to examine the particular subquestion "What does it mean to be a human being?" Though most psychologists avoid addressing this question, they answer it nonetheless, inevitably, but then only implicitly. For every psychology is necessarily also a perspective, however presupposed, about what it means to be human. Some imply that to be human is to be an organism, a biochemical compound or a physiological system, or a neural network. Other psychologies imply that to be human is to be a conditioned response, a moment in an ongoing causal chain of stimulus–response mechanisms, driven by contingencies of reinforcements. Others view the human as an information-processing system, computationally applying programmatic rules to bits of information.

But such perspectives focus only on the anonymous profile of human being, that is, lacking the essentially human act of owning one's own existence. Therefore, they are at best theories of the *infra-human* order – and necessarily unable to explicate the meaning of our being *human* in particular. To understand the specifically human, we must extend our inquiry beyond presuppositions limited to the subhuman level.

When I reached adolescence, I expected I would soon work out profound and normative answers to these questions that would serve to guide my life's journey. It has taken many more years than I expected to discern satisfying answers. Indeed, they are still "works in progress" – but more about those in the final section. Before examining "where the path leads," it is appropriate to consider the steps that led me there. The next three sections portray that journey as three "movements": my early social-cultural context, my university education, and my professional position. For each, I will describe my own particular history, and note how it also reveals the biographical impact of one's social development.

It would be appropriate to preface that description with a brief reflection on the nature of this relationship between individual development and one's socio-cultural situation. For human beings, the world is not something to which we are merely mechanistically or objectively related. But neither is it a merely subjective construct. Our world is always that within which we are *situated*. To be situated means to be engaged there, to have an intrinsic involvement with a network of experienced, or lived, meanings. This relationship is essentially different from the merely extrinsic relation of things, such as billiard balls which, bumping into each other, impact each other merely causally rather than meaningfully. As experienced, our social world is a meaningful *dimension* of our lives. In other words, it is *both* within the horizon of this meaningful social world that we enact our lived experience, *and* it is through our lived experience that the meaning of our situatedness is concretized. Far from negating the reality of lived experience, our social world, as its context or situation, *dimensionalizes* it.

First movement: My early social-cultural world

My earliest social world was that of my family, into which I was born on April 4, 1952. Two idiosyncratic features of that familial background were uniquely formative. First, I was the oldest of eight children. It seemed from an early age that I was a "teacher": inveterately inviting my siblings to ponder whatever nook of the world I found fascinating that day (including the experiential rudiments of botany, geology, astronomy, biology, chemistry, math, economics). For me, it was fun to share the thrill of understanding something that had been invisible before. Though I did not imagine teaching as my profession until my late twenties, in hindsight I see that I've always been one.

Second, my father worked for the CIA, and so we traveled and lived in many different parts of the world. Indeed, I was born on a tropical island in the Pacific (Saipan) which, at that time, was not a part of any nation. Not only did we live in many different countries, but we also got to experience a wide variety of transport, from camels to elephants, and a plethora of unusual events, from typhoons to sandstorms. I think we may even have been among the first Americans to be shot at by the (then) Viet Cong (in early 1953).

Growing up in such a variegated socio-cultural milieu freed me from the standard American society for much my childhood. I even went years without watching TV during those supposedly "golden years of television." But it also opened me to so many other ways of engaging the world. My child's eye view rendered many of these differences utterly beguiling. I'll never forget, for example, coming upon a little hut in the remote mountains in Greece, and discovering it packed with precious religious icons, left there as a place of prayer for roaming shepherds. So much gold, silver, jewels, and no locks – and no theft!

My first "calling" (as one's "vocations" were identified then) surely arose from those experiences. When I was six, I decided I would become a missionary. Father Damian, who had worked with lepers in Hawaii, became my model after I'd read a biography about him. I wanted to go to the strangest, most remote, most different people on earth. I was a very finicky eater then, and anticipated I would be nauseated by the different foods I imagined I'd have to eat (bugs! snakes! rats!). But somehow I cheerfully accepted even that most gruesome prerequisite, so compelling was my calling. A couple years later, I read books by Tom Dooley about his experience as a medical doctor in Indochina, and realized it was not necessary to be a missionary to fulfill the truest aspect of that calling: to be with and be of service to the Other. As an older child with increasing knowledge, my sense of my future continued evolving: Peace Corps, State Department, Foreign Service, diplomat. In each I understood myself to be a citizen of the world, and that the entire range of world culture, no matter how different, was of value.

Of course, living in many places and cultures is a double-edged experience: it opens one to an enriching range of meaning, but at the price that one has no real "home base" from which to grow and against which to chart one's trajectory. Though I wouldn't have traded my childhood for a more sedentary one, I was keenly aware of how my early life as a "homeless wanderer" deprived me of a deep sense of belonging to a "place." To the question "Where are you from?" I typically reply, "No place, really." Having no place to which I belonged, I felt an odd nostalgia – of longing for the home I never had. While others bemoan that they "can never go home again" my lament is of a more primal absence. Home, for me, would be "where you make it." But such self-creating, by definition, lacks the essential character of being rooted in a transcendentally pre-existing order of things.

Returning to the US as a 13-year-old, settling into suburbia (outside Washington, DC) felt very strange indeed. Winning a scholarship to an elite high school (St. John's) compounded my growing sense of alienation from the dominant culture. With a precocious adolescent distantiation and criticality, I situated myself on the periphery, gazing with the scorn of a Nietzschean steppenwolf. Novels such as Hesse's *Beneath the Wheel*, Joyce's *Portrait of the Artist as a Young Man*, Dostoyevsky's *Notes from Underground*, Steinbeck's *Winter of Our Discontent*, and Salinger's *Catcher in the Rye* showed that I was not alone. Then I discovered sociology and philosophy and a whole language of alienation. Paul Goodman's *Growing Up Absurd* was a true godsend. And Camus, and Sartre. Not only was I not alone, but I also felt justified to scoff at the bourgeois aspirations of a materialistically decadent but spiritually vacuous culture (or, as Laing said so pithily, "the fibrillating heartland of a senescent civilization"). Ah, the easy certitudes of youth!

In looking for an alternative to the western metaphysical tradition, I also looked to the east, as so many of my contemporaries and intellectual heroes were doing. (Or, in some cases, had for a long time: Thoreau, Schopenhauer, Jung, to name only a few.) I was inspired by some works of Alan Watts on Hinduism, Taoism, and Buddhism, and especially by his deliciously clever yet profound unraveling, through the Vedic tradition, of the "taboo against knowing who you are" (Watts, 1966). I was intrigued, but a deeper understanding would have to wait much longer.

As the 1960s continued their tumultuous unfolding, a whole counterculture began to rise and politics revealed a depth of latent meaningful problematics I was absolutely struck to discover. Following President Kennedy's assassination, the "liberal enlightenment" interregnum between the conservative 1950s and the radical 1960s unraveled, bequeathing the pressing problems of racism, sexism and war for the next generation to overcome. Though young, I was galvanized, and eager to do whatever I could to help. The twin assassinations of Martin Luther King and Robert Kennedy in 1968 attuned an era that would be multilayered with urgency, iconoclasm, cynicism, ecstasy, consciousness raising, and a keen sense of the absurd. I skipped school to join protest marches, surrounded the White House, and did what I could to shame Nixon for the blood on his hands.

Second movement: My education as a psychologist

And then it was time to go to college, on a tidal wave of radicalized students, in the months after Kent State. As a National Merit scholar I could select from many good schools. My high school had semi-realistic pretensions of being a feeder to the Ivy League, but I chose Michigan State, precisely because it was the opposite of my high school: it was big, public, open (and coed). I wanted a place where I could explore widely. And I did, changing majors seven times, dropping out three times. MSU was big enough to accommodate all my rambunctiousness, even a period of literal homelessness; even, at 19 years, dropping out and hitchhiking to Haight-Ashbury with 20 dollars and no plans. (It was great.) Those were the days when a loose-knit "Woodstock Nation" made almost anything possible. Even, eventually, ending segregation. And a war. And sexism.

Academically, I explored purely for the sake of learning what I wanted to learn, with no thought of "careers" at the end of it. An innovative program within Michigan State allowed students to design their own majors. I gravitated to history and philosophy of science. I found how much I disagreed with Descartes and Newton, how naive Popper and Hempel were, and how much I disdained the logical empiricism of the Vienna Circle. Then I discovered Thomas Kuhn and his vision of paradigmatic change, and acquired a perspective that clarified a lot. Then Michael Polanyi, and Stephen Toulmin, and now I had a powerful critique of the naive reductionism of positivism.

From there, I returned to my old inspiration – existentialism – and saw it within this larger intellectual history as a decisive alternative to the dehumanization embedded within positivism. Not only was it an exhilarating call to live one's own humanness, but as phenomenology it was also a way for intellectual thought to retrieve itself from the "dustbowl" of abstract empiricism and recover living experience as the basis for genuine philosophizing. In this vein, I read more deeply in my old favorites – Sartre, Kierkegaard, and Nietzsche – but now also discovered the formative insights of Merleau-Ponty, Husserl, and Heidegger. I'd run out of courses and then independent studies in this vein. My education at that point was primarily sitting before library shelves, pulling down and imbibing everything I could find about this existential-phenomenological philosophy.

My next leap was to discover how existential-phenomenological philosophy was being appropriated within psychology. The books of Rollo May and R.D. Laing touched me deeply, as they made it very apparent just how profoundly we could understand the living experiences of a human being, and human suffering. I devoured May's *Man's Search for Himself* and R.D. Laing's *The Divided Self* so thoroughly that the copies fell apart in my hands. Then I read everything else they'd written. Roaming through caverns in the library I also found the *Review of Existential Psychology and Psychiatry* – a journal published since the early 1960s filled with evocative writing by existential psychologists, psychiatrists and philosophers at the forward edge of this movement. Weeks of sitting before that stack followed.

And then I found a teacher – Marian Kinget, already elderly, but still spry physically and mentally. She was the only humanistic psychologist in the 100-member department at Michigan State. In fact, by her reckoning, she taught the first course in humanistic psychology at any American university. In Belgium, she'd studied at Louvain University (home of the Husserl archives and a world center for phenomenology). After emigrating to the US, she worked with Carl Rogers and also had her own psychotherapy private practice. She thus brought a richly layered background to her courses. I took both her undergraduate lecture course and her graduate seminar. In addition to working our way through the main thinkers, Kinget was developing her own original psychology of human being, which culminated the following year in her book *On Being Human* (1975).

In mid-1974, I suddenly realized I could graduate with a degree in psychology, if I just took the required Intro Psych course (the one psych course I had never been drawn to). I did and soon found myself faced with the question "What next?" Several months of living on a communal farm followed, during which I thought I knew enough to outline my "first book" – whose envisaged title was "Nothingness, Freedom and Love." This interlude showed me that I really wanted to study more existential-phenomenological psychology. Kinget had already pointed me toward Duquesne University as its epicenter. They had a 12-month MA program as well as a separate PhD program. I figured another year's study sounded just right, and off I went to Pittsburgh (with all my worldly possessions still able to fit in the back seat of my little car).

In the weeks before classes began, I read everything I could by the Duquesne faculty. Ironically, it was only then that I read Amedeo Giorgi's work. I'd previously seen his articles in *Review of Existential Psychology and Psychiatry*, but had skipped over them because they had titles like "Phenomenology and Experimental Psychology." I'd thought, "Experimental psychology? That's what we're trying to get away from!" Now I began to appreciate what his project was really about: his aim was not to include phenomenology within the experimental tradition, but to demonstrate that a phenomenological psychology was, in its own way, as methodologically rigorous as experimental psychology, and that it could meet the legitimate demands of science without falling prey to the fatal reductionism of experimental psychology (e.g., Aanstoos, 1996b; Giorgi, 1970; Wertz and Aanstoos, 1999). He was enlarging the meaning of science. This was a heady claim: a frontal assault on the tradition. Giorgi thematized the key significance of "approach": how a discipline (in this case, psychology) "approached" its own subject matter. Such "meta" issues all too often remain submerged within the practice of "normal science" and certainly had been presupposed by psychology's uncritical conception of itself along the lines of a natural science.

And then the academic year began, and I learned that I was to be Giorgi's graduate assistant. And I found my second mentor. By the time I arrived at Duquesne in 1975, he had earned a well-deserved reputation for developing an alternative foundation for psychology as a genuinely human science by establishing a "middle ground" between the antimonies of a natural science psychology and a nonscientific psychology. Already by the mid-1970s I had come to see that much of the larger "alternative" movement within psychology (known loosely as "humanistic psychology") was unsophisticated with regard to these issues of philosophical foundations – and thus tended to accept one side or the other of the antimony without realizing it was doing so. For some, reforming psychology to become more humanistic meant simply addressing previously neglected content areas (love, creativity, spirituality, etc.), but researching these by means of the same natural science methods of mainstream psychology: experimental. On the other hand, there were reformers who considered the very project of a scientific psychology to be the source of psychology's enduring problem, and sought instead to refound psychology as a humanities-based discipline. The Duquesne project was, instead, to retain for psychology a scientific foundation, but to revision the very sense of science, by discerning its criteria in their essential breadth, so that it could more faithfully study psychology's own subject matter. The goal of the Duquesne project was to research psychological life as it was lived, without reducing it to putative mechanisms for the sake of fitting into the "Procrustean bed" of a pre-existing methodological regime. And the means to do so was an originally developed empirical phenomenological methodology, based on the qualitative analysis of descriptive data, informed by Husserl's method of epoche and eidetic intuition, adapted to a psychological level of analysis. (see Aanstoos, 1983b, 1983c; Giorgi, 1975, 1983, 1985; van Kaam, 1966; Wertz, 1983).

Such a project engaged my own history quite deeply. On the one hand, I had become increasingly pessimistic about the prospects of an authentic psychology within the purview of science, yet on the other hand, from the time I first read him, I also resonated with Husserl's call for phenomenology as "rigorous science." On the "third hand," though, I also felt that I understood Husserl's pessimistic assessment, at the end of his life, that his dream of such a "rigorous science" was "over." I think what he meant was not that it was impossible for phenomenology to meet the requisites of "science," but rather that it was not going to be accepted as having done so by the larger scientific community (Aanstoos, 1999a). (And, in that regard, he has largely been proven right.) But, in the mid-1970s, riding the still potent wave of the 1960s zeitgeist, it seemed that almost anything was possible. I admired Giorgi for his earnest effort to get scientific psychology to recognize the legitimacy of a phenomenological approach. And I was happy to have the chance to help that project. We pursued this work optimistically. Giorgi, Fred Wertz and I even presented a symposium to the Division of Experimental Psychology at the APA convention, in the hope of demonstrating the value of this prospect to the very hardcore of the mainstream (Aanstoos, 1985a). I recall my delight when, as the session began, I noticed how large our audience was. But, once the questions began, it became clear that most of them were actually humanistic psychologists who had followed us to the experimentalists' program, and that the audience we had tried to reach did not turn out in the numbers we had hoped. By the mid-1980s I even published a short piece in the *American Psychologist*, depicting the possibility of psychology as a "human science" as a response to a previous article which had argued that C.P. Snow's vision of "two cultures" (science and humanities) constituted an inevitable divide for psychology. My own position was that this divide was factually accurate, but not essentially so, that it was only inevitable as long as psychology sought to found itself along the lines of the natural sciences, but could, in principle, be overcome by an alternative human science foundation (Aanstoos, 1985b). This argument was the same one Giorgi had been making for years (e.g., Giorgi, 1976) in the face of various assertions of psychology's regrettable disunity. I advanced this thesis again later in *American Psychologist* with regard to the topic of memory in particular (Aanstoos, 1991).

When I arrived at Duquesne in 1975, this dialogue between human science and natural science approaches was primarily carried out by phenomenologists in relation to behaviorism, which had dominated mainstream academic psychology for several decades, and in relation to psychoanalysis, which was dominant in clinical psychology. But, as a result of my previous work at Michigan State, I saw the importance of the rising cognitive paradigm in psychology, and realized it was already supplanting behaviorism as psychology's leading approach. In other words, the paradigmatic revolution advocated by humanistic psychology since the late 1950s was now underway, but the emergent new governing paradigm was not to be humanistic, but cognitive, psychology. There are many reasons for that result, but I think the most central one is that cognitivism offered psychology the opportunity to recover "the higher mental functions" excluded by behaviorism while retaining the mechanistic basis presupposed by a natural science approach. Their new "computer model" (Simon and Newell, 1964) successfully displaced behaviorism's older "telephone switchboard model." While revolutionary in terms of contents, this change was atavistic in terms of approach. In other words, old wine was poured into shiny new bottles, thereby co-opting the growing opposition to behaviorism's exclusionary taboos without disturbing the scientific foundations.

I decided that phenomenology's quest to establish psychology's appropriate foundations would have to include an engagement with cognitive psychology. Therefore (now continuing on in the doctoral program), I undertook for my dissertation research a study of thinking (Aanstoos, 1982), long recognized as both the most important yet also most difficult of all psychological phenomena. I decided to study thinking as it is exemplified during chess playing because, from its beginning, cognitive psychology had itself identified chess playing as the "type case" for the demonstration of their new paradigm. Indeed, chess playing had become so important a task for their efforts that by 1978 it had become known as the "fruit fly" of that field.

My results (Aanstoos, 1983a, 1985c, 1986) demonstrated striking differences from the computer simulation models of thought. Thinking's capacity to grasp the particulars in terms of an ongoing, general understanding of the game situation as a whole stood in marked contrast to the "constructed from bits" approach of the computational models. Previous critiques of the computer models had mainly argued they could not be good simulations because they could not play expert chess, but the chess programs were improving rapidly, and were already attaining expert status by the end of the 1970s. My research made clear that the very improvements in computer play (which rested on faster computations of more possible variations) were misguided as simulations: better play achieved by faster "construction from bits" simply compensated for, rather than ameliorated, the fundamental difference with human thought.

Regrettably, the cognitivist paradigm had a momentum that was not to be stopped. But its impact has not been wholly negative. It has succeeded in reopening the "black box" into which behaviorism had locked away consciousness. And this resurgence of interest in consciousness presents the next generation of psychologists with rich opportunities. Also, though the information processing model has critically limiting philosophical presuppositions (Aanstoos, 1987b), it has been the timely paradigm for illustrating the late 20th century as a period of the triumph of a technological attitude in popular culture (Aanstoos, 2001a).

Third movement: My professional world

During the last three years I was a doctoral student, I held an instructor position at a branch campus of the Pennsylvania State University. My students were typically the sons and daughters of steel mill workers, often the first generation in their families to attend college. Though not the most academic I'd encountered, they were infused with "the spirit of Pittsburgh": a "shot and a beer" mill town of people who melted iron for a living, giving a hard day's work for a hard day's pay, and for whom life was very real. Their eastern and southern European immigrant grandparents had stood up to Carnegie and his private army of Pinkertons at his peak in the 1890s and they had been fighting Big Steel for workers' rights ever since. Used to climbing uphill and making the most of opportunities, higher education was not something they took for granted, and genuine learning was an experience to be treasured. It was with them that I found myself as a teacher.

As I was completing my dissertation research and could anticipate my PhD, I knew I wanted to continue with college teaching. While with my students, I never felt that I was "working." It wasn't a "job," it was a pleasure, and getting paid for it never ceases to amaze me. To earn a living by sharing ideas I treasure with students and (through my writing) with colleagues suited me so perfectly I couldn't imagine preferring anything else.

But I realized I would rather be on the faculty of a program (like Duquesne's) that was dedicated to a kindred vision of psychology as a human science, rather than a program (like Penn State's) where I would be the only one with such a vision, amongst colleagues who took for granted the natural science foundation for psychology. Ah, but such programs are few and far between, so openings are infrequent. Instead, I found a wonderful receptivity from a department in an elite liberal arts university near Seattle. Though most of the faculty knew little about phenomenology, they wanted more, and invited me to join their faculty in order to develop this approach as the future of the department. Then Penn State offered me a tenure track position as well. And by then I had come to love Pittsburgh. Its spirit had deeply infused my own. Not only its spirit – I was also held there in an endearing nest of friends, colleagues, and a happy everyday life. So, to leave, or to stay, that was the question.

Just then, serendipity (synchronicity?) gently intervened. Sitting in a stall at the faculty men's room between classes, I chanced to notice, there at my feet, a left behind copy of the *Chronicle of Higher Ed* – the other academic newspaper that carried announcements of position openings (I had only been looking for them in the *APA Monitor*). Though I had already completed my own search, and had only to make my decision, I was curious to see what I might find, and flipped it open. In my selectivity of where I'd like to move, I'd never looked at ads for positions in the deep South, but this time I chanced to see the ad for West Georgia. Stunningly unique, it read something like: wanted: existential, phenomenological, transpersonal, hermeneutic, post-modern, Buddhist, Gestalt psychologist. A week later, I went to a conference in New Orleans (the annual meeting of the Southeastern Psychological Association) to present my research on a symposium there. The other panelists were faculty from West Georgia – Mike Arons and Bob Masek. They'd also brought about 15 of their graduate students. Their presentations on hermeneutic and dialogical phenomenology were extraordinary and my subsequent socializing with their students showed me clearly that West Georgia was another place for kindred spirits. I applied, and was offered the position there.

Ah, but then the necessity to choose really became evident! What shall I do? Shall I stay in Pittsburgh (the place I loved most in the world), or move to Seattle (a great place with a department eager for me to bring phenomenology), or to rural Georgia (though the deep South evoked an almost visceral repulsion of old stereotypes for me, it was a program of kindred spirits). Each path would open a very different life, but which one was mine? Since I didn't know, I knew not to choose until I did know. I asked each to give me more time to decide, and they did so, very generously, all the way to June. Finally, while soaking in a warm bath, it came to me quite clearly: my path was to go to West Georgia.

The West Georgia undergrad and graduate psychology programs had been revisioned in 1968 when Mike Arons was appointed its new chair. After his doctorate on creativity at the Sorbonne under Paul Ricoeur, Arons had worked at Brandeis with Abraham Maslow. He brought a deep understanding of contemporary continental thought (existentialism, phenomenology, hermeneutics) and the cutting edge of developments in American humanistic psychology. Along with several new faculty (most especially Jim Klee), he began a program in humanistic psychology at West Georgia.

The orientation of this program included the same philosophical bases as Duquesne's, but these were incorporated into a larger and more loosely confederated potpourri of humanistic thought. By the early 1980s humanistic psychology in America had had almost a generation to develop, and it had grown two "wings" which I colloquially identify as "east coast" and "west coast." The "east coast" wing was that imported from Europe, imbued with the contemporary continental philosophy of existential phenomenology, and the phenomenological psychology that had emerged from that philosophical anthropology. The "west coast" wing was the more "homespun" humanistic psychology that had emerged in the 1960s, through the work of psychologists such as Carl Rogers, Abraham Maslow, Fritz Perls, the Esalen group and the human potential movement more generally. At Duquesne, we had tended to be a little "puristic" about the rigorousness of our approach to psychology, and so tended to be concerned about being identified with the larger, but less philosophically sophisticated, humanistic movement. But, at West Georgia, I found a place where these wings not only co-existed, but were cross-pollinating in fertile ways. Indeed, many streams of thought were coursing through the program, including transpersonal psychology, Asian spiritual philosophies, and postmodernism. Given that the early 1980s were culturally a period of neoconservatism, the humanistic psychology movement nationally was entering a phase of retrenchment (particularly disconcerting after two decades of explosive growth). Therefore, it seemed to me to be very timely for the various strands to come together and intertwine. The West Georgia program offered the optimal occasion for such a development.

This desire to bring together the various currents has characterized my dialogue with a range of post-positivistic methodologies (e.g., Aanstoos, 1987a). It has also guided my professional work with organizations especially with the Division of Humanistic Psychology of the APA and with the Human Science Research Association. In the former, I served as division president (1997 to 1998) and as editor of the division's journal, *The Humanistic Psychologist* (1985 to 2002). In the latter, I served as an early program chair

(1984), and helped guide its inclusive vision (e.g., Aanstoos, 1990a). In my own research, I've brought phenomenological methods to bear on topics from spirituality (Aanstoos, 1993) to sexuality (Aanstoos, 2001b). And I have brought phenomenology into dialogue with such approaches as Jungian thought (Aanstoos, 1999b), Buddhism (Aanstoos, 1998, 1999b), postmodernism (Aanstoos, 1990b), and ecopsychology (Aanstoos, 1996a). I remain firmly convinced that a psychology adequate to the subject matter of human existence is possible, and necessary (Aanstoos, 2003).

Coda: "What is the point of the trip?"

Having now spent the past 23 years at West Georgia (though it seems more like six or seven), I have gathered my answers to the "big questions" with which I began this journey. First, some "answers" about the process itself. There has been a certain sort of coherence to the trip. This coherence is not the substantive constellation of an independent mental ego but a coherent flow. The postmodernist philosophies and the Asian spiritual traditions have it right: there is no separate self. It is right for us to move beyond that modernist illusion, just as we need to deconstruct the entire edifice of objectivism. But postmodernism overshoots the mark of its accurate refutation of the modernist self by claiming in turn that the self is dispersed so completely that it is only its representational narratives that cohere. My life has shown me that it is not necessary to choose between these two horns of the dilemma: either meaningful coherence as a thing ("subject") or no coherence. Instead, there is meaning, but not as objectified in a "self" as a thing; rather, it is autochthonous to lived experience itself. It is as an emergent, intrinsic, property that experience is meaningful, rather than arbitrarily constructed. Such meaningfulness arises not from any underlying or absolutist foundation – the modernist pipedream (shared by the fundamentalists who loathe postmodernism). But neither is its appearance limited to the (always subsequent) representational circumscription of signifiers. Experience itself flows. The symphony is not that of singular or dispersed subjects as mental egos. The symphony inheres in the musicality of experience itself: its pulsations, its rhythms, its flow.

And it isn't only "my" experience that is flowing. It is all flow. Being-as-a-whole is flowing. From the pre-Socratics' ontology, to the Buddha's vision of transiency, to Lao-Tzu's grasp of the Tao, to Heidegger's notion of being-in-time, great thinkers and mystics have long understood a nondual vision of Being. But this understanding is not a conceptual one. We can benefit by a radical reflection: a reflection that reflects the pre-reflective by a deep inquiry into its own origins. Ultimately, however, it is lived experience that provides the richest manifestation of the nonduality of Being-as-a-whole.

My own experiences of Being-as-a-whole began in early childhood, but fully blossomed only in midlife. I vividly recall the day when, as a 5-year old, I decided to find out what the biggest number was. I knew how to count – simply go on to the next number – so I figured that if I just kept counting until there was no "next number" I would then have found the biggest number. So, sitting on that green cement floor of the screen porch, I started counting, and counting, and counting. All afternoon. Well into the thousands, it finally struck me – very powerfully – that no matter what number I was on it would always be possible to add one more to it. An enchanting glimpse of infinity opened before me. I saw a vision of wholeness: the numbers were no longer separate bits, chained together sequentially, for there was nothing outside the "chain." It was breathtaking. A few months later I was standing, barefoot, on the concrete floor of the basement, the sun shining in through the window of the back door. And, suddenly, the sunshine, the floor, the room, and me were no longer separate "bits" but instantiations of the whole, which I felt with a sense of profound well-being. Not only were numbers revelatory of an infinite wholeness, but so was the everyday world. Another few months later, winter now, I was running on the asphalt parking lot at school. The nuns had repeatedly warned us "Don't run, don't run," but who listens to such admonitions at that age? But the asphalt was ice covered, and now my feet slipped and I went flying through the air, horizontally, with my head falling backward, back toward that hard paved surface. Without hesitating, I called out to my "guardian angel" to save me. And somehow, in the next instant, I was again standing on my feet. Ah! Not only was the everyday world a seamless whole, but even spiritual being was not segregated from this nonduality.

These experiences, of course, are those of a young child. I do think that period (say three to six) is a particularly apt time to experience Being-as-a-whole. Midlife is the next crucially sensitive developmental period in which the person is susceptible to the rupture of egoic life by the dynamic ground of Being. For me, two journeys provided the optimum context: to India at age 40, and to Thailand at age 45. Serendipitously well-timed, my trip to India came unexpectedly as an invitation to give a lecture series. I went early, and spent some time in a Tibetan monastery there (Drepung Loseling, their rebuilt version of the big monastery destroyed by the Chinese in Lhasa). While practicing daily meditation with the monks, I found myself drawn to a particular notion in Tibetan Buddhism: *sunyata*, or emptiness (Aanstoos, 1998). Like most deep spiritual insights, the basic idea is easy to state, but difficult to truly realize. This notion of *sunyata* was first formulated by Nagarjuna, as an alternative to the twin shibboleths of absolutism and nihilism.

In Buddhism, the basic premises have to do with the nature of suffering, its source and the possibilities of its cessation. Nagarjuna understood that suffering was rooted in our reifying tendency to posit permanence, where the nature of reality is actually impermanence:

> Human suffering arises because people posit and identify with a substantial, unchanging ego at the core of the flux of experience. By identifying with this supposedly permanent self, we enter into the state of ignorance known as subject–object dualism. Such dualism is characterized by craving, aversion and delusion, which combine to produce suffering. (Zimmerman, 1993, p.254)

But how to overcome this very ingrained tendency? Through the experience of emptiness, or *sunyata*. "One who is in harmony with emptiness is in harmony with all things" said Nagarjuna. And why is that? Because this understanding is demonstrated by a life based on non-clinging, or non-attachment. And onto what does this liberation from hypostatized concepts of somethingness deliver us? What is its soteriological value? With the realization of emptiness, we gain an intuitive awareness of the intimate interrelatedness of phenomena, in which one grasps the holistic and contextual nature of experience.

Thich Nhat Hanh (1997) demonstrates this notion very simply as he performs wonderfully instructive deconstructions of our sense of independent entities. Following his example, we may begin with any simple "thing" – such as a tree. Looking more closely we see that the tree does not present itself as a thing-in-itself, but as a tree growing from a ground, sucking up water dropped from clouds, energized by sun, blown by wind, etc. So that to even "see" a "tree" means we see no thing, but rather the simultaneous arising of a whole panoply. An inter-being.

With these fresh insights in mind, I embarked next on a train trip across the Indian subcontinent. Wanting to "go native," I had not done as other westerners do and reserved a first-class air-conditioned sleeper car. No, I waited on the platform with the locals for the end of the train to pull up, so I could board one of the unreserved third-class cars. As these car doors opened, I was dismayed to see that every one of them was already jammed with passengers. As I stared blankly, wondering what to do, hundreds around me rushed every one of those cars, and pushed into them. So I did the same, and found myself shoved into the crowded car. By the time the train began moving again, there was no room even to stand: we were packed so tightly that everyone was just leaning into the people around them. Then I noticed the very strong stench of urine, and realized I was positioned near the hole in the floor that served as the "bathroom" for this car. (A small hole, evidently frequently missed on a moving train.) As a reactive wave of disgust swept over me, I remembered the lesson of *sunyata*: this smell is a sensation, its meaning is neither good nor bad in itself, rather it is as a node of being-as-a-whole that it is at all. With that understanding, I felt fine with it. Next, I noticed who I was squashed into: an old woman, with bugs crawling out of her hair and open sores on her arms. Again, a visceral revulsion, but it was again followed by the same insight: no inherent "thing" here either, but a meaningfulness reflective of the whole of being. With that, compassion replaced revulsion, and I was again fine. Then, after traveling for hours through the tropical heat, the train simply stopped, in the middle of the night, in the middle of nowhere. And stayed stopped for what seemed like hours. Now there was no air circulating through the windows, and the hot, tightly packed car was becoming quite stifling. As I was once more succumbing to the tendency to reify this experience, I remembered instead that this also was a moment in the dependent co-origination of the whole, and was truly fine with it being just as it was. And then, the ultimate lesson. A band of machete-wielding fanatics burst through the door and boarded our car. (In the sectarian turmoil then roiling Hindu–Moslem relations in India, I had heard that a train car full of people had just the month before been hacked to death by machete-wielding fanatics.) I very rationally pondered if there was any way for me to get out of that car, and quickly realized there wasn't (the only exit being the door from which they were now entering). At that point, I grasped that this moment was the opportunity to deeply realize *sunyata*: that even life and death (my life and death) are no inherent thing, but moments in the unfolding of being-as-a-whole. And with that insight a deep calm settled over the scene. It was not a dissociation – I could see everything very perceptively (even how dull those machetes were). As it happened, they did not want to kill us all – only one (whom they took off the train, for a final act, out of our sight). And eventually the train started to move again, air flowed again, we got to Madras, I got to stand on my own again, and life went on. Someone said "it was the train from hell," but I always thought it "the train from heaven" for the lesson it gave me.

India was full of such lessons, as was my subsequent trip to Thailand five years later. While there, I stayed in a village of the Karen tribe, in very northern Thailand. They are still relatively remote (the previous visit by an outsider to their village was five years before). They live a sustainable way of life, and have been doing so for over two thousand years. Their attunement to the natural world around them is truly impressive and deeply inspiring, as is their extraordinary good nature. Many incidents were profoundly impactful for me, but one will have to suffice. While walking one day with the village headman through the jungle, I asked if the leaves of these very tall deciduous trees ever turned different colors. Yes, he said, they would turn red in about a month. Struck by the imagination of this huge forest filled with red leaves, I exclaimed, "That must be really beautiful!" Surprised by his apparent reluctance to agree, I pressed him, "Well, don't you think they're especially beautiful then?" In reply, he simply said, "They're beautiful when they're red, they're beautiful when they're green. Why do you pick one color and say 'that's the beautiful one'?" Ah! Yes, indeed, why do we pick one color as the beautiful one? Well, of course, I could reply, "Well they're green 11 months of the year, but red only one month, so it's rare, and therefore beautiful." But such a perspective stands apart from the immediate perception. Every moment, when fully engaged, is the fulfillment of the whole in its own, fully beautiful way.

And that, I believe, is "the point of the trip": to be the place of awareness of being-as-a-whole. To be that lighted clearing, the sheltering place, the sanctuary, within which Being manifests itself. Within this actual, experienced, living moment. And as eternity.

References

Aanstoos, C.M. (1982) *A Phenomenological Study of Thinking as it is Exemplified during Chess Playing*. Ann Arbor: University Microfilms (also abstracted in Dissertation Abstracts International, 43, 2726-B).

Aanstoos, C.M. (1983a) "A phenomenological study of thinking." In A. Giorgi, A. Barton and C. Maes (eds) *Duquesne Studies in Phenomenological Psychology*, Vol. 4. Pittsburgh: Duquesne University Press.

Aanstoos, C.M. (1983b) "The think aloud method in descriptive research." *Journal of Phenomenological Psychology 14*, 150–190.

Aanstoos, C.M. (1983c) "What is phenomenological psychology?" *West Georgia Review 15*, 14–19.

Aanstoos, C.M. (1985a) "Findings and implications of a descriptive approach to thinking." Paper presented to the meeting of the American Psychological Association (sponsored by Division 3). Los Angeles, August.

Aanstoos, C.M. (1985b) "Psychology as a human science." *American Psychologist 40*, 1417–1418.

Aanstoos, C.M. (1985c) "The structure of thinking in chess." In A. Giorgi (ed) *Phenomenology and Psychological Research*. Pittsburgh: Duquesne University Press.

Aanstoos, C.M. (1986) "Phenomenology and the psychology of thinking." In P. Ashworth, A. Giorgi and A. de Koning (eds) *Qualitative Research in Psychology*. Pittsburgh: Duquesne University Press.

Aanstoos, C.M. (1987a) "A comparative survey of human science psychologies." *Methods 1*, 2, 1–36.

Aanstoos, C.M. (1987b) "Information processing and the phenomenology of thinking." In D. Welton and H. Silverman (eds) *Critical and Dialectical Phenomenology*. Albany: State University of New York Press.

Aanstoos, C.M. (1989) "Toward a phenomenology of spiritual experience." Paper presented to the meeting of the American Psychological Association (sponsored by Division 36), New Orleans, August.

Aanstoos, C.M. (1990a) "A brief history of the Human Science Research Conference." *Journal of Humanistic Psychology 30*, 137–145.

Aanstoos, C.M. (1990b) "Preface." *Psychology and Postmodernity*. Special issue of *Humanistic Psychologist 18*, 2–4.

Aanstoos, C.M. (1991) "Experimental psychology and the challenge of real life." *American Psychologist 46*, 77–78.

Aanstoos, C.M. (1993) "Toward a phenomenology of spiritual experience." *Journal of the Psychology of Religion 1*, 81–90.

Aanstoos, C.M. (1996a) "Ecopsychology: An interview with Theodore Roszak." *Humanistic Psychologist 24*, 155–174.

Aanstoos, C.M. (1996b) "Reflections and visions: An interview with Amedeo Giorgi." *Humanistic Psychologist 24*, 3–27.

Aanstoos, C.M. (1998) "Freedom, nothingness and love." Presidential address presented to the meeting of the American Psychological Association (sponsored by Division 32). San Francisco, August.

Aanstoos, C.M. (1999a) "Husserl and transcendental subjectivity." Paper presented to the meeting of the Symposium for Qualitative Research, Perugia, Italy, August.

Aanstoos, C.M. (1999b) "Jung, Buddhism and phenomenology." Invited lecture presented to the C.G. Jung Society of Atlanta, September 18.

Aanstoos, C.M. (2001a) "Cognitive science and technological culture: A humanistic response." In K. Schneider, J. Bugental and F. Pearson (eds) *Handbook of Humanistic Psychology*. Los Angeles: Sage.

Aanstoos, C.M. (2001b) "Phenomenology of sexuality." In P. Kleinplatz (ed) *New Directions in Sex Therapy*. New York: Brunner/Mazel.

Aanstoos, C.M. (2003) "The relevance of humanistic psychology." *Journal of Humanistic Psychology 43*, 121–132.

Giorgi, A. (1970) *Psychology as a Human Science*. New York: Harper & Row.

Giorgi, A. (1975) "An application of phenomenological method in psychology." In A. Giorgi, C. Fischer and E. Murray (eds) *Duquesne Studies in Phenomenological Psychology*, Vol. 2. Pittsburgh: Duquesne University Press.

Giorgi, A. (1976) "Phenomenology and the foundations of psychology." In W. Arnold (ed) *1975 Nebraska Symposium on Motivation: Conceptual Foundations of Psychology*. Lincoln: University of Nebraska Press.

Giorgi, A. (1983) "Concerning the possibility of phenomenological psychological research." *Journal of Phenomenological Psychology 14*, 129–169.

Giorgi, A. (ed) (1985) *Phenomenology and Psychological Research*. Pittsburgh: Duquesne University Press.

Hanh, T.N. (1997) *The Heart of Understanding*. Delhi: Nice.

Kinget, M. (1975) *On Being Human: A Systematic View*. New York: Harcourt Brace Jovanovich.

Simon, H.A. and Newell, A. (1964) "Information processing in computers and man." *American Scientist 52*, 281–300.

van Kaam, A. (1966) *Existential Foundations of Psychology*. Pittsburgh: Duquesne University Press.

Watts, A. (1966) *The Book: On the Taboo against Knowing Who You Are*. New York: Collier.

Wertz, F.J. (1983) "The constituents of descriptive psychological reflection." *Human Studies 8*, 35–51.

Wertz, F. and Aanstoos, C.M. (1999) "Amedeo Giorgi and the project of a human science." In D. Moss (ed) *Humanistic and Transpersonal Psychology: A Historical and Biographical Sourcebook*. Westport, CT: Greenwood Press.

Zimmerman, M. (1993) "Heidegger, Buddhism and deep ecology." In C. Guignon (ed) *The Cambridge Companion to Heidegger*. Cambridge: Cambridge University Press.

CHAPTER 8

Moving On By Backing Away

John Shotter

The problems arising through a misinterpretation of our forms of language have the character of depth. They are deep disquietudes; their roots are as deep in us as the forms of our language and their significance is as great as the importance of our language.

(Wittgenstein, 1953, no.111)

What is most difficult here is to put this indefiniteness, correctly and unfalsified, into words.

(Wittgenstein, 1953, p.227)

Nothing is so difficult as not deceiving oneself.

(Wittgenstein, 1980, p.34)

George Yancy originally asked me to contribute toward this volume as one of the originators of the movement in psychology and social theory known as social constructionism. However, I have to say that for me, social constructionism has been a way station on the way to somewhere else. I have always been concerned with the larger social conditions of our lives together, and with our unresponsiveness to the obvious misery and injustices occurring all around us; and, once I had overcome my entrancement with the sheer mystery and amazingness of things and turned toward more everyday practicalities, my first forays into the social and behavioral sciences were with the aim in mind of being more responsive to such troubles and injustices. It came as a shock to me to realize that the very activity of pursuing good aims with a good will could still (unintentionally) result in the production of social and moral disasters (Scott, 1998; Shotter, 2004). The very activity of becoming an "expert," a "scholar," an "academic," an "intellectual," leads us so easily into a contempt for ordinary people, and into ignoring of the fact that all our claims to special knowledge – which we want to "give back" to "them" through lectures and special plans for their betterment – have had their origins in *their* activities, and in those of their predecessors. Without the benefit *their* company in *our* endeavors, our claims as experts would be completely unintelligible.

Our immersion in this ongoing stream of collective life, our spontaneous responsiveness to events and to the activities of others around us apart from anything that we might do consciously and deliberately, is crucial. Indeed, our wanting and doing occurs, and can only occur, within this larger context of the spontaneously occurring activity between us all. It is all that just goes on, that just happens to us, over and above our wanting and doing, that has been ignored. To think we can have the kind of masterful and possessive agency dreamed of by Descartes is dangerously to deceive ourselves. Many versions of social constructionism still seem to me to be deeply "infected" with the Cartesianism that in fact they aim to overcome. Hence, in recent times I have begun to look beyond current versions of social constructionism, toward the surrounding circumstances that, on the one hand, make such a movement possible, but on the other, enable it to hide its own social and historical origins. Many social constructionists have still not yet moved on from a world of dead, mechanically structured activities to a world of living, embodied beings, spontaneously responsive to each other. In an earlier book, *Social Accountability and Selfhood* (Shotter, 1984), in an effort to overcome the deadhand of the mechanistic approach to human affairs, I called my approach a *social ecological* one, and it is to that approach that I feel I have now returned.

Reflected in the comments above are two themes which run through my life, just as much in my daily life as in my intellectual and academic life: One is the gradual emergence of disquiet arising within the context of a passionate commitment to something which at first I think is "it," is ideal. Hence my title: moving on by backing away – a (trial and error?) process by which we can in fact slowly improve our actions while lacking a determinate goal at which to aim. The other is the instant arousal in me of indignation at injustice, whether inflicted on my own person or on others. The second, I guess, is my motivation for the passion expressed in the first. I have always felt the need to search for a place to be where injustice is not the norm, a place where I do not have continually to justify my own very existence to others – a dream, clearly, shared by many of us (Sennett, 2003).

Early influences

Grammar school (1949 to 1953 and 1954 to 1956)

An early incident will characterize the issue here. Aged 12 years, I was among a small group of boys "allowed" into the local grammar school in virtue of having passed the 11-plus exam (IQ tests) established by the post-war Labour government. The other boys in that year's intake had attended the fee-paying preparatory school, we hadn't. The headmaster took us on one side: "You boys are part of a special experiment. You ought not to be here, so you had better be on your best behavior." Clearly, I never felt "at home" in that school and I left it at 15 to work as an engineering apprentice in an aircraft factory, but returned to it later, to study mathematics and physics.

At the aircraft factory (1953 to 1954)

In the preface to *Cultural Politics of Everyday Life* (Shotter, 1993a, pp.xi–xii) I wrote of my experiences at the aircraft factory, for they were deeply formative in two ways. One was to do with the bodily "feels," so to speak, that one can get while filing metals – which I had to do in the apprentice's workshop. Even now, 40-odd years later, I can remember the oily slipperiness of brass, the way soft aluminum tore and clogged the file, the hard crumbliness of cast iron, the utterly intransigent nature of stainless steel, but the yielding friendliness of mild steel such that file and material seemed to have been made for each other. It was as if, with the file, I could "feel into" the very crystalline structure of the metals themselves. Hammering was different, and revealed different properties within the materials. Other tools worked to reveal yet further characteristics. But the other memory is a continuation of my "wrong social class" experience at school. Our humiliation began at 7.30am, when we thousand or so workers had to troop in through a single, little door at the back of the factory, jostling and pushing each other to make sure we clocked in on time, as every minute late cost us 15 minutes pay. While the "staff" (management, drawing office, administrative, and other such personnel) and the Royal Air Force Officer customers, came in ("sauntered in" we thought) through big double doors at the front, up imposing steps at 9.00am. But more than that, while "they" had their lunch on a mezzanine floor raised five feet above "us" in the lunch room, and had waitress service and white tablecloths, "we" buttered our sliced bread straight from the paper packet on the Formica top of the table... and so on, and so on. But it wasn't simply that they "looked down on 'us,'" it was that "they" treated us as like "about-to-be-naughty children".

Such incidents as these were paradigmatic of the thousand other small daily "hidden injuries of class" (Sennett and Cobb, 1972), or "degradation ceremonies" (Garfinkel, 1956) that were then – in the 1950s (and for the next decade) – an integral part of the British industrial scene, marked, as it then was, by a large number of strikes and a general level of anger, resentment and widespread bloody-mindedness expressed by all.

Looking back upon these little degradations, later, I was intrigued to realize that, while "we" on the workshop floor had "gone on" about these and other little incidents almost continually, the staff had seemed impervious to the fact that our anger was occasioned by their behavior, their "perks" (why should they care, they deserved them didn't they?). As I came to realize, that is a part of the phenomenology of power: those who have it are least aware of it, for the world "offers no resistance" to them and their desires. Only those without such power are aware of its workings "in" the resistance they meet in trying to realize their desires. The event that occasioned this thought occurred when I noticed a cleaner in the corridor outside my lecturer's room in my first university, brushing an absolutely spotless, gleaming floor as I walked by. I wonder "Why?" Of course! As soon as I peeked back after turning the corner, he had stopped. Had I that much power?

But I was intrigued also in the aircraft factory by the fact that, when workers had returned to the workshop floor after a brush with management, seething with anger, and everyone had said "Oh, you've just got to complain about that," no one ever did. In the end, it seemed too trivial, and one knew it would be useless. To complain, for instance, about the windows in the men's toilets – put there so that the foreman could see that what was being done there was being done properly, and not wasting time – to complain just by saying "Well, I don't like being looked at those times," seemed both inadequate to the anger, and unlikely to be effective. But what else could one say? Our rage was impotent rage; we didn't even know where our anger came from, so to speak. There seemed to be no adequate language within which to express why we had become so angry, to explain why these little degradations mattered so much to us. And this, I suspect, made us even more angry, for we also became angry at ourselves, for trivializing ourselves at being so bothered by such trivial things... or at not being sufficiently linguistically eloquent to express what we felt needed expression.

It was hard to realize – and to sustain one's excitement at the fact – that the factory was in the business of building some of the most amazing engineering triumphs of the day. I have great admiration for engineers, and I still have; some of their feats are truly heroic (as well as some of their "mistakes") – no doubt about it – but I left after one year, to return to school to become a mathematician, so that I too could become one of the "staff," and have some say in the "making" of things. I was sixteen at the time. Then, I never thought that I would be writing on communication and the role of bodily feelings in its conduct in ways which in fact connects these two memories, in two different ways.

One way is to do with how (a) the "feeling into" the hidden inner structure of materials *through* the use of a tool like a file, connects with (b) sensing the (also supposedly hidden) inner structure of the social world *through* the use of words-as-prosthetic-devices. The other is to do with how (a) our lack of words then to express how and why these "trivial" things mattered so much to us, connects with (b) how we still do not quite understand how to articulate the way these small things work to influence us in our feelings as to 'who' we are, i.e., to influence us "in" our identities, and how legitimately to counter them. Nor do we quite understand how it is that, if one feels oneself reduced as a person, one feels oneself as living in a reduced world.

Indeed, as an aside here, although I'm convinced that we human beings are the *makers* both of ourselves and what we take our realities to be, the kind of "constructionism" of interest to me has always been much more of the "river-bed" than of the "river" (see Wittgenstein, 1969, nos 95, 96 and 97), i.e., to do with that aspect of our lives which goes on between us unconsciously and spontaneously, rather then cognitively and deliberately. Indeed, with apologies for the "sexist" (and "Enlightenment") terminology within which it was then framed, I set the scene for my overall project in an earlier 1975 book as follows:

> Men have created and are still creating the characteristics of their own humanity. It has been produced, not as a result of evolutionary processes – processes that produce changes of a biological kind – for men seem to have stayed biologically constant for some time. Its development must be considered to be a historical, cultural one, a matter not of natural processes but of human imagination, choice and effort. And in "inheriting" this manmade nature, this "second nature," men's children do not inherit it genetically like blue eyes, but like the houses and cities, the tools and other more material artifacts they have fashioned, and besides teaching them skills at using these they teach them skills at fashioning more. Children "inherit" their humanity, then, in a process of communication which takes place after birth... What has been overlooked in modern psychology, especially in its more extreme mechanistic-behavioristic manifestations as a natural science of behavior, is that man is not simply a being immersed directly in nature but

is a being *in a culture* in nature. Thus people must not be treated like organisms that respond directly in relation to their position in the world, but as rather special organic forms which deal with nature in terms of their knowledge of the "position" in a culture; that is, in terms of a knowledge of the part their actions play in relation to the part played by other people's actions in maintaining (or progressing) the culture. (Shotter, 1975, pp.13–14).

And my overall project has changed very little since.

My first attempt at a university degree (1956 to 1957)

There is a whole episode to my life of great passion and anguish, of failure in one sense but success in another, that I am going to pass over pretty quickly, as its relevance to my subsequent intellectual work (although deep) is difficult to judge.

After studying mathematics and physics at school from age 17 to 19, I went in 1956 to Bristol University to study Pure Mathematics. Having read Bertrand Russell (1917), I thought mathematics was the royal road to absolute truth, and also, naively, to a just world. But it was not only the year of the Suez crisis in Britain – with students marching the streets, as if in a rehearsal for Paris 1968 – but also the year in which British theatre began again to flourish. Peter O'Toole had just graduated from the Old Vic Theatre school in Bristol, and I saw every one of his appearances – in Beckett's *Waiting for Godot*, Shakespeare's *Hamlet*, Osborne's *Look Back in Anger*, and (as Arthur Dolittle) in Shaw's *Pygmalion*. I was captivated by the theater, and got myself involved doing the lighting in a student production of Arthur Miller's *Death of a Salesman*. The student who taught me this skill was John Barrett, who at that time was a psychology student (and later a faculty member of the Psychology department there at Bristol). Barrett also gave me the psychological lowdown on Willy Loman. Wow! I had not met this kind of stuff before. This got me much closer to real life and to problems of injustice than mathematics ever could. My passion for mathematics disappeared as my passion for the theater grew. Psychology was the subject I must pursue, I thought. As a result, at the end of the year, I failed all my maths exams and had to leave Bristol to do two years National Service in the Royal Air Force (RAF). My success at this time was in meeting my wife-to-be, Ann, to whom I was married in 1959, and who saw me through the deep anguish and unhappiness of those times. We were married for 38 years, but as two very ambitious and independent people, oriented always to "the-yet-further," we finally parted to pursue our personal careers; not, however, before having two children of our own, and adopting two more.

Electronics in National Service, and in the Phonetics Department at University College, London (1959 to 1963)

As a consequence of taking "aptitude tests," I was assigned in the RAF to be trained in radar. But before I could go to the Radar School, I had to do six weeks of "basic training." This was a nightmare. Why it is thought that continual humiliation and degradation builds character among those continually humiliated and degraded beats me – sooner or later they get their revenge (no matter what Festinger's 1962 *Cognitive Dissonance* might predict).

But all things pass, and in 1959, I began to work as an electronics technician in the Phonetics Department in University College, London – a department that once had as its head Professor Daniel Jones (1881–1967), who was famous for being the originator of received pronunciation (RP), and (so I was told) for being the model for Professor Higgins in Shaw's *Pygmalion*. At the time, besides all the purely phonetic research, there were a number of electronic projects: both speech analysis (with the hope of building a speech-recognizer-typewriter) and speech synthesis, as well as an experiment on "auto-correlation" – in which white noise was fed directly into one ear, and after a slight delay (10 msecs or so) into the other ear, to give rise to the experience of the noise as coming from a specific *direction*. Amazing stuff, and I learnt a great deal from it all. There is something very special about *living* processes that, it still seems to me, simply cannot be captured in a priori notions of the relations between cause and effect. Some other kinds of relations, still quite mysterious to us, are at work (see Liberman *et al.*, 1967).

During this time, I was very fortunate in being introduced to Basil Bernstein, who had just then begun his work on "speech codes" (Bernstein, 1971). Basil had a passion I appreciated (and I mourn his passing). He introduced me – with "You must read this" – to G.H. Mead (1934), Ernst Cassirer (1953, 1955, 1957), and Luria (1961). The Luria stuff was especially important. Working with children in Moscow, brain damaged due to starvation during World War II, he was showing the power of speech to mediate the development of voluntary movement where none had previously existed. As Luria (1961) put it: "What [the child] could do only with adult help, he is [later] able to do unassisted. This fact becomes the basic law in the child's development" (p.2). This became the basic theme in all my subsequent work.

My research program: Its background and current directions

Overall, my research is marked by two major themes:

1. Negatively, I have been trying to express, not just the technical inadequacy of the Cartesian mechanistic paradigm in the human and behavior sciences, but its pernicious moral effects – the undermining of our intrinsic human relatedness, both to each other as well as to our surroundings.

2. But positively, since around 1980, in relation to the concept of "joint action," I have been exploring the philosophical, empirical, and methodological consequences of the (essentially Vicoian and Vygotskian) assumption that, as living embodies being, we cannot help but be spontaneously responsive to both the others and othernesses in our surroundings. In this work, I have focused most intensely on the writings of (initially) Vygotsky and Vico, especially on Wittgenstein, but also (more recently) on Voloshinov and Bakhtin, as well as on Gadamer and Merleau-Ponty.

Let me comment on the negative aspects of my research program first. Two major themes in Cartesianism have always bothered me. One is to do with Descartes' (1968) pronouncement that his aim is to seek a "practical philosophy" which, if we had it, then "knowing the power and the effects of fire, water, air, the stars, the heavens and all the other bodies that surround us...we might put them in the same way to all the uses for which they are appropriate, and thereby make ourselves, as it were, masters and possessors of nature" (p.78). Just to be an unconfused participant in the world along with others has always seemed to me to be a good enough aim in life. The aim of mastery and possession is an overweening arrogance. The other theme that bothered me was Descartes' (1968) determination "to speak only of what would happen in a new world, if God were to create...enough matter to compose it, and if he were to agitate diversely and confusedly the different parts of this matter, and afterwards did no more than...to let her act according to his established laws" (p.62). We can find these themes reflected in, say, Hull's (1943) claim that a scientific psychology must start with "colorless, atomic movements." But to take this as a starting point for understanding the complexity of people's behavior always seemed to me an aspect of the craziness that a strict adherence to "rationality" can induce. For this is to deny not only the *wholistic* nature of our experience of our shared lives with those around us, but also whatever pre-existing character it *must* have for us, if we are to experience ourselves (at least to an extent) as living in a common world.

More recently, it has occurred to me that we need to add another Cartesian theme: the belief that the goal of our research into our own human affairs *must be* to identify a single central God-like agency, a "system of rules," that is responsible for the order observable in our lives. Our belief that this is so arises, I think, also from Descartes' writings. Although he thinks of himself, because of his doubts, as an imperfect being, he can still nonetheless find within himself certain things, *perfections*, which he cannot even conceive of doubting. And it is on the basis of these perfections that he feels able to follow the "general rule that the things we conceive very clearly and distinctly are all true" (p.54). But from whence could such a confidence issue? "It must have been put into me by a being whose nature was truly more perfect than mine and which even had in itself all the perfections of which I could only have an idea, that is to say, in a single word, which was God" (Descartes, 1968, p.55).

Thus this claim – that it is the work of an other or of an otherness within himself, more perfect than himself – is crucial in providing Descartes with the foundational point of departure for all his other claims to truth. It enables him to locate within himself a certain, a priori "ordered necessity," a self-discovered inner certainty, against which all the apparent contingencies of life may be judged. As imperfectly intellectual beings, it is only through God's agency (i.e., the workings in us of a reality utterly independent of our opinions about it) that we can find within ourselves both certain basic undeniable truths, and a capacity for reasoning, thus to grasp in certain basic respects the nature of the world around us. Thus, the compulsion we currently feel in the human sciences to seek single systematic *theories* to *explain* the particular action before us as one instance of a general, underlying, hidden scheme of things, is still to seek a single God-like being located somewhere *beyond* our everyday lives together. This is a major distraction standing in the way of our being able to help ourselves to refine, elaborate, and develop our own everyday lives in the course of our living of them.

I turn now to the more positive aspects of my research program. After an initial excursion in the computer simulation of language acquisition, I then turned to an approach fundamentally influenced by Vygotsky (and Luria), and later, more and more, by Wittgenstein's later philosophy (see Shotter, 1970). In general, my stance toward all these problems can be described as *social constructionist* (Gergen, 1982; Gergen and Davis, 1985; Harré, 1983), although in my 1984 book (Shotter, 1984), I called my approach *social ecology*, and, as mentioned above, I would now like to return to that designation. For what strikes me as wrong with many current social constructionist approaches is their still Cartesian, (post) structuralist, dualistic approach to language and to our surroundings – as if we have only an *external* relationship to them both, rather than having our very being *within them*. They still take the referential-representational function of language as central, and, so to speak, merely reverse its representational direction – i.e., instead of being *of* reality, they are taken as being *constitutive* of our realities. Instead, I have taken the central function of language to be of a relationally responsive kind. It is in being directly responsive to the bodily expressions of others that we enter into one or another kind of living relationship with them.

In my two 1993 books, I explored what I then called a *rhetorical-responsive* approach to language (which, I now call, variously, relationally responsive or expressive responsive, according to the relevant context) – concerned with studying that dimension of everyday, spontaneous but contested interpersonal language use, that works to "construct" or "constitute" the style of our social relations, the grammars of our forms of life; and how these in turn, are formative of our different experiences of both ourselves as individuals, and of the supposed "realities" surrounding us (Shotter, 1993a, 1993b).

The main influences upon my thought then were drawn from Wittgenstein, Vico, Vygotsky, Mead, Bakhtin, Billig, and MacIntyre. Then my main interest was in what could be called "traditions of argumentation," and in how viewing social life as constituting such a living tradition – rather than a static structure – opens up a whole new range of phenomena for study. In particular, it brought into focus that aspect of cultural politics to do with those activities in which people are able to play a part in the constructing of their own way of life: being able to voice (or not, as the case may be) the character of one's own concerns, and have them taken seriously by others around one, is an essential part of being a citizen and having a sense of belonging in one's society.

More recently, I have moved away from *argumentation* and *debate* as a source of cultural change and growth, and – under the influence of Bakhtin, Merleau-Ponty, and that aspect of Wittgenstein's work to do with our spontaneous reactions – toward both a much more complex but more practical, nonreflective form of social change. Influenced at first by Bakhtin's (1981, 1984, 1986) *dialogic* notions, but now also by Merleau-Ponty's (1968) *chiasmic* notions, I have begun a whole new *descriptive, participatory* approach to an understanding of social life – drawing heavily on Wittgenstein's "poetic" methods of inquiry. Central here is the concept of "real presences" (Levy-Bruhl, 1926; Steiner, 1989), a concept very similar in intent to Raymond William's (1977) "Structures of feeling" (see Shotter, 2003). Recently, this work has resulted not only in the outlining of a new set of methods for action research – the methods of a "social poetics" which focuses on the new responses that can function as "the prototypes for new language-games" (Wittgenstein) – but also on new styles of writing: participatory ("with-ness") writing rather than representational ("about-ness") writing (Shotter, 1998).

Beginnings (1964 to 1984)

Originally, back in 1964 to 1965, my research was on the computer simulation of language learning – with a computer model in which a "mother" who already knew a set of "linguistic" rules transmitted them to a "child." My first published paper is in *Nature* upon this topic (Shotter, 1966). However, through difficulties arising from within this project, I came to realize that it was *not the following of rules* that made linguistic meaning possible for people, but *being able to mean* – due to people's spontaneous living, bodily responsivity – *that made it possible for people to follow rules*. Rule following is a consequence of meaning, not its cause. In this, I was influenced by a phrase in Vygotsky (1962), in which he noted that "consciousness and control appear only at a late stage in the development of a [higher mental] function, after it has been used and practiced unconsciously and spontaneously" (p.90). I switched to the video-tape study of the interactive activities between actual mothers and children. At that time, in 1975, I outlined my research project as attempting to understand the question: "What is it in the everyday interaction with the others around one that makes it possible for us to develop into morally autonomous *persons*?" I was trying to understand what enabled the shift from acting in response to events in one's circumstances, to acting in response to events occurring within oneself – to events occurring in oneself as a result (as I would say later) of events occurring within one's own inner dialogues. In the studies I did in the 1970s, I began to map out arguments for ways of interpreting observations made in the video-tape studies, as relevant to that question.

During this time, I was David Wood's PhD supervisor. Besides the whole Vygotsky interest, we were especially interested in an approach to analyzing problem solving strategies in terms of Jakobson, Fant and Halle's (1952) *distinctive features*. Wood was later to publish with Jerome Bruner, the famous "scaffolding" paper. Strangely, however, there is no mention in this paper of Vygotsky, even though Wood's original study was developed as a study of Vygotsky's ZPD, and Bruner wrote the Introduction to the 1962 translation of Vygotsky's *Thought and Language*.

Besides Vygotsky (1962), central influences at this time came from Dewey's (1896) "The Concept of the Reflex Arc in Psychology," and from Dreyfus's (1967) "Why Computers must have Bodies in order to be Intelligent," while the work of John Macmurray (1957, 1961) and of Charles Taylor (1971) was also important in emphasizing the moral dimension. I first outlined all these concerns (Shotter, 1970), in relation to George Kelly's (1955) psychology of personal constructs.

I continued these themes in my 1975 book, *Images of Man in Psychological Research*. Central to it is the distinction between behavior and action, between events that are caused to happen outside of our agency to control, and events which we as agents make happen. This distinction is crucial, not only in our everyday lives, in which we hold each other accountable for our actions, but in science, where it is fundamental. For scientists unable to discriminate between just happening events and those happening only in accord with their manipulations would be unable to do experiments to test their theories. People's responsibility for their actions is, thus, basic: it cannot be "explained" causally. Thus as I saw it then, this meant that psychology could not be a natural science of behavior, but must be a moral science of action. This is still a point of importance, for it means that weighing, counting, and measuring cannot simply be taken as so basic that we can root our claims about human psychology in their results as they stand. As social activities, they are all still dependent on shared human judgments occurring with shared forms of life.

In the 1975 book, I had talked vaguely of people being "positioned" in social life in some way, and of their actions being understood only socially and culturally, in terms of the part they played in maintaining, developing, and transmitting their group's culture in their actions. In 1977, this lead to another book, with Alan Gauld as first author, outlining an *hermeneutical* approach to psychological investigations, i.e., the claim that *interpretation* was central to all our understandings of each other's activities. Central to that book were two topics that have remained central in all subsequent work:

1. All human activities work in terms of *anticipations*, they "point to" or "relate to" aspects in their surroundings "other than" themselves.

2. To the extent that all human activities occur and have their meaning within a larger whole, not only must others understand their meaning in terms of their relations "within" that whole (i.e., meaning is a relational notion), but that complex meanings can be "played out" or "specified" between people, step by step, over a period of time.

I soon began to realize that the distinction between action and behavior, between events happening within and outside of our agency to control, was not at all clear cut. For there are many events that, while they occur only within and as a result of human involvements, occur without any of those involved having any clear sense of having directly produced them, let alone of having intended them. Further, the notion of understanding set out in the 1977 book was, to the extent that it focused on interpretations, an inter-individualistic, cognitive notion. It depended on events occurring within the heads of individuals. I needed to return to the beginnings occasioned in me by Vygotsky, Dreyfus, and Dewey.

Thus, in articles written between 1978 and 1980, I introduced the term "joint action" (stolen from Blummer, 1965/1966) to account for a special "third" form of spontaneous social activity (i.e., activity that cannot be accounted as either individual *action* done for a reason, or as *behavior* with an outside cause), activity that cannot be attributed to any of the individuals involved in it, but which is itself productive not only of the "situation" that they are in, but also provides them with resources for their continued action within it.

While the notion of "joint action" remains central to my whole research program, my conception of social life at large has gradually grown more complex. In my 1984 book, I began to talk of everyday social life as possessing a "moral ecology" – as if people acted from within a landscape of ethically defined but still contestable rights and duties. That landscape contained a "political economy of developmental opportunities," with certain regions of it containing more opportunities than others, with different people having differential access to such opportunities. I also explored further the whole social ontology of a world in which it was possible for human actions to make a real difference to its future – a world of becoming rather than merely of being.

Cultural politics (1984 to 1990)

What became of interest to me was why it was so difficult to introduce the study of "joint action" and other "developmental" processes into psychology as a discipline. Habits of thought within the discipline itself seem to render them "rationally invisible," few seemed to see these issues as important.

In developing the theme of joint action, I began to use it not only to provide a critique of the (one-way, monological) methodology in experimental psychology, but also to provide a positive account of people's social development – with the eventual aim of giving a comprehensive account of human personhood, i.e., what it is to have a *voice* in influencing the conditions of one's life. My work was focused on the nature of disciplinary writing and research, and the way in which it worked to silence important marginal "voices."

This work led to my appointment in 1987, as a full professor, to one of the three directorships of a new General Social Sciences program with special reference to language, thinking, perception and culture, in the Rijksuniversiteit Utrecht, The Netherlands (Bryan Turner was appointed to the Sociology chair). The overall theme of the Utrecht program was citizenship and development, and it was thought, and I agreed, that this should be the main thrust of my work there. It has continued to be a main focus of my work ever since. It was at this point that I began to reorient away from academic psychology (and my critique of its misformulation of its problems) and toward the communication discipline.

Influenced both by events within the interdisciplinary program in which I was involved and on the continent of Europe itself, my work took a more practice-situated turn. My original way of formulating the problems to do with self-determination and moral autonomy was still far too general and abstract, insufficiently political or historical, and too centered in ahistorical, individualistic, systematic Enlightenment notions centered around "the nature of Man." Further, theoretical work both on the nature of deconstruction and rhetoric in literary theory, upon historical traditions of argumentation in moral philosophy, and upon Bakhtin's (1986) notion of utterance, voice, and speech genres, have lead to a new, rich, and active field of problems to do not just with personhood but with identity and belonging, with issues of citizenship, and that aspect of politics present in interpersonal relations to do with "whose" way of life is the one that is currently being developed in an interaction.

These more practical concerns led me to focus on that special kind of knowledge – knowledge that is neither theoretical nor technical, but which is a third kind of knowledge – the kind of knowledge one has *from within* a way of life, to do with knowing how to conduct oneself prudently within it. It is to the nature of this third kind of (cultural-participatory) knowledge that I have given most of my attention in recent years.

"Real presences" in the unnoticed background and consciousness (1991 to 2002)

Levy-Bruhl (1926) and Cassirer (1957), in their studies of mythical thought, call those influences that, although inaudible and invisible to all others at the moment of their emergence are nonetheless influential in the behavior of unique individuals in certain special circumstances, "presences." Rather than providing an objective knowledge of a situation or circumstance, such presences seem to function as expressive personages, as if, in their silence and invisibility, they still had a voice and a face, a physiognomy expressive of their meaning. George Steiner (1984, 1989), more concerned to describe the power of a literary text to create – in our responsive, interactive reading of it – a felt meaning, calls such agentic influences "real presences."

In the past, two great realms of activity have occupied our attention in the social sciences, in social theory, and in philosophy: the realms of action and behavior. Action can be studied and explained in terms of an individual's (culturally conditioned) reasons for his or her actions, while in the study of behavior we seek the (natural) causes of an individual's movements. But between these two great realms containing a mixture of both cultural and natural influences is another great realm, activity of a third kind, *sui generis*. In Vygotskian developmental psychology, it occurs in a region called the zone of proximal development (ZPD), but this is not to give it its full importance as the "inexpressible" background flow of everyday practices "against which whatever [we] could express has its meaning" (Wittgenstein, 1980, p.16).

Its complex, mixed, *chiasmic* character arises out of the fact that, as soon as a second living human being spontaneously responds to the activities of a first, what the second does cannot be accounted as wholly their own – for they act in a way partly "shaped" by the first's actions (while the first's actions, in being addressed to the second person, were also responsive to their very presence). Thus what happens between people, between you and me, is neither wholly yours nor mine, but ours – but neither wholly ours either, for we must be responsive to those over there too. In other words, the results of joint action are public property, so to speak. But more than that, such activity is always intrinsically creative, for people's activities are not only uniquely responsive to each other's, but also to particular events occurring in the rest of their surroundings. Such *chiasmically* structured activity is thus full of unique, "first-time" forms of interaction which, if those involved in them continue to be responsive to them, can be developed into, to use a Wittgensteinian term, new "forms of life." It is in this sphere of social practices that my work has its application for, rather than theories of their nature, I have focused on certain special methods for their development – methods, but not a methodology, got from following Wittgenstein's (1953) methods in his philosophical investigations.

What is so special about these methods is that they work in terms of what Wittgenstein (1953) calls "reminders" – philosophical utterances that, if uttered to onself at the appropriate moment on encountering a difficulty in one's involvements, "move" or "direct" one to act in a particular way.

The importance of such self-directed utterances – such "inner speech," in Vygotsky's (1962) terms – can be understood in relation to two of his claims: (a) that our "higher" mental processes are developed from our learning how to marshal, deploy, and direct our already (biologically provided) "lower" mental processes so as to "orchestrate" them into complex sequences; (b) that a spoken word – which might later become a symbol, i.e., have a representational function – "at first plays the role of means in forming a concept" (p.56). This is because in their expressive-responsive function, words spoken to oneself can enable one to direct one's attention to an event, select distinctive features within it, and to interrelate such features with others in other events.

As I see it, there is a direct connection between Wittgenstein's (1953) philosophical methods of investigation and inquiry and the part played in them by the power of the living, human voice, and the methods we all as parents and teachers use in helping our children "grow into the intellectual life of those around them" (Vygotsky, 1978, p.88), as outlined by Vygotsky. Thus, Wittgenstein's (1953) methods should not be thought of as methods of research aimed at discovering already existing facts, but as concerned with exploring possible next steps in the development of our already existing forms of life.

Important academic involvements (1991 to 2003)

It was also during my time in Utrecht that Ken Gergen invited me to start with him the Sage series Inquiries in Social Constructionism. I had first met Ken in 1979 at the British Psychological Society "Models of Man" Conference (Chapman and Jones, 1980). We immediately fell in with each other, as we were both being heavily attacked, he in America, me in England, as dangerous "heretics," bent on destroying (as our attackers saw it) the scientific credentials psychology had worked so hard to achieve. Although we do not always agree, and often have different agendas, and want to apply our work in different spheres, Ken and Mary Gergen have always been staunch friends and allies in times of need. Let me add here that Rom Harré has also provided this kind of encouragement in dark times (see Shotter, 1990, for an account of his work and my relation to it).

I first came to the Department of Communication at the University of New Hampshire (UNH) in 1991. The original enticement was an offer to help begin a graduate program here. That, unfortunately, was overtaken by the financial stringencies that struck the university about that time. Thus my supervision of PhD research, instead of continuing at UNH, was cut short. However, while at UNH, my scholarly writing continued, and I was blessed there by a couple of enthusiastic colleagues in social constructionism – both strong scholars in their own right: Sheila McNamee and Jack Lannamann. I was also able to do some collaborative work within the research projects of other colleagues.

One of these arose out of *Conversational Realities* (Shotter, 1993b), in which I discussed extensively a dialogical approach to social scientific research. In 1992, Professor Bjorn Gustavsen, originally an industrial relations lawyer but at this time the director of the Worklife Research Institutes of both Norway and Sweden, published *Dialogue and Development* (Gustavsen, 1992). He outlined a way out of the adversarial strife between unions and management in European work life, using more dialogical forms of enterprise development. He was also the architect of the Swedish "Learning Regions" project, based in the idea of "dialogue conferences" amongst regional stakeholders, as well as other similar Norwegian projects. He contacted me, and this has been one of my main research involvements in recent years.

Another set of involvements has been in the medical sphere. Together with Dr. Arlene M. Katz in the Harvard Department of Social Medicine, we have published a number of papers on diagnostic interviewing, mentorship programs, and psychotherapy. Of particular importance here, I think, is her work with a "Council of Elders," who functioned as "consultants" to young doctors training in geriatrics, helping the "consultants" to orient these doctors toward aspects of health care for the aged they might otherwise overlook (see Katz *et al.*, 2000). Following the leads provided by Wittgenstein's (1953) philosophical methods, we have begun to develop what we call the methods of "a social poetics," a set of methods that works by focusing on unique and fleeting but nonetheless striking moments to which participants involved in an interaction respond – moments that Bakhtin (1993) calls "once-occurrent events of Being" (p.2). These methods make visible the *uniqueness* of another person's life, what *matters* to them. For this is the kind of understanding that is required by practitioners who face everyday the practical task of deciding how to treat *this* particular person. Working with Dr. Ann L. Cunliffe, then from the Whittemore Business School at UNH (and now working in California), we showed how these methods – for the refinement and elaboration of people practices *from within* the practices themselves – could be applied to management (see especially Shotter and Cunliffe, 2003).

Consciousness (2002 to 2003)

To return to my present scholarly work on the implications of our embedding in an unbroken background stream of spontaneously responsive bodily activity, I have finished a long rough first draft, of a paper entitled "Spontaneous Responsiveness, Chiasmic Relations, and Consciousness: Inside the Realm of Living Expression." I explore the relevance of (chiasmically) intertwined activity for an understanding of consciousness (Shotter, 2002 – see also Shotter, in press). I suggest that our ways of talking are not just simply a matter of representing or picturing a state of affairs, so that how others act in relation to what we say is a matter, always, of *interpretation*, a matter of inference or hypothesis formation. Rather, an important aspect of people's verbal communication is their possession of the *right*, as first-person agents, to *express* themselves, to make certain expressive bodily movements. Such expressions are living movements which, as elaborations of our natural, spontaneously expressed responses to events occurring around us, work in a *gestural* fashion to communicate *our own unique* orientation, our own unique relations to our surroundings. Further, in not being simply changes in the position of our bodies in space, but *physiognomic* changes within our bodies themselves, such gestures "point" for others to aspects of what we call our "inner lives."

What marks this work is that it makes no attempt to answer (to me, the seeming metaphysical question) "What *is* consciousness?" It is oriented more toward the kind of exploration of consciousness that Nagel (1982) set out in his famous paper: "What is it like to be a Bat?" In setting out the question in this form, he opens up the possibility that "there is something that it is like to *be* that organism – something that it is like *for* the organism" (p.392). For, as Nagel realizes, when we confront other *living* beings, we confront beings which, *in relation to us*, clearly have "a life of their own." What I think Nagel misses in that paper is that there is a clear difference between questions like: "What is it like to be a bat?" and "What is it like to be a mathematician?" or even, "What is it like to be a blind or a deaf person?" We can ask mathematicians, blind persons, and deaf persons to *tell* us of their lives in a way that we cannot ask bats. They can at least try to tell us of the nature of *their* world (according to their own degree of eloquence) in *their own terms*. The question now is what kind of stance – ethical and otherwise – is required if we are to open ourselves to them *as they tell us of themselves*, and allow their otherness to enter us and to make us other than we already are.

Concluding remarks

I have charted a course that has stretched over nearly 50 years – but clearly, it is not over yet. My hardback copy of Wittgenstein's *Investigations* (now held together by duct tape), has "Nottingham 1968" inscribed inside the front cover. But even now, it is still not a matter of me thinking that I am at last beginning to understand it fully and authentically. Something else is at work. At last I am beginning to see how the remarks in it can indeed work, at crucial moments in one's own involvements, as "reminders." Like Vygotsky's (1962) "inner speech" that we can use to *instruct* ourselves in the conduct of complex actions, so we can use Wittgenstein's words (his utterances, his "voice") in the same way. They can halt us in our tracks (halt the spontaneous, routine flow of action), then direct our attention, not only to previously unnoticed features of our immediate surroundings, but also to links and connections between them and other important aspects of our lives.

More so, his methods get us *up close* to the details that matter to us in our lives; put us, so to speak, so closely "in touch" with them that we can get a feel for how we can "go on" in our practical affairs with a sure sense of where our next step is coming from and going to: "In order to see more clearly," he remarks in commenting on the complexity of what occurs, even in the simple activity of describing an array of colored squares, "here as in countless similar cases, we must focus on the details of what goes on; must look at them *from close to*" (Wittgenstein, 1953, no.51). When we do, it is in terms of everyday details, accessible to all of us, that he is able to bring out into the light of day distinctions of importance to us, distinctions that we do in fact use without being aware it. Not troubling to pay such close attention, we can easily ignore such facts, jumping to false conclusions as to how we *must* be acting to accomplish such achievements. It is this aspect of Wittgenstein's work, its ability to enable us to get "inside" the "moment of acting," that makes it so powerful in relation to my concerns – along with Vygotsky, Vico, Bakhtin, Merleau-Ponty, and others I have mentioned.

Our academic and scholarly training to do with human affairs, I now feel, has been and still is wrongly oriented. In being modeled on "scientific" styles of inquiry, it orients us toward focusing on an already determined set of fundamental entities, and on the merely causal relations between them. This, as indicated with respect to our inquiries into communication, leads us to ask questions only about the patterns discernable in completed actions. In other words, it orients us toward the scene of inquiry at much too late a stage, and then leads us to look in the wrong direction, with the wrong attitude. We only arrive on the scene *after* we have passed our exams and adopted certain already agreed upon *versions* of what is supposed to be occurring out in the world between us – officially, everything of importance *is hidden* in the heads of individuals. But then, not content with that, we *look back* toward past accomplishments, toward already existing actualities to find a causal pattern in them, seeing them as mechanisms external to ourselves, rather than looking *forward* toward the new possibilities provided to us *from within* our relational involvements. We do all this with the wrong attitude. For we seek a *static, dead picture*, a theoretical representation, of a phenomenon, rather than a living sense of it as an active, authoritative and action-guiding agency in our lives.

Clearly, what I have been trying to do in my allusive, linguistic gesturing above, is to outline the character of something-yet-to-be-achieved, something about which I still feel disquiet, a something-not-right with how we currently *are* with ourselves. In short, my life has been, and still is, a process of moving on by backing away.

References

Bakhtin, M.M. (1981) *The Dialogical Imagination*, ed M. Holquist, trans C. Emerson and M. Holquist. Austin: University of Texas Press.

Bakhtin, M.M. (1984) *Problems of Dostoevsky's Poetics*, ed and trans C. Emerson. Minneapolis: University of Michigan Press.

Bakhtin, M.M. (1986) *Speech Genres and Other Late Essays*, trans V.W. McGee. Austin: University of Texas Press.

Bakhtin, M.M. (1993) *Toward a Philosophy of the Act*, trans and notes V. Lianpov, ed M. Holquist. Austin: University of Texas Press.

Bernstein, B. (1971) *Class, Codes and Control*, Vol. 1. London: Routledge and Kegan Paul.

Blummer, H. (1965/1966) "Sociological implications of the thought of George Herbert Mead." *American Journal of Sociology 71*, 535–544.

Cassirer, E. (1953) *The Philosophy of Symbolic Forms, Vol. 1: Language.* New Haven: University of Yale Press.

Cassirer, E. (1955) *The Philosophy of Symbolic Forms, Vol. 2: Mythical Thought.* New Haven: University of Yale Press.

Cassirer, E. (1957) *The Philosophy of Symbolic Forms: Vol. 3: The Phenomenology of Knowledge.* New Haven: University of Yale Press.

Chapman, A.J. and Jones, D.M. (eds) (1980) *Models of Man*. Leicester: British Psychological Society.

Descartes, R. (1968) *Discourse on Method and Other Writings*. Trans. with introduction F.E. Sutcliffe. Harmondsworth: Penguin.

Dewey, J. (1896) "The concept of the reflex arc in psychology." *Psychological Revue 3*, 13–32. Reprinted in W. Dennis (ed) *Readings in the History of Psychology*. New York: Appleton-Century-Crofts, 1944.

Dreyfus, H.L. (1967) "Why computers must have bodies in order to be intelligent." *Review of Metaphysics 21*, 13–21.

Festinger, L. (1962) *A Theory of Cognitive Dissonance*. Stanford, CA: University of Stanford Press.

Garfinkel, H. (1956) "Conditions for successful degradation ceremonies." *American Journal of Sociology 61*, 420–424.

Gauld, A. and Shotter, J. (1977) *Human Action and its Psychological Investigation*. London: Routledge and Kegan Paul.

Gergen, K.J. (1982) *Toward Transformation in Social Knowledge*. New York: Springer.

Gergen, K.J. and Davis, K.E (eds) (1985) *The Social Construction of the Person*. New York: Springer Verlag.

Gustavsen, B. (1992) *Dialogue and Development: Theory of Communication, Action Research and the Restructuring of Working Life*. Van Assen, Netherlands: Gorcum.

Harré, R. (1986) "The social construction of selves." In K. Yardley and T. Honess (eds) *Self and Identity*. Chichester: Wiley.

Hull, C.L. (1943) *Principles of Behavior*. New York: Appleton-Century-Crofts.

Jakobson, R., Fant, C.G.M. and Halle, M. (1952) *Preliminaries to Speech Analysis: The Distinctive Features and their Correlates*. Cambridge, MA: MIT Press. (MIT Acoustics Laboratory Technical Report 13.)

Katz, A.M., Conant, L., Inui, T., Baron, D. and Bor, D. (2000) "A council of elders: Creating a community of care." *Social Science and Medicine 50*, 851–860.

Kelly, G.A. (1955) *The Psychology of Personal Constructs*, Vols 1 and 2. New York: W.W. Norton.

Levy-Bruhl, L. (1926) *How Natives Think (Les Fonctions Mentales dans les Sociétés Inférieurs)*, trans L.A. Clare. London: George Allen and Unwin.

Liberman, A.M., Cooper, F.S., Shankweiler, D.P. and Studdart-Kennedy, M. (1967) "Perception of the speech code." *Psychology Review 74*, 431–461.

Luria, A.R. (1961) *Speech and the Regulation of Behaviour*. London: Pergamon Press.

Macmurray, J. (1957) *The Self as Agent*. London: Faber and Faber.

Macmurray, J. (1961) *Persons in Relation*. London: Faber and Faber.

Mead, G.H. (1934) *Mind, Self and Society*. Chicago, IL: University of Chicago Press.

Merleau-Ponty, M. (1968) *The Visible and the Invisible*. Ed C. Lefort, trans. A. Lingis. Evanston, IL: Northwestern University Press.

Nagel, T. (1982) "What is it like to be a bat?" Reprinted in D. Hofstadter and D.C. Dennett (eds) *The Mind's I: Fantasies and Reflections on Self and Soul*. New York: Bantam Books. First published in *Philosophical Review 83*, 435–451, 1974.

Russell, B. (1917) *Mysticism and Logic, and Other Essays*. London: George Allen and Unwin.

Scott, J.C. (1998) *Seeing Like a State: How Certain Schemes to Improve the Human Condition Have Failed*. New Haven: University of Yale Press.

Sennett, R. (2003) *Respect in a World of Inequality*. New York: Norton.

Sennett, R. and Cobb, J. (1972) *The Hidden Injuries of Class*. Cambridge: Cambridge University Press.

Shotter, J. (1966) "The existence of the crossroads policemen." *Nature 211*, 343–345.

Shotter, J. (1970) "Men, the man-makers: George Kelly and the psychology of personal constructs." In D. Bannister (ed) *Perspectives in Personal Construct Theory*. London and New York: Academic Press.

Shotter, J. (1975) *Images of Man in Psychological Research*. London: Methuen.

Shotter, J. (1980) "Action, joint action, and intentionality." In M. Brenner (ed) *The Structure of Action*. Oxford: Blackwell.

Shotter, J. (1984) *Social Accountability and Selfhood*. Oxford: Blackwell.

Shotter, J. (1990) "Rom Harré: Realism and the turn to social constructionism." In R. Bhaskar (ed) *Harré and his Critics: Essays in Honour of Rom Harré with his Commentary on Them*. Oxford: Blackwell.

Shotter, J. (1993a) *Cultural Politics of Everyday Life: Social Constructionism, Rhetoric, and Knowing of the Third Kind*. Milton Keynes: Open University Press.

Shotter, J. (1993b) *Conversational Realities: Constructing Life through Language*. London: Sage.

Shotter, J. (1998) "Telling of (not about) other voices: 'real presences' within a text." *Concepts and Transformations 3*, 77–96.

Shotter, J. (2002) "Spontaneous responsiveness, chiasmic relations, and consciousness: Inside the realm of living expression." http://pubpages.unh.edu/~jds/Consciousness.htm

Shotter, J. (2003) "Real presences: Meaning as living movement in a participatory world." *Theory and Psychology 13*, 4, 435–468.

Shotter, J. (2004) "The manufacture of personhood, and the institutionalization of mutual humiliation." *Concepts and Transformations 9*, 1, 1–38.

Shotter, J. (in press) "Vygotsky and consciousness as *con-scientia*, as witnessable knowing along with others." *Theory and Psychology*.

Shotter, J. and Cunliffe, A.L. (2003) "The manager as practical author: Everyday conversations for action." In D. Holman and R. Thorpe (eds) *Management and Language*. London: Sage.

Steiner, G. (1984) "'Critic'/'Reader'." In *George Steiner: A Reader*. Harmondsworth: Penguin.

Steiner, G. (1989) *Real Presences*. Chicago, IL: University of Chicago Press.

Taylor, C. (1971) "Interpretation and the science of man." *Review of Metaphysics 34*, 1–51.

Vygotsky, L.S. (1962) *Thought and Language*. Ed and trans E. Hanfmann and G. Vakar. Cambridge, MA: MIT Press.

Vygotsky, L.S. (1966) "Development of the higher mental functions." In A.N. Leont'ev, A.R. Luria and A. Smirnov (eds) *Psychological Research in the USSR*. Moscow: Progress Publishers.

Vygotsky, L.S. (1978) *Mind in Society: The Development of Higher Psychological Processes*. Eds M. Cole, V. John-Steiner, S. Scribner and E. Souberman. Cambridge, MA: Harvard University Press.

Vygotsky, L.S. (1986) *Thought and Language*, trans. A. Kozulin. Cambridge, MA: MIT Press.

Williams, R. (1977) *Marxism and Literature*. Oxford: Oxford University Press.

Wittgenstein, L. (1953) *Philosophical Investigations*, trans. G.E.M. Anscombe. Oxford: Blackwell.

Wittgenstein, L. (1969) *On Certainty*. Ed G.E.M. Anscombe and G.H. von Wright, trans. Dennis Paul and G.E.M. Anscombe. Oxford: Blackwell.

Wittgenstein, L. (1980) *Culture and Value*, trans. P. Winch. Oxford: Blackwell.

Wittgenstein, L. (1981) *Zettel*, 2nd edn. Eds G.E.M. Anscombe and G.H.V. Wright. Oxford: Blackwell.

Wood, D., Bruner, J.S. and Ross, G. (1976) "The role of tutoring in problem solving." *Journal of Child Psychology and Psychiatry 17*, 89–100.

CHAPTER 9

Living with Authority in "The Between"

Hendrika Vande Kemp

Introduction: How I became a collector of kaleidoscopes

Visitors to my home often notice my kaleidoscopes. Several of the scopes are works of art, but I treasure them as "transitional objects" (Winnicott, 1953) and "symbolic object lessons" that represent several interrelated aspects of my life and work. The first three scopes were gifts from my doctoral student Barbara Eurich-Rascoe. I had used kaleidoscopes to challenge an image of psychotheological integration presented by the neuropsychologist Malcolm Jeeves in a series of lectures at Fuller Theological Seminary in January 1995. Jeeves regarded the integration of psychological facts and theological knowledge as analogous to the eye's integration of the images from a stereoscope.[1] I approached the class with toy kaleidoscopes and teleidoscopes to provide a sensory object lesson; challenged the students to think of the various "facts" emerging from psychological research as mere chips in a kaleidoscope which might or might not be visible or relevant in any particular clinical or life situation represented by the latest twist of the scope; and suggested that they take the repetitious perspectives of a teleidoscopic view as an example of the tunnel vision resulting from fixation on a discrete decontextualized "fact." Barbara was enchanted by this metaphor and, to thank me for my help in the completion of her dissertation, presented me with three kaleidoscopes carefully selected with the help of her husband and two daughters. These scopes symbolize our postmodern, feminist construction of the world (Eurich-Rascoe and Vande Kemp, 1997),[2] as well as the multidimensionality of our relationship (Eurich-Rascoe, 2000). That summer, I composed a poem applying the distortions of lenses and light to our imprecise knowledge of the Other.

Totally unaware of this kaleidoscope story, the psychology students at Fuller who selected my farewell gift in 2001 presented me with a fourth kaleidoscope, inspired by a quotation from Salvador Minuchin which I routinely recited in the family therapy class:

> We live our lives like chips in a kaleidoscope, always part of patterns that are larger than ourselves and somehow more than the sum of their parts. Our individual epistemology usually blinds us to this kaleidoscopic self, and that is unfortunate because, when we look at human beings from this perspective, whole new possibilities open up for exploring behavior and alleviating pain. (Minuchin, 1984, p.2)

Over the years, I've found that numerous scholars in various disciplines have articulated similar views. The philosopher John Macmurray wrote in his published Gifford Lectures:

> Individual independence is an illusion; and the independent individual, the isolated self, a nonentity. In ourselves we are nothing; and when we turn our eyes inward in search of ourselves we find a vacuum... It is only in relation to others that we exist as persons; we are invested with significance by others who have need of us; and borrow our reality from those who care for us. (Macmurray, [1961] 1979, p.211)

Macmurray echoes the words of the theologian Emil Brunner as they're summarized by Paul Jewett (n.d.): "The isolated individual is an abstraction of the reason which is severed from the word of God" (p.13). These men articulated in philosophical-theological terms what Minuchin asserted in his efforts to expose the lie that constitutes the American myth of individualism. Minuchin and Fishman (1981) argued that the concept of the "single, unattached adult" is nonsensical: "Nowhere among living organisms can one find 'unattachment,' yet it exists in our human typologies" (p.14). We are always "persons-in-relation" (Macmurray, [1961] 1979) and individuals in relationship constantly influence each other in patterns that structure and maintain stable relationships, patterns that psychologists mislabel and reify as "traits" or "personality factors." Sullivan (1953) defined personality as "the relatively enduring pattern of recurrent interpersonal situations which characterize a human life," which manifests itself "only in interpersonal relationships, whether real or illusory" (p.111). It follows logically that "personality disorder consists of the pursuit of a particular, stable interpersonal position in relation to real or imagined others in ways that publicly violate the residual rules of a culture" (Carson, 1969, p.232). Such definitions are empowering in that they define personality and psychopathology in terms of observable interaction sequences rather than hypothetical, unobservable, and reified traits; and because they recognize the essential role and power of the real or imagined other as a context and stimulus for interpersonal behavior. Because interpersonal fields are constantly shifting, Sullivan ([1950] 1964) regarded "personality" as a mythological attribution, mere illusion (p.221).

My kaleidoscopes concretize the reason why this chapter was so difficult to write. In part I struggle to define "work," which includes not just publications but also every class taught; every dissertation chaired; every student mentored; every therapy client healed; every toddler nurtured on Sunday mornings; every seminary student under the care of our presbytery committee; meals prepared and parties hosted; colorful stitches on linen and canvas; and the quality of myriad familial, collegial, and friendly relationships. I struggle to tell a story that changes with each telling, in a new moment of space and time, to a new audience, flowing out of a transitory interpersonal context. I live and work in constant awareness of my derivation from others:

> We may or may not live *for* others, but whether we like it or not, we do live *from* others... Giving, we permit others to be derived from us; receiving, we accept derivation from them. Gratitude is the acknowledgment of derivation; courtesy an expression of it... Derivation is one of the primary forms of co-inherence. (Shideler, 1962, pp.48, 68)

How can *I* show gratitude with courtesy? In a state of reverie, I entertain a kaleidoscopic parade of images. I welcome guests to a grand celebration, a party in a cozy pub located in illusory space and out of ordinary time in that spiritual world so lovingly described by Charles Williams. The party guests include "ghosts," but this pub is no haunted house. Attendees include not only those whose living presence influenced me – both living and dead – but also the multitude of writers who've shaped my life and my work only through their ideas. They include Christians (both Protestant and Catholic), Jews, and atheists from a host of disciplines – my personal "cloud of witnesses" (Hebrews 12:1, RSV), shapers of my unique living faith. Inklings C.S. Lewis, J.R.R. Tolkien, and Charles Williams entertain at their usual table, in witty exchange with Dorothy Sayers.[3] In the corner near the hazy antique looking glass, Harry Stack Sullivan, Charles Cooley, and George Herbert Mead discuss the role of reflected appraisals in the development of the self (Sullivan, 1953). Under the spider's web in another corner, Emil Brunner and Martin

Buber speak of their debt to Ferdinand Ebner, as Maurice Friedman, John Macmurray, Ivan Boszormenyi-Nagy, and Paul Johnson look on. Near the soothing fire, Søren Kierkegaard, Paul Tillich, and R.D. Laing probe the complexities of existential anxiety, as Igor Caruso nods in assent. Nearby, Carl Jung, Harry Guntrip, Anton Boisen, Frank Lake, Morton Kelsey, and Henri Nouwen discuss the role of religion in psychotherapy. E.B. Holt, Franz Brentano, Paul W. Pruyser, D.W. Winnicott, Norman Cameron, and Ann Magaret exchange ideas about subsistents, immanent objectivity, and illusory space. I've invited all those whose ideas have influenced me – some may come only to express dismay at the way I've transformed their ideas.

Neither camera nor teleidoscope scanning the pub will capture the essence of my world, especially that rich world of internalized relationships perceived only by "the inner eye." My internal world is richly interpersonal: Alone, I can be "in relationship" with internalized loved ones, with an author explaining ideas to me, with the characters in a novel, or with a psychotherapy client who has unwittingly facilitated my personal and professional growth. Psychologists tend to interpret aloneness as lack of object relatedness, thus failing to recognize the rich relational potential of solitude, which is ultimately the only place in which we can encounter God. The Christian life follows a pattern of "moving alternately from solitude to community," what William Ernest Hocking (1912) "called the 'law of alternation,' as the devoted seeker moves back and forth from inner solitude of meditation and prayer to outgoing meeting with others in fellowship and service" (quoted in Johnson, 1957, p.125). David Bakan (1966) referred to this as "the duality of human existence," the balance between agency and communion that constitutes the dialectic of Self and Person in Macmurray's (1957, 1979) work and that figures so prominently in interpersonal, object-relational, and family psychologies.

Life, work, and the liberal arts[4]

I'm not sure just when my intellectual curiosity began, but I do know that I took to my liberal arts education at Hope College as a fish takes to water, and that my professional life constitutes a "working out" of an interdisciplinary consciousness. My writings represent a broad range of subjects, a wide variety of "methods," and the wearing of various professional hats. Each writing project has left me subtly changed. I emerged from the interviews that formed the data for my qualitative master's thesis sensitized to the dynamics of genetic epistemology and keenly aware of the truth that reasonable people disagree and that "no one can possibly do more than decide what to believe" (Williams, [1930] 1980b, p.113) – although it was many years before I found those words in the mouth of Charles Williams's humble archdeacon and found in Williams himself a ghostly spiritual mentor. My deep affinity for Williams's thought inspired me to integrate literature, psychology, and theology in an analysis of his novels. I'm a member of the Southern California C.S. Lewis Society (SCCSLS), and have co-led three summer workshops for them at St. Andrew's Priory in Valyermo, CA on "Till We Have Faces: The Meaning of Spiritual and Emotional Wholeness" (with Peter Schakel 1983), "The Four Loves in the Life and Writings of C.S. Lewis" (with Nancy-Lou Patterson 1989), and "Archetypes and End-Time Myths in the Fiction of Charles Williams" (with Charles Huttar 2000). I've also spoken to monthly gatherings of the group on the novels of Charles Williams, "A Genogram for C.S. Lewis," "My Love Affair with J.R.R. Tolkien" and "Peter Wimsey and Harriet Vane: A Comedy of Manners." I've used my favorite fiction as the basis for philosophical reflection questions in the history of psychology, for assessments in family therapy, and to focus the discussion of the relationship between sanctification and psychological growth. Several of these papers have been published in the SCCSLS newsletter, *The Lamp-Post* (see Atkinson, 1991; Dalfiume, 1991; Okiyama, 1991; Pfeiffer, 1991; Steigenga, 1983; Vande Kemp, 1987, 1999; Wilmot, 1991).

Obviously, The Inklings facilitated a link between my leisure hours and my professional activities. But the writer who first opened my heart to the power of story was the Dutch schoolmaster and children's author W.G. van de Hulst, who defined a good children's book as "a mirror in which the child sees the truths of heaven and earth, together; and sees them better, truer, sharper than in life itself." The "story must echo the child's own heart. Then the child will learn to read" (ver Kaaden, 1994, p.61, my translation). Van de Hulst clearly distinguished between fantasy and distortions of reality, and I found both his fantasy and his reality so enchanting that I'm thoroughly baffled by Christians who make realism a "test" of orthodoxy in the creative arts, as does Francis Schaeffer (1976) in his rejection of romantic and abstract art, and Karl Barth ([1956] 1986) in his elevation of Mozart's classical music to "truth" and his dismissal of Beethoven in an essay that strikes me as an aesthetic in search of a theology. Even as a child I knew there was a realm "between reality and fantasy" (to use Winnicott's classic phrase), and Pruyser (1983) spoke for me when he argued that both religion and art are constituted in the illusionistic world of tutored fantasy that lies between the autistic and realistic worlds.

Barth was mistaken, not in regarding music as an expression of "truth," but in privileging Mozart's perception.

Despite such unorthodox thoughts, I take as seriously as most Presbyterians the Apostle Paul's injunction to "Let all things be done decently and in order" (1 Corinthians 14:40, KJV). I relish the ordering of facts that constitutes my work as historical sleuth. I worked as historian and reference librarian in preparing the annotated bibliography, *Psychology and Theology in Western Thought, 1672–1965*, a process producing material that set the agenda for two decades of future research in the psychology of religion, work that I was able to share with my colleagues in the history of psychology in a wonderful *Festschrift* celebration honoring the life and work of John Popplestone and Marion White McPherson – founders of the Archives of the History of American Psychology – in April 2000, just weeks before Marion's death.

I first became a topical historian in my doctoral dissertation on pre-Freudian dream theories. As I cataloged hundreds of dreams for the appendix, I practiced a type of research phenomenology that affected my life by activating my previously dormant dream memory and imagination, and since then I have filled hundreds of pages of dream journals. I am rather envious of my dream creativity, and proud to have published a comforting dream, three creative dreams, and a poem interpreting one of Joseph's dreams from my unique psycho-theological vantage point, in Presbyterian fashion fitting the words into a sestina.

In the biographer's role, I've consistently encountered the commingling of my life and my work. My research on Robert Brodie MacLeod led me to Mary Shideler, my dearest spiritual friend and mentor, who vastly enhanced my understanding of Charles Williams. My investigation into the life of Diana Baumrind brought forth not only a deep mutual respect but also my recognition of the many values we shared despite her allegiance to dialectical materialism and mine to evangelical Christianity. I was prepared for this insight by my dissertation chair Howard Gadlin who wondered how a nice Christian girl like me wound up working with an atheist. The Baumrind project brought healing at a time when I was smarting over the insinuation by a powerful academic authority that my ethical commitments "biased" me, disqualifying me for a project he was assigning. I knew that I had achieved scholarly neutrality, and that the hurtful comment was motivated by envy and by fear that I would speak the truth and reveal institutional secrets. I found it a simple joy to write a detailed obituary of Virginia Staudt Sexton, and thus to honor a respected colleague, friend, and surprise dream visitor. I ached with empathy while writing my piece on Harry Stack Sullivan. I began with an interest in psychologists who struggled with mental illness – as Sullivan apparently did in late adolescence – and soon yearned to understand the pain of a closeted homosexual psychiatrist in the 1920s and 1930s. In the course of my research on Sullivan and his dear friend Clara Thompson, I crossed scholarly paths with Calvin Saxton, who has profoundly changed my personal life through his love, thus giving me my own experience of being "surprised by joy" (Lewis, 1955).

Feminism trickled into my life and my work very gradually. In graduate school, my focus was on surviving as a Christian in a secular environment, and I merely observed my activist feminist peers. I arrived at Fuller in time to witness the heated debates triggered by the publication of Paul Jewett's (1975) *Man as Male and Female* and Harold Lindsell's (1976) *The Battle for the Bible*. I gradually absorbed the influence of various persons and events at Fuller, and I tackled feminist theology and feminist psychology simultaneously, assimilating and developing the perspectives evident in the book chapter on feminism and humanism (Vande Kemp and Anderson, 1999). I served on committees to develop items on gender issues in course evaluations, formulate a maternity leave policy, and draft *Suggestions for Using Gender Neutral Language*; and I boycotted the men-only University Club which was regularly used for seminary faculty functions. I taught Fuller's first seminars on Child Abuse and Domestic Violence and supervised the Stop Abusive Family Environments clinic. As chair of the curriculum committee, I facilitated the development of courses on Women in Therapy and the Psychology of Women/Gender. I introduced students to significant women in the history of psychology; wrote sketches on Flanders Dunbar, Diana Baumrind, Virginia Sexton, and Alexandra Adler; encouraged student research on eminent women; had students observe the work of major female family therapists; assigned reading from the brilliant writing of Lorna Benjamin (1974, 1996) and other female textbook authors; encouraged research on the contributions of women to the psychology of religion (Vande Kemp *et al.*, 2001); and chaired dissertations on domestic violence, child abuse, and gender issues. In 1983, I became the first woman to obtain tenure at Fuller, despite the obstructive efforts and envious comments of various male colleagues. The environment in the Graduate School of Psychology (SOP) was not a nurturing one for its women faculty, and friends humorously classified my survival there as an instance of "the perseverance of the saints."[5] This attribution has me musing on the subtle distinction between "perseverance" as a mark of sanctity and a virtue valued by positive psychologists and the "per*sev*erance" or "perseveration" that constitute signs of psychopathology. During my 25 years at Fuller, 10 of my female colleagues in the SOP left, either because working circumstances were too difficult or because it was clear they would not be approved for tenure or promotion. Each farewell represented a potential loss of friendship which we prevented by forming the Former Fuller Faculty Club of which I became an honorary charter member. Eventually, I found my feminist voice and was able to help students discover theirs (Eurich-Rascoe, 2000; Eurich-Rascoe and Vande Kemp, 1997), but this merely served to increase the silencing efforts at Fuller.

Therapist and client, healer and healed

> If there is any posture that disturbs a suffering man or woman, it is aloofness. No one can help anyone without becoming involved, without entering with his whole person into the painful situation, without taking the risk of becoming hurt, wounded or even destroyed in the process. (Nouwen, 1972, pp.71–72)

Eurich-Rascoe (2000) spoke of our relationship as one that involved "using, finding, [and] giving a voice" (p.345). This has often been my function as a psychotherapist, and psychotherapists helped me find my voice. Short psychotherapy experiences in college and graduate school paved the way for real healing later. I began psychoanalytic psychotherapy in 1979 when the deaths of a special graduate student supervisee and a Fuller alumnus surfaced my own grief at the loss of my parents and the early loss of country, family, and friends when we emigrated from the Netherlands. In the next 20 years, I experienced numerous losses in my personal life that included my brother, several Fuller colleagues and alumni/ae, a very dear college friend,[6] and a graduate school buddy. When my colleague and friend Lucy Bregman presented a series of lectures at Fuller in 1989 on "Death in the Midst of Life" (Bregman, 1992), I designed a course on death and dying that included the taboo topics of therapist death and suicide, and later I wrote an article focused on the death of siblings and friends that sensitized me to the special grief of gay men and war buddies.

In July of 1989, my life changed drastically as I sustained a head injury when my car was hit by an 18-wheel truck. A neurologist prescribed antidepressant medications for the post-traumatic headaches, and in 1990 I was hospitalized for a manic episode triggered by the medications. Memories of this time remain nightmarish, and I vividly remember writing the manuscripts that became "Character Armor or the Armor of Faith? Reflections on Psychologies of Suffering" and "Adrift in Pain: Anchored by Grace." I found it difficult to focus on intellectual discourse when pain was the absolute center of my experience. The hardest piece I ever wrote, measured in terms of sheer physical and mental agony, was "G. Stanley Hall and the Clark School of Religious Psychology." Extended periods of reading or writing exacerbated my back pain, fatigue, and the never-ending post-traumatic headaches. I was frequently overwhelmed by the challenge of verifying historical facts and ensuring accuracy of names and dates when I routinely transposed letters and numbers. I completed the article only because my editor Ludy Benjamin Jr. graciously extended the deadline and because my psychotherapist Charles Barr and my new neurologist Greg Gorman revealed God to me through their Christ-like love. I used my traumatic experience to evaluate the success of the scientist-practitioner model in actually addressing patient needs. As I adapted to my "invisible disability," I revived an integration seminar on Psychological and Theological Aspects of Physical Disability with the help of theologian Ray Anderson and student Gail Nagel. I also led an informal small group of disabled women which one of them dubbed "The Red Cross Club," and became an advocate for disabled Fuller students. These experiences culminated in the collaborative writing of "ADA Accommodation of Therapists with Disabilities in Clinical Training" (Vande Kemp *et al.*, 2003).

I felt exposed in writing my personal narratives of suffering and pain: it's much easier to submit intellectual "works" for peer review than to imagine those peers judging one's life and person. I see now how vulnerable and exposed our clients feel when therapists tell their story, as I told Deborah's story in "Psychotherapy and Redemption: A Tribute to a Dying Mom." My first marital therapy case dragged me and my cotherapist, Guillermo Bernal, into the courts and exposed deep disagreements between us. Our wrestling with the case resulted in a publication (Bernal and Vande Kemp, 1976) and a lifelong friendship, and it was Guillermo who later introduced me personally to contextual family therapist Ivan Boszormenyi-Nagy.

Deborah touched me personally in her own inimitable way, but many psychotherapy clients have affected me profoundly and changed my life and work irrevocably. Their strongest effect has been on my person as each client has revealed to me a new layer of my capacity for what Martin Buber ([1954] 1957) described as "imagining the real," to imagine what the other is "at this very moment wishing, feeling, perceiving, thinking, and not as a detached content but in his very reality" in such a way that "the character of what is imagined is joined to the act of imagining" (p.103). Buber thus applies imagination not to the realm of fantasy and creativity, but to "the particular real person who confronts me, whom I can attempt to make present to myself just in this way, and not otherwise, in his wholeness, unity, and uniqueness, and with his dynamic center which realizes all these things ever anew" (p.110). I gradually discovered such imagination in myself, especially in my intuitive grasp for the meaning of dream symbols and intrusive fantasies in clients with schizotypal tendencies.

For Buber, the psychological was merely "the hidden accompaniment to the conversation itself...whose meaning is to be found neither in one of the two partners, nor in both together, but only in their dialogue itself, in this 'between' which they live together" (p.106). Truth in the interhuman realm requires that persons "communicate themselves to one another as what they are...on letting no *seeming* creep in between" (pp.107–108). Such truth leads to healing, which "comes from connectedness itself. Each person's presence, directness and immediacy characterize the moment in which two people genuinely care about each other's side" (Boszormenyi-Nagy and Krasner, 1986, pp.33, 73). In such moments of mutuality – which Buber (1958) characterized as "I–Thou" relationship – we comprehend what Jesus meant when he said "I am the truth," for in these encounters we can see in ourselves the image of God in which we were created. I believe God created me to be a woman of authority, living life in the various spaces between me and my significant others.

Becoming a woman of authority

I cannot single out any one of my works as "most important to date." But I suspect my "work in progress," presented in nascent form at George Fox University in November 2000, will ultimately prove to be of the greatest significance. I am increasingly preoccupied with issues of agency and intentionality that challenge the worldview inherent in virtually all psychological models of interpersonal behavior, and explored these issues in a preliminary way in a recent book chapter on "Power in Interpersonal and Family Relationships." My professional awareness of this issue grew in part out of more than a decade of research using Lorna Benjamin's (1974) "Structural Analysis of Social Behavior" (SASB) to study family dynamics and family therapy process, and integrating family theories with interpersonal psychology.[7] Later, I taught clinical seminars on personality disorders from Benjamin's (1996) textbook in which she translates formal diagnostic criteria into codable interpersonal behaviors. It became increasingly evident to me, as I examined and re-examined the "intentionality" codes connected to various psychopathologies, that many persons try to live out the illusion that there is no sphere of autonomy. In their version of the world "if I am not in control, I am being controlled." Such persons target all their behavior at retaining freedom from control and achieving control over others. They further believe that "if you are not under my control, you are out of control" – not grasping that I may simply be under *my own* control. All other interpersonal theorists depict the interpersonal world as if this misperception is in fact the truth: they regard autonomy merely as a point midway between control and submission, rather than as an entirely different sort of relationship to self and others. Benjamin offers a way for us to think about the kind of "personal authority" that is central to a tradition that begins with Friedrich Nietzsche and culminates in the work of C.G. Jung, writers who assume that personal authority is achieved only after the person has the courage to face head on the facts about the self and others. Thus, authority arises from truth, which in turn emerges from encounter, with God and with other persons. Emil Brunner (1943) argued that "the Biblical conception of truth is: truth as encounter" (p.7). And Jewett (n.d.) wrote: "To know about *God* does not mean merely to *know* about God, but to be *personally encountered* of him" (p.7). God "communicates to us the secret of his person in a free act of self-disclosure" (p.7), which ultimately requires of us, not an increase in our knowledge, but the transformation of our persons-in-relation:

> Only when we have real address from without, confronting us "as that which absolutely commands us," the divine word, requiring absolute obedience, are we compelled to render a decision. Only when the continuity between the divine and the inner self is questioned, only when the address does not come "*from* me," but "*to* me," is decision (*Entscheidung*) possible as *de*-cision (Ent*scheidung*), a break with my way of existence as evil, "self-abandonment in despair of myself," which is the newly given possibility of the divine address of justification. But such address is possible only in the personal dimension. There can be speech only between two persons...[the true act of faith is] an encounter in which God challenges me to a decision. (Jewett, n.d., pp.10–11)

In the realm of the I–Thou, truth is not a matter of correct thinking or the empirical determination of facts: it is a matter of responding to God's call. We become persons of authority only in our solitary confrontation with God's address, in our uniqueness: God knows us by name, and created each of us to be in a unique relationship with us. Thus, it is "only when a [we have] fully accepted [our] individual way [that we are] able to will, to *choose consciously*, all that [t]his way may bring" (Luke, n.d., p.24). Such autonomy was manifest in Jesus Christ, whose teaching "made a deep impression on [the Jews] because, unlike the scribes, he taught them with authority" (Mark 1:22, NJB). In fact, in the authorized translation this authority endows *power*: "they were astonished at his doctrine: for his word was with power" (Luke 4:32, KJV).

In my clinical seminars, I explored with students what this kind of authority, mapped as autonomy on SASB, means for issues with which the Fuller faculty were struggling: the question of how to encourage "character formation" in students (character is a reflection of autonomy and authentic self-disclosure, and thus cannot be instilled through a process of control and submission); the challenge to create "community" between faculty and students (community involves free give and take, nurturance and succorance, and authentic self-disclosure and affirmation, and it cannot exist in a climate of control that expects submission); encouraging respect and mutuality among faculty and between faculty and students (which cannot emerge in an atmosphere that suppresses autonomy and free choice). Students and I also explored tentatively some ways that SASB might help us to understand a variety of theological constructs related to free will and to human relationships with the divine.

These ideas crystalized after I had suffered for several years the abuses of a dean who constantly tried to control me and to attack my being: one of my colleagues justified this as a reaction to my being "out of control." I eventually recognized this as a form of the lie that equated "out of their control" with "out of control." The leaders in the Graduate School of Psychology, and at Fuller's higher levels, could not tolerate persons with personal authority, and they were creating for students an atmosphere that in fact contradicted all their stated goals. This diametrically opposed my lived philosophy of education (see Eurich-Rascoe, 2000). As I struggled with decisions about my future at Fuller, I was asked to co-lead the summer workshop on Charles Williams for the Southern California C.S. Lewis Society. I re-read *The Place of the Lion* (Williams, [1933] 1980a) and was deeply moved by Williams's description of the mystical experience that confronted Anthony Durrant with the choices leading to personal authority, about which Helen Luke wrote:

> [W]hen we say that a man has authority in his particular field of knowledge we mean that he has penetrated imaginatively to the heart of his subject, not that he simply has information about it. To have authority in this sense over oneself therefore means, not that a man is rigidly controlling himself according to a set of rules, but that he has achieved real self-knowledge, which includes conscious and unconscious areas of the psyche, and he has therefore become a creator. (Luke, n.d., p.26)

Here we see again an unexpected role for the imagination, as it "imagines the real" within ourselves and gives rise to personal authority. We find such authority in many of the characters in Charles Williams's novels, and all of them recognize that personal authority is intertwined with "*living* in love" (which contrasts with merely *being* in love): "In the final analysis existence *in* love and knowledge *of* love are the same" (Brunner, 1943, p.64). Rabbi Heschel (1973) asserted that "it is impossible to find Truth without being in love" (p.45), and it is not by accident that there is a Christian "theology of romantic love" (Shideler, 1962) based on the assumption that there is a precise analogy between Christian experience and "the vivid personal experience of being in love" (p.1). Truth and love are intertwined, and that interconnection applies not just to psychotherapy, but also to education, as Parker Palmer (1983) spelled out in *To Know as We are Known*: "The act of knowing *is* an act of love, the act of entering and embracing the reality of the other, of allowing the other to enter and embrace our own" (p.8). Nouwen (1972) believed that such compassionate knowing was the "core and even the nature of authority" (p.40).

I was aware for several years before I left Fuller that there was no longer a place for me in terms of my work – my colleagues had little interest in the historical and philosophical-theoretical aspects of the integration of psychology and theology. By the time I left I also knew there was no place for *me* as a person. I was subjected to constant attacks on my *being* and my definition of reality that could have illustrated R.D. Laing's (1965) poignant essay on "Mystification, Confusion, and Conflict" or his chapter on "False and Untenable Positions" (1969, pp.107–131). When I decided to leave Fuller, my therapist opined with prescience that only after leaving would I understand how much this oppressive work community was influencing my personal life. Three years later I find myself thriving in love, and replying to Rabbi Heschel (1973): "But you cannot find Love until you are free to live authentically." Love blossoms in "the between," not in untenable tenured positions.

Perspective on power and its sources

As I continue to clarify my understanding of authority and intentionality, I realize that my ideas about interpersonal power represent a unique and very personal integration of several theoretical traditions whose common elements are seldom recognized. My perspective is in part that of a clinical psychologist with 25 years of experience as a teacher of family psychology, family therapy, and interpersonal psychology, and of a psychotherapist applying these theories in practice. Like many family psychologists, I've struggled to integrate the individualistic focus of mainstream psychology with the dyadic emphasis of social and interpersonal psychology and the triadic emphasis of family psychology. I have encouraged my students to develop comprehensive theoretical frameworks which allow free movement from therapy with individuals to therapy with couples and families. The focus on the integration of psychology and Christian theology at Fuller forced me to articulate psychological theories consistent with my interpretation of Protestant Christian theology and elaborate enough to describe the complex nature of human relationships: individuals are embedded in dyadic relationships which are embedded in a series of overlapping larger systems. To understand all these levels of being persons-in-relation requires intrapersonal, interpersonal, familial, social, and political theories. Over the years I incorporated these into the schemas I taught in the classroom.

But my journey began during my college years, when I first questioned individually focused Calvinist theology, and gradually realized that it was quite inconsistent with the realities of my life as the eighth of ten children in a Dutch family closely intertwined with two extended families. I first encountered the notion that individuals emerge from and are shaped by society in 1967, in my freshman course at Hope College on An Introduction to Liberal Education. In this course the philosopher D. Ivan Dykstra introduced the notions of "community and interpersonality" with selections from the writings of several social scientists who explored the relationship between individuals and society. In summarizing the work of John Dewey, Dykstra (n.d.) described the agentic power that must be wrested out of the interpersonal matrix: "Individuality in a social and moral sense is something to be wrought out. It means initiative, inventiveness, varied resourcefulness, assumption of responsibility in choice of belief and conduct. These are not gifts, but achievements" (pp.194–195).

As a college sophomore, I was devastated by reading *Escape from Freedom*, Erich Fromm's (1941) analysis of the authoritarian personality of which Martin Luther and John Calvin were prime examples. I was left with agonizing questions regarding agency and relationships to authority and was not yet equipped to recognize that Fromm implicitly refused to recognize our inherent interdependence, a refusal typically manifested in what feminist psychologists (Kaplan, 1983) now label as "independent" and "restricted" personalities – persons who live as if the myth of individualism were true and personal agency could be unrestricted by the agency of others, when in fact others constantly affect our lives by their choices. I felt the very painful personal consequences of this philosophical error every time someone confidently assured me that I was single by choice. I chose, in my personal relationships, not to place or be placed in untenable positions, and often wondered how my choice could be responsible for the decision of others "not to love," for their choice to run from the adventure of authentic relatedness.[8] I wondered how these observers thought one could manipulate another into loving, authentic relatedness by employing the various untenable positions that constitute the game of "courtship." I've always known instinctively that "persons-in-relation" must remain agentic selves, and find that this is true in my relationship with Calvin.

As a sophomore I encountered Martin Buber's (1958) assertion, in *I and Thou*, that "a person makes his appearance by entering into relation with other persons" (p.62). This was my first exposure to neo-personalist theology, with its emphasis on persons-in-relation and the authority bestowing power of authentic interpersonal relatedness. I see that reading now as a foretaste of glory.

In graduate school at the University of Massachusetts in Amherst, two courses kindled my interpersonal awareness. One was a seminar on family therapy, the first such course ever taught in a graduate program in clinical psychology. Although it would be many years before I fully comprehended the freedom-restricting implications of family dynamics, I began to understand the power of the family's influence in shaping both my sense of self-as-agent and my style of being a person-in-relation. The second influential course was a seminar on interpersonal psychotherapy taught by Sheldon Cashdan (1973), who approached the interpersonal from the framework of "symbolic action" and dramaturgical theory, a variation on the symbolic interactionism of George Herbert Mead (1934); the theories of symbolic action developed by the literary critic Kenneth Burke (1952, 1957); and the highly interpersonal behaviorism of Norman Cameron and Ann Magaret (1951). Symbolic interactionists focus on entire interaction sequences as they are symbolized, and emphasize how internalized actions become actions that can be transformed through rehearsal and empathic role taking in order to increase our interpersonal power:

> In Mead's model the self arises out of a parliament of selves in which the self takes into account the attitudes of other selves toward the self. This is necessary because in situations which are problematic the self cannot act without the help of other selves. To act with others we need to put ourselves in their place, as they need to put themselves in our place. (Duncan, [1968] 1993, p.181)

Here, again, I encountered the assertion that the power of individual agents is limited by the agency of others, which places genuine limits on our powers of self-determination. Yet the assertion is coupled with the wisdom that interpersonal power and responsibility and personal agency can all be enhanced through empathic role taking, or "imagining the real" (Buber, 1957, pp.103, 110). And ultimately, in authentic interpersonal relationships we begin to see ourselves as God sees us, to imagine the reality of the image of God in us.

Afterthoughts

It is difficult to tell one's story to an unidentified audience – the task itself takes place in the illusory realm, where the audience is imagined, if not entirely imaginary. As I finish this version of my story, I can't help thinking of Sullivan's "fantastic auditor" (1944, p.5) or "illusory critic" (1964, p.214) whose presence shapes our social perception in the direction of the consensually validated. In telling my story, I seek affirmation and confirmation and fear disconfirmation, disqualification, and alienation. In my life and in my work I strive to respond to others so that the self reflected in my appraisal of them spurs them to imagine how God sees them, created in God's image as God's beloved children. As a psychotherapist, I become God's image bearer so that my clients can learn to imagine God's love and grace. And in that process I am transformed as I learn to see my clients – even when they are broken, fallen persons – as men and women created in the image of God, and fallen from it. In the end, what is central to my life and my work is a truth beautifully expressed in the song sung by Jean Valjean, Fantine, and Eponine just before the Finale in *Les Misérables* (Boubil, Kertzmer, Natel, 1987):

> And remember the truth that once was spoken
> To love another person is to see the face of God!

Notes

1   In the published work Jeeves (1997, pp.230–233) employs a considerably more nuanced visual processing analogy.

2   In order to save space, I reference only the works of others or my joint works with others. Readers interested in my publications will find a curriculum vitae posted at http://members.cox.net/hendrika/HVIT.htm or http://members.cox.net/hendrika/HVIT.pdf.

3   The pub is inspired by the regular meetings of the Inklings at the *Eagle and Child* (nicknamed *The Bird and Baby*), and the guests might partake of a comforting high tea.

4   An outline of this section was previously published in 1999 as "A Psychologist Writes" in *Theology, News and Notes 46*, 4, 19–21.

5   The doctrine of the *perseverance* of the saints actually refers to eternal salvation and appears in section 6.094 of the *Westminster Confession of Faith* (1647) and is also clearly stated in the *Canons of Dort* (1618–1619).

6   Lynda Dethmers Sittser died in a car accident along with her mother-in-law and her 4-year-old daughter. Her husband wrote a moving account of his response to this grief experience (Sittser, 1998).

7   I am grateful to Clinton McLemore, one of my early colleagues at Fuller, who first introduced me to Benjamin's work and the Sullivanian interpersonal tradition.

8   The anxieties related to intimacy and relatedness are explored in a 1997 lecture at Wheaton College, and the doctoral dissertation by Anwar (2002) which reflects my thinking as much as it does hers.

References

Anwar, F. (2002) "Anxieties of intimacy and aloneness and the courage to be in relation." *Dissertation Abstracts International 63*, 01B, 514.

Atkinson, B. (1991) "From facelessness to devine identity: An analysis of C.S. Lewis's Till We Have Faces." *The Lamp-Post 15*, 1, 21–30.

Bakan, D. (1966) *The Duality of Human Existence. An Essay on Psychology and Religion.* Chicago: Rand McNally.

Barth, K. [1956] (1986) *Wolfgang Amadeus Mozart,* trans. C.K. Pott. Grand Rapids, MI: William B. Eerdmans. (Original work published 1956.)

Benjamin, L.S. (1974) "Structural Analysis of Social Behavior." *Psychological Review 81*, 392–425.

Benjamin, L.S. (1996) *Interpersonal Diagnosis and Treatment of Personality Disorders,* 2nd edn. New York: Guilford Press.

Bernal, G. and Vande Kemp, H. (1976) "Marital therapy: Experiential perspectives of two developing clinicians." *Family Therapy 3*, 109–122.

Boszormenyi-Nagy, I. and Krasner, B. (1986) *Between Give and Take: A Clinical Guide to Contextual Therapy.* New York: Brunner/Mazel.

Boubil, A., Kertzmer, H. and Natel, J.-M. (1987) "Finale from Les Miserables." Music by C.-M. Schonberg.

Bregman, L. (1992) *Death in the Midst of Life: Perspectives on Death from Christianity and Depth Psychology.* Grand Rapids, MI: Baker Book House.

Brunner, E. (1943) *The Divine–Human Encounter,* trans A.W. Loos. Philadelphia: Westminster Press.

Buber, M. [1954] (1957) "Elements of the interhuman", trans R.G. Smith. *Psychiatry 20*, 105–113. (Original work published 1954.)

Buber, M. (1958) *I and Thou,* 2nd edn, trans R.G. Smith. New York: Charles Scribner's Sons.

Burke, K. (1952) *A Grammar of Motives.* New York: Prentice-Hall.

Burke, K. (1957) *The Philosophy of Literary Form: Studies in Symbolic Action.* New York: Vintage Books.

Cameron, N. and Magaret, A. (1951) *Behavior Pathology.* Boston: Houghton Mifflin.

Carson, R.C. (1969) *Interaction Concepts of Personality.* Chicago: Aldine.

Cashdan, S. (1973) *Interactional Psychotherapy: Stages and Strategies in Behavioral Change.* New York: Grune and Stratton.

Dalfiume, L. (1991) "The position of C.S. Lewis on selected philosophical issues as found in *The Pilgrim's Regress.*" *The Lamp-Post 15,* 3, 13–19.

Duncan, H. [1968] (1993) "Symbols in society." In B. Brummett (ed) *Landmark Essays on Kenneth Burke.* Davis, CA: Hermagoras Press. (Original work published 1968.)

Dykstra, D.I. (ed) (n.d.) *An Introduction to Liberal Education: A Book of Readings Compiled for a Freshman Course at Hope College, Holland, Michigan.* Holland, MI: Hope College, Department of Philosophy.

Eurich-Rascoe, B. (2000) "Hendrika Vande Kemp as mentor: Using, finding, giving a voice." *Journal of Psychology and Christianity 19,* 345–354.

Eurich-Rascoe, B.L. and Vande Kemp, H. (1997) *Femininity and Shame: Women and Men Giving Voice to the Feminine.* Lanham, MD: University Press of America.

Fromm, E. (1941) *Escape from Freedom.* New York: Holt, Rinehart and Winston.

Heschel, A.J. (1973) *A Passion for Truth.* New York: Farrar, Straus and Girioux.

Hocking, W.E. (1912) *The Meaning of God in Human Experience: A Philosophic Study of Religion.* New Haven, CT: Yale University Press.

Jeeves, M.A. (1997) *Human Nature at the Millennium: Reflections on the Integration of Psychology and Christianity.* Grand Rapids, MI: Baker Books.

Jewett, P.K. (n.d.) "Theology and the dimension of the personal." In *Theology I. Occasional Bulletins. Doctrine of God.* Unpublished course materials. Pasadena, CA: Fuller Theological Seminary.

Jewett, P.K. (1975) *Man as Male and Female: A Study in Sexual Relationships from a Theological Point of View.* Grand Rapids, MI: William B. Eerdmans.

Johnson, P.E. (1957) *Personality and Religion.* New York: Abingdon Press.

Kaplan, M. (1983) "A woman's view of DSM-III." *American Psychologist 38,* 786–792.

Laing, R.D. (1965) "Mystification, confusion, and conflict." In I. Boszormenyi-Nagy and J.L. Framo (eds) *Intensive Family Therapy: Theoretical and Practical Aspects.* New York: Harper & Row/Hoeber Medical Division.

Laing, R.D. [1961] (1969) *Self and Others.* New York: Pantheon Books. (Original work published 1961.)

Lewis, C.S. (1955) *Surprised by Joy: The Shape of my Early Life.* London: Geoffrey Bles.

Lindsell, H. (1976) *The Battle for the Bible.* Grand Rapids, MI: Zondervan.

Luke, H. (n.d.) *Through Defeat to Joy: The Novels of Charles Williams in the Light of Jungian Thought.* Three Rivers, MI: Apple Farm.

Macmurray, J. (1957) *The Self as Agent.* London: Faber and Faber.

Macmurray, J. [1961] (1979) *Persons in Relation.* Atlantic Highlands, NJ: Humanities Press. (Original work published 1961.)

Mead, G.H. (1934) *Mind, Self and Society from the Standpoint of a Social Behaviorist,* ed C.W. Morris. Chicago: University of Chicago Press.

Minuchin, S. (1984) *Family Kaleidoscope: Images of Violence and Healing.* Cambridge, MA: Harvard University Press.

Minuchin, S. and Fishman, H.C. (1981) *Family Therapy Techniques.* Cambridge, MA: Harvard University Press.

Nouwen, H. (1972) *The Wounded Healer: Ministry in Contemporary Society.* New York: Doubleday.

Okiyama, S.L. (1991) "Till We Have Faces: A book review." *The Lamp-Post 15,* 1, 15–20.

Palmer, P. (1983) *To Know As We Are Known: A Spirituality of Education.* San Francisco: Harper & Row.

Pfeiffer, B.J. (1991) "A psychodynamic/family systems analysis of the Vanaukens' relationship as described in *A Severe Mercy.*" *The Lamp-Post 15,* 3, 20–28.

Pruyser, P.W. (1983) *The Play of the Imagination: Toward a Psychoanalysis of Culture.* New York: International Universities Press.

Schaeffer, F.A. (1976) *How Should We Then Live? The Rise and Decline of Western Thought and Culture.* Old Tappan, NJ: Fleming H. Revell.

Shideler, M.M. (1962) *The Theology of Romantic Love: A Study in the Writings of Charles Williams.* New York: Harper.

Sittser, G.L. (1998) *A Grace Disguised: How the Soul Grows through Loss.* Grand Rapids, MI: Zondervan.

Steigenga, J.J. (1983) "Through a veil of tears: Reflections on C.S. Lewis's *Till We Have Faces.*" *The Lamp-Post 7,* 1, 13–15, 25.

Sullivan, H.S. (1944) "The language of schizophrenia." In J.S. Kahanin (ed) *Language and Thought in Schizophrenia: Collected Papers.* Berkeley: University of California Press.

Sullivan, H.S. (1953) *The Interpersonal Theory of Psychiatry,* eds H. Swick Perry and M. Ladd Gawell. New York: Norton.

Sullivan, H.S. [1950] (1964) "The illusion of personal individuality." In H. Swick Perry (ed) *The Fusion of Psychiatry and Social Science.* New York: Norton. (Original work published 1950.)

Vande Kemp, H. (1987) "Relational ethics in the novels of Charles Williams." *Family Process 26,* 283–294. (Reprinted in 1993 in *The Lamp-Post 17,* 1, 8–19.)

Vande Kemp, H. (1991) "Lord Peter Wimsey in the novel/comedy of manners: Courtesy, Intimacy, and the Courage to Be." *The Lamp-Post 15,* 3, 3–12.

Vande Kemp, H. and Anderson, T.L. (1999) "Humanistic psychology and feminist psychology." In D. Moss (ed) *Humanistic and Transpersonal Psychology: Historical and Biographical Sourcebook.* New York: Greenwood Press.

Vande Kemp, H., Chen, J.C., Nagel Erickson, G. and Friesen, N. (2003) "ADA accommodation of therapists with disabilities in clinical training." In M.E. Banks (ed) *Women with Visible and Invisible Disabilities: Multiple Intersections, Multiple Issues, Multiple Therapies.* New York: Haworth Press.

Vande Kemp, H., Wiseman, R., Friesen, N. and Young, C. (2001) "Women's contributions to psychology and religion: Historical and contemporary data." *Journal of Psychology and Christianity 20,* 109–131.

ver Kaaden, D. (1994) *Zoeken naar de ziel: Leven en werk van W.G. van de Hulst [In Search of the Spirit: The Life and Work of W.G. van de Hulst].* Nijkerk: Callenbach.

Williams, C. [1930] (1980b) *War in Heaven.* Grand Rapids, MI: Wm.B. Eerdmans. (Original work published 1930.)

Williams, C. [1933] (1980a) *The Place of the Lion.* Grand Rapids, MI: Wm.B. Eerdmans. (Original work published 1933.)

Wilmot, M.H. (1991) "A brief analysis of C.S. Lewis's *Till We have Faces.*" *The Lamp-Post 15,* 3, 3–12.

Winnicott, D.W. (1953) "Transitional objects and transitional phenomena." *International Journal of Psychoanalysis 34,* 89–97.

CHAPTER 10

The Personal/Psychological and the Pursuit of a Profession

Adelbert H. Jenkins

We mark with light in the memory the few interviews we have had...with souls that made our souls wiser; that spoke what we thought; that told us what we knew; that gave us leave to be what we inly were.

R.W. Emerson, "An Address", quoted in Atkinson, 1950, p.82

While there are obviously a number of entries into a narrative regarding one's personal development, I will start with the present moment, some 40 years after having earned my doctoral degree, and see how I got here. I have come to the point where I would describe myself as a humanistically oriented psychologist. The term "humanistic" in psychology is rather broad and I mean it in a rather specific, philosophical sense. I have aligned myself with the "teleologic" philosophical perspective of Joseph Rychlak (1994), a framework which he calls "logical learning theory." His is a view which sees the human individual as necessarily being a psychological "agent" in the world. In taking this perspective, I favor a view in psychology that portrays the person as active in engaging the surrounding world. I have found this view generally satisfying in organizing my personal experience as an African-American man and my functioning as a theoretical and clinical psychologist. I have also found it useful in evolving my views on spirituality. In this brief narrative, I will blend a sequence of selected chronological events from my life and some of the associated evolution of my thinking with quotes from the writing of some of the scholars who have influenced me along the way. Hopefully, these choices will heighten what I shall later define as an "introspective" point of view, a view from the inside of my experience as it were, perhaps making it easier for the reader to join me on the journey.

Beginnings

I grew up in Cleveland, Ohio, a major industrial city and an important lake port, home to major steel companies and the many small spin-off industries turning that steel into finished products. I came to adolescence in post-World War II America when the nation was entering the height of its sense of global importance. At this time, Cleveland was relatively moderate racially as compared to most major US cities. African-American children were not systematically excluded from public schools in predominantly white neighborhoods and one of the first fairly effective "fair employment practices" laws in a major US city was in place.

My parents were both social workers raised in the North, my mother having been born and raised in Cleveland. While, like most of our family, they had been spared the rawest indignities of southern racism, their experiences in living in various parts of the country gave them a full recognition of the continued precariousness of African-Americans' social situation in this society. However, they were hardworking and believed in the "American dream." They concurred with the idea that it was up to individuals to prepare themselves for social equality through education and hard work. To get the full benefit of Cleveland's public school system we moved into a predominantly white and Jewish neighborhood with good schools, and my parents closely monitored my educational progress. They were definitely in favor of integrating into the society, and they saw to it that I was exposed to the general culture, but we kept in close contact with the African-American community as well. We maintained our ties to my mother's large, mostly working-class extended family, and throughout my childhood we attended the concerts of prominent African-American artists of the day. Being an able reader from early on, I did well in my kindergarten through 12th grade public school years. As I approached questions of career choice in high school, my parents suggested that I consider psychology as a potentially rewarding avenue of professional service and I went off to college with that goal in mind.

College awakenings

While I did not go too far from home to college geographically, I began to travel, with my generation, quite a distance from my conservative parents in some aspects of my political values. Antioch College, in southern Ohio, was an academically strong school noted for its socially progressive point of view. I majored in psychology with a philosophy minor. In my American Philosophy course, among other thinkers I was very much attracted to the writing of Ralph Waldo Emerson. For one thing I was attracted to Emerson's almost devout attitude towards nature and his similarly reverent stance toward the potential of human beings as children of God.

> If a man is at heart just, then in so far is he God... Wherever a man comes, there comes revolution... Man is the wonderworker. He is seen amid miracles. ("An Address," from Atkinson, 1950, pp.68, 80)

And granted this, one should trust oneself if one is to come fully into one's own:

> Whoso would be a man, must be a nonconformist... Insist on yourself; never imitate. ("Self-Reliance," from Atkinson, 1950, pp.148, 166)

This was rather heady stuff for someone who had been brought up in a sober, pretty strict home atmosphere and given rather conventional standards of right and wrong. It was not that I became particularly rebellious in my behavior. It was rather that Emerson opened up my imagination. For one thing, consistent with the generally free-thinking atmosphere on the Antioch campus, his thought helped me to a more liberal perspective on my religious attitudes:

> Good is positive. Evil is merely privative, not absolute: it is like cold, which is the privation of heat. ("An Address," from Atkinson, 1950, p.69)

Even more, I felt intrigued by his portrayal of the human situation:

> At present, man applies to nature but half his force... His relation to nature, his power over it, is through the understanding, as by manure; the economic use of fire, wind, water...; steam,...chemical agriculture; the repairs of the human body by the dentist and the surgeon. This is such a resumption of power as if a banished king should buy his territories inch by inch, instead of vaulting at once into his throne. (*Nature*, from Atkinson, 1950, p.40)

This seemed an ennobled portrait of human potential and it supported my secular occupational ambitions to help people to a sense of their own capacity. In developmental perspective I can see that my fascination with the transcendentalists may have reflected not just an unfolding independence of thinking, but also the beginnings of something of an *individualist* orientation in my thinking. In any event, my interests in philosophy blended with my continuing love of psychology and I went on to graduate school to get clinical training.

Graduate school

My training at Michigan was psychoanalytic in perspective. The thing that had always attracted me to a psychoanalytic approach was the concern with subjective experience and the power of unconscious psychological processes. This articulated with the fact that I had been an introspective only child and was captivated by the imaginative depictions of human experience to be found in good literature. Psychoanalysis took the depths and pluralities of human psychological experience seriously without dismissing individual idiosyncracy as being merely the random by-product – the exhaust, so to speak – of a "machine ready to run," as the "father" of behaviorism in psychology, John Watson, put it. The fact that Freud originally attempted to build a comprehensive model of the human personality on his study of the process of dreaming was intriguing to me because he proposed that the peculiar phenomena of dreaming, experienced by everyone, were ordered and *meaningful* and in that sense were the indication of the thoroughgoing purposefulness of mental life in the efforts to come to terms with living.

When I entered graduate school, the particular aspect of psychoanalytic theory that I became interested in, "ego psychology," was in its heyday. This view emphasized the idea that the child is born with basic mental capacities which are adaptively functional in a rudimentary way before there is conflictual interaction with the world. Thus, some aspects of ego functioning are "conflict free" from the beginning. Adopting such a view enabled psychoanalytically oriented psychologists to better integrate their theoretical interests with the work of academic, non-psychoanalytic experimental psychologists.

This emphasis on the reality negotiating processes in everyday life also gave psychoanalysis a more solid footing as a general theory of personality. This helped expand its relevance beyond the purview of the clinic. From a clinical standpoint one of the most important aspects of a focus on ego functions for me was that the primary emphasis was taken off the ubiquitous primitive fantasies hidden in the human psyche and placed on describing how well the individual handles the task of coping with personal needs. Thus, behavior is seen as maladaptive, not because an individual has Oedipal wishes (for example, a boy may want to kill his father) – everyone does according to the theory. The psychopathology lies in the individual's inability to manage these feelings in ways that let him or her get on with the tasks of developing into a mature person.

I think that probably one of the reasons that ego psychology was a particularly influential theoretical paradigm in the US was because it championed "ego autonomy" as the goal of development. That is, an ideal in this paradigm was that of achieving relative independence from the continuing press of instinctual drive derivatives on the one hand and the demands of environmental constraints on the other. This psychoanalytic ideal was fully consistent with a foundational US cultural myth regarding the special possibilities for individual freedom inherent in the "American dream" (Weinstein, 1996). This longstanding cultural value undoubtedly gained particular validation from America's post-World War II rise to pre-eminence in the world. Looking back on it now, I think my interest in ego psychology not only reflected my interest in mastering an important intellectual topic but was also a part of the continuing evolution of the individualist trend in my thinking.

Beginning a career

The beginning years of my professional career were spent honing my clinical skills in psychodynamically oriented psychiatric settings. With PhD in hand in the early 1960s I came to New York City for postdoctoral clinical training and then a staff position at the Albert Einstein College of Medicine and its affiliated city hospital. Some of the top psychoanalytic psychiatrists were on the attending staff of this training hospital, and a very smart crop of young doctors, some of whom were destined to become prominent in their own right, were in the psychiatric residency program. This was a very stimulating intellectual atmosphere. We immersed ourselves in our work and engaged in the task of honing our professional expertise. Further, in a liberal spirit (for that time) as a team of psychologists, psychiatrists, social workers, and nurses, we were on a color-blind humanitarian mission to bring the fruits of psychoanalytic wisdom to the predominantly working-class, mixed race catchment area served by the hospital. However, as I look back in narrative hindsight, I'm afraid there was a degree of (quite unconscious) class elitism in our stance – which was not different from other well-meaning and well-run professional settings around the country, incidentally. This led to a kind of "top-down" quality in the service we offered. That is, based on our grounding in an overarching theory, we felt we really knew (more than previous generations) what to do to solve that set of human problems related to mental disorder. In fact, however, although we were perhaps a bit more sophisticated than previous generations of "helping professionals" in some ways, I think we were unwittingly still not really in touch with a large segment of our clientele. We still came from, or aspired to, a different social class status than many of our clients and were removed from them experientially in subtle ways.

"The times they are a-changin'"

I make these points to direct my discussion to the idea that during this time, in the mid- to late 1960s, as I was attempting to develop my skills as a teacher and a professional, Bob Dylan's generation was trying to call our attention to a wider social context. To some degree we felt ourselves to be a part of that. The civil rights movement, which had been evolving since my college days, seemed to my black and white colleagues to be bringing, finally, the promise for genuine equality; the US appeared to be waking up to the persistence of racial injustice. In that context, we middle-class professionals bought into the idea that true integration was just around the corner. But because of our social distance from the community, even many black professionals failed to realize how many people in the black community, for example, did not feel fully a part of this promise. When the protest for rights came to a full boil, most of us in the middle class, white and black alike, were caught off guard. The culturally nationalist tones of that protest became strident and had an impact on many young African-American professionals. We formed separate "caucuses" in the larger, predominantly white associations to which we belonged and began to think about ways that we could make our disciplines and our own professional functioning more directly useful to the African-American community.

I joined the Association of Black Psychologists (ABPsi) at its founding in 1968 and became an officer in the New York City chapter soon after that. The national organization was successful in the early years in pressuring the large American Psychological Association (APA) to recognize the dearth of African-American psychologists. It worked with ABPsi to provide support for recruiting African-American students and training them at the doctoral level to serve the community as scholars and practitioners. After a few years, however, a more separatist spirit emerged within ABPsi. Influential people in the organization felt that even the appearance of a close association with the APA simply replayed a kind of subservience to the white cultural dominance which had ill-served the African-American community. ABPsi stopped holding its national meetings in conjunction with the APA convention. The Association also took on a strongly "Afrocentric" orientation (Jones, 2004; Myers, 1988;

White and Parham, 1990). Although I maintained my membership in ABPsi, I remained more intellectually engaged with APA and became a founding member of the APA Division of Ethnic Minority Psychology.

The New York University years

I had left the Einstein staff in 1967 and joined the faculty in the Psychology Division of one of New York University Medical Center's affiliate hospitals, the famous Bellevue Hospital. After several years at the Medical Center I joined the Faculty of Arts and Science psychology department at the Washington Square campus of NYU in the department's graduate and undergraduate programs, where I have been ever since. I had married in 1969 and our son was born at about the time that I made the move to the Arts and Science campus of NYU. As I settled into family life and the new job, my career orientation took a decided shift toward being a teacher and scholar, rather than primarily a clinical practitioner.

Psychology and African-Americans

I immersed myself in some of the literature that was coming out at that time about the history of social science descriptions of African-Americans (Guthrie, 1976; Thomas and Sillen, 1972). In the critical intellectual climate toward the social sciences that prevailed around many African-American scholars it was not surprising that some of them chose the Afrocentric route, abandoning Western perspectives in psychology entirely. I felt that this was a possible intellectual path to take, but my view was that there were still frameworks within contemporary Western psychology that could be used to give a fuller and fairer assessment of African-Americans. In fact my interests in the ego psychological aspects of psychodynamic theory – how one copes with stress – probably had laid the groundwork for my belief that there were conceptions in traditional psychology that were relevant to the direction I wanted to take.

From "competence" to humanism

In my first efforts at addressing some of these issues, I stayed close to the psychodynamic intellectual tradition that I was familiar with. I was particularly interested in the psychologist Robert White's (1963) concept of psychological "competence," which is basically an ego psychological point of view. White developed his view that organisms, particularly the higher mammals, demonstrate an innate striving to interact "effectively" with their environments. This kind of behavior was different from those activities prompted to deal with the arousal of biological drives. On this view, it is primarily when peremptory drives are satisfied and quiescent that the neonate is able to attend to various objects in the world – a rattle, a teddy bear – and respond to and evaluate these items in their own right. In so doing the child's interactions lead to pleasing *effects*, repeated and expanded contact with the world. Such "effectance behavior" leads to ever greater skills in achieving these effects. With maturation and continued activity the child develops wider ranges of effectiveness and actual "competence" in dealing with the physical and social world. This continually evolving process in people is postulated as operative in all cultural contexts, although the form and modes of its expression are, of course, heavily culturally determined.

In my original view, the idea of universal human competence strivings seemed like a good model for expanding the social science perspective regarding African-Americans. If all persons could be seen as basically competent, in White's sense of the term, then this certainly applied to African-Americans. Granted such a universal assumption, the focus could be taken off the putative inferiority of blacks and placed on the circumstances in the social world which distorted the development and functioning of their competence motivation. However, while the competence notion was an appealing one in the effort to provide a more positive perspective on the psychological situation of African-Americans, it began to be clear to me that it was really not complex enough as an overarching concept to capture the various facets of psychological functioning that I wanted to deal with. Towards the end of the 1970s, after a sabbatical semester during which I wrote the first draft of a proposed book, I came across the work of Joseph Rychlak, a clinically trained psychologist with philosophical interests (1968), who had just published his humanistic critique of extant psychology (1977). Part of the appeal of this perspective was probably that it allowed me to return to my interests in theoretical and philosophical issues, latent since college days. His framework of "rigorous humanism" was a general psychological perspective which provided me with the depth and breadth that I was looking for to ground my efforts.

In taking on this broadly philosophical approach to psychology, I came to a clearer articulation of why trends in psychological research have served the study of African-Americans so poorly. I proposed that it was not just that there have been racist trends, as such, in social science which mirror and support the attitudes and practices of the broader society. In addition, I argued that a major problem with psychological characterizations of African-Americans had been that human beings in general have not been seen as taking an active, coping stance in life. When people ordinarily are not seen as proactive beings, the tendency not to see active and creative features in the behavior of blacks follows naturally. This image of humankind was, more and more, being labeled as a "mechanistic" view of the person. Such a framework portrays the human individual as a passive being whose responses are primarily determined either by environmental factors or by internal physiological and constitutional states. While the behaviorist position had been most clearly identified with the mechanistic tradition, even classical Freudian theory showed clear evidence of such a direction in the efforts to develop a "metapsychology" delineating the basic forces driving human functioning (Holt, 1972).

However, a number of theorists from a variety of theoretical perspectives were beginning to express the need for a new way of conceptualizing the human being (Chein, 1972; Maslow, 1968; Sarbin, 1977). In a broad opening statement in the first chapter of her book the noted counseling psychologist, Leona Tyler (1978) maintained: "In psychology fresh winds are blowing, sweeping away overly restrictive assumptions, dusting off concepts that had been covered over and neglected, picking up and juxtaposing separate ideas to produce novel combinations... Pluralism is the order of the day" (p.1). This expression was quite compatible with the direction in which my thinking was moving.

Psychological agency

A notion of the "psychological agent" is central to systematic humanistic psychological accounts. "The tie binding all humanists is [the] assumption that the individual 'makes a difference' or contributes to the flow of events" (Rychlak, 1976, p.128). I had been impressed by the thinking of my colleague at NYU, the late Isidore Chein (1972), who proposed a view of agency which he counterposed to the traditional psychological view of humankind in the passive, mechanistic voice. Chein's humanistic view, portrayed the human individual as "an active, responsible agent, not simply a helpless, powerless reagent" (Chein, 1972, p.6). The human being in this active image is one "who actively does something with regard to some of the things that happen to [him or her], a being who...seeks to shape [the] environment rather than passively permit [himself or herself] to be shaped by the latter, a being, in short, who insists on injecting [himself or herself] into the causal process of the [surrounding] world" (p.6). Rychlak's definition of agency provided the ground for broader philosophical connections.

In the logical learning theory (LLT) framework, an "agent" is designated as a being who can behave so as to go along with, add to, oppose or disregard sociocultural and/or biological stimulations (Rychlak, 1994). Key ideas that elucidate this definition are, first, that subjectively held intentions are as important as "objective" environmental contingencies in governing the way people behave. Thus, the human individual is an important causal factor in his/her own life. This is a "teleological" or "telic" perspective on human behavior with a *final cause* implication, in Aristotelian terminology, because it emphasizes that human behavior is always governed in part by the goal or end the actor has in mind. As we try to understand the intentions that contribute to an individual's actions, we necessarily take an "introspective" point of view on that person's life that is, a view from the *actor's* perspective. A second point is that human mentality from birth is actively structuring, not simply passively reactive, as it "comes at" experience. We actively organize the world into meaningful units and then relate mentally to the "reality" that we have constructed. As the psychoanalyst, Marshall Edelson, put it: "While 'real' external reality may be presumed to exist independently of its apprehension, it cannot be known except symbolically – as part...of psychic reality" (1971, p.27). This is consistent with recent "constructivist" and even "narrativist" approaches to knowledge (Fay, 1996; Howard, 1991; Sarbin, 1986; Schafer, 1992). Third, and of particular importance for the way I have used this framework, "dialectical" thinking, the innate capacity to imagine alternative or opposing conceptions of life situations, is frequently used by people to guide their behavior. With this capacity, people have an independent ability to determine the meaning of a given situation. In principle, they can fashion conceptions of a situation that are contradictory to those given by the tradition of a particular authority. A key feature of this dialectic capacity in human activity is the *imaginative* power available to human mentality that can provide perspectives leading to new understanding and behavior. This way of thinking complements the capacity that we have to define our constructions of the world in denotative, straightforward and unambiguous terms in order to negotiate our circumstances (a "demonstrative" mode of thought, in Aristotelian terms).

Rychlak's discussion of agency showed the relevance of a systematic, philosophically grounded approach to psychology and deepened the conception for me of the nature of the individual's efforts at mastery and competence in adapting to the world. I found it rather easy to bridge over to this perspective from my interests in psychoanalytic ego psychology because Rychlak was an appreciative scholar of what he described as the teleological and humanistic aspects in Freudian theory (Cameron and Rychlak, 1985). In addition, the LLT framework allowed me to put the work of some of those who were my favorite psychoanalytic writers at that time into a broader context. For example, a prominent psychoanalyst, Roy Schafer, introduced what he called an "action language" for psychoanalysis in which he tried to present what can be called "humanistic" aspects of psychoanalysis in a systematic reframing (1976). He noted that "the person as agent has always stood at the center of psychoanalytic understanding" (1976, p.361). In his view, psychoanalytic theory proposes that all mental acts such as wishing, believing, or expressing emotions, whether in conscious or unconscious mode, are "actions." That is, they are intentional and purposeful – therefore *meaningful* – human activities. From the LLT view, this is a final cause formulation in which behavior is seen as being carried out for the sake of goals (i.e., reasons) which the individual frames in or out of awareness (Jenkins, 1992).

To take another example, an attractive feature of Marshall Edelson's work was his effort to recognize that psychoanalytic theory was best cast in non-reductive terms (1971). The human is clearly a biological being, but she or he is more. The human being is also a *symbolizing* animal:

> [The human being] symbolizes the invisible...[she or he] alone is able...in the absence of "anything" to imagine "something," in the presence of "that which is" to imagine and act in terms of "that which is not," and in any situation to imagine alternatives and their possible consequences. (Edelson, 1971, p.25)

In the above idea of "imagining alternatives" one can see the notion of dialectic thinking. In this process, the actor is not seen as standing outside the world of events. She or he carries out dialectic cognitive activities in the situation where she or he is engaged. The actor can set intentions which guide actions, perhaps in accord with, perhaps in opposition to, received wisdom. This is a central aspect of the *psychological* conception of "free will" in LLT and what turned out to be an illuminating idea for me (Jenkins, 1997; Rychlak, 1979). Psychologically speaking, "free will" rests on this basic human dialectical symbolizing capacity; the ability to contribute a necessary component of the conceptual grounds for defining the meaning of a situation and its possible implications. In this view, the "freedom" in the *free will* term is the option for alternative conceptions of the given experience – *prior* to the agent's affirmation that "this" as opposed to "that" is so. Having decided, the individual proceeds to act "wilfully" or intentionally – that is, "for the sake of" – furthering the meanings of such a conception.

My earlier interests in "ego functioning" were obviously changing with my growing humanistic interests because the latter perspective put more weight on notions of the "self." This evolution in my thinking, away from the classical psychoanalytic structures of personality, allowed me to appreciate some of the late 20th-century developments in psychoanalytic formulations (e.g., Kohut, 1977; Mitchell, 1993). Of importance for this discussion, it provided a particularly relevant context for considerations of ethnicity, since issues of "self" and "self-concept" have been major areas of research with respect to people of color.

Humanism and African-Americans

My use of the LLT framework, then, allowed me to recast my notions of competence and bring these ideas to the situation of African-Americans and people of color in America (e.g., Jenkins, 1982, 1989, 1990). It allowed me to draw a richer portrait of African-Americans as having developed their "human qualities" by actively and intentionally bringing to their lives dialectically conceived ideas of their competence at variance with the judgments made of them by the majority society.

Earlier, I mentioned a link between humanistic psychological principles and the scope that literary scholars have used to achieve their insights. One of my favorite illustrations of this point can be seen in Ellison's famous work *Invisible Man* (1952). In the opening passages of the novel, the family of an old black man is gathered around his deathbed. He calls his son (the father of the protagonist of the novel) close to him and says:

> "Son...I never told you, but our life is a war and I have been a traitor all my born days, a spy in the enemy's country ever since I give up my gun back in the Reconstruction. Live with your head in the lion's mouth. I want you to overcome 'em with yeses, undermine 'em with grins, agree 'em to death and destruction, let 'em swoller you till they...bust wide open... Learn it to the younguns," he whispered fiercely; then he died.

The writer continues:

> They thought the old man had gone out of his mind. *He had been the meekest of men.* (Ellison, 1952, pp.19–20; italics added)

In my view the old man had taken a dialectically imaginative perspective on his situation throughout his life without anyone being quite aware of it. That is to say, recognizing fully the nature of his oppressive circumstances, he had acted in seeming submission to those circumstances; but, at the same time, he had constructed an opposing mental perspective on the racial situation. With fully crafted intentions, he had found ways during his life to express those ends. This was his way of sustaining his human qualities "despite and in rejection of the obstacles and meannesses" (Ellison, 1964) that had been imposed upon him. And he was urgently trying to pass that strategy on to his family as a part of his legacy. Consistent with a general humanistic position on agency, the episode illustrates that one cannot understand the behavior without understanding the *intent* that contributes to the behavior. We cannot understand the way this man acts unless we take an "introspective" or "first-person" view, a look "through his eyes," as it were. To recognize the intentional, purposive quality in people's behavior is to recognize the *active* role of the person – a being who seeks "to shape his environment rather than passively permit himself to be shaped by the latter" – which I have been stressing here.

The theoretical emphasis that I have come to place on agency seems to continue and elaborate my earlier career interests in effective ego functioning and ego autonomy. However, this lifelong concern with "competent" and masterful action obviously foregrounds the study of the *individual* in society. In recent years, I have become more aware of the extent to which such a perspective has to be culturally contextualized. An increasing number of writers in both the social sciences and literature have noted the value placed in Western society (especially upper- and middle-class American society) on achieving an autonomous, almost transcendent sense of self (e.g., Cushman, 1995; Sampson, 1988; Weinstein, 1996). Such a sense of personhood emphasizes separateness from others, independent hegemony of action, and the primacy of one's own "rights." This is an indigenous cultural notion in the West, not universally shared among world cultures. It contrasts with the notion of self found in most other cultures in the world where individuality is ideally experienced as being embedded in social relationships in the "collective." My emphasis on "agency" might be seen as advocating the Western cultural preference on "self-contained individualism" (Sampson, 1988) as the ideal for humanity. However, that is not the point. My view is that psychological agency, as I have come to understand it, is a *process* of human functioning which operates in various societal settings to develop and sustain the cultural *form* that emerges, whether that be a collectivistic or more individualistic manifestation (Jenkins, 2001). Most people are adapted to their culture. Nevertheless, I submit that they live *proactively* – as agents – to fashion and sustain their culture's tenets; and, of course, people are in turn greatly shaped and enabled by the social mechanisms that are created. While I insist on the irreducible contribution of intentional action guided by a dialectically functioning imagination in human beings, such a process can only function and derive meaning within a social and physical context. That is, beings can only become persons within a human social context. However, human development cannot be accounted for solely in terms of the cultural/environmental surround.

There are trends in the social science literature that I have used to support this position. Gurin and Epps (1975) studied African-American students at historically black colleges at the height of the general student activism of the late 1960s. They found that some students were quite able to combine high personal occupational aspirations with strong commitments to collective action for group advancement. In some ways, those students were a more effective and motivated group than students who only emphasized either individual aspirations or collective commitments during their college years. More recently, Kagitcibasi (1996) has discussed the value of an "autonomous-relational" perspective in the sense of self in which one develops the individual skill and sense of autonomy for functioning capably in the modern workplace world while at the same time maintaining a supportive emotional relatedness to one's family and group.

Concluding thoughts

Thus, the humanistic perspective has come to be an organizing one for my personal as well as my professional thinking. As I noted in the opening paragraph, that includes my perspective on religious and spiritual matters as well, so I will end this chapter with a brief commentary in that regard. In my early adult years my religious commitment, while still a part of me, remained in the background of my daily living. When my wife and I became parents, we decided to upgrade our rather dormant religiosity and become active church members to provide a context for religious education for our child. In our son's elementary school years we joined New York's Riverside Church when its famous activist preacher, William Sloane Coffin, was the Senior Minister. Riverside is an interracial, interfaith community, which under Coffin's leadership tended to be politically liberal. It was made up of interesting and inquiring people, for the most part, who did not just accept dogma blindly. It was not only intellectually and spiritually stimulating for us, but also provided the kind of religious experience for our son that we were looking for.

Now that our son has his own independent adult life we have become less active there. However, the messages I took from my fellowship in that congregation fit the humanistic perspectives that I was developing in my professional work. Most people (including some humanists) think of the term "humanism" as being necessarily linked to the word "secular." It is as if putting questions about the nature of human experience at the center of intellectual investigation is antithetical to spiritual endeavors. I think quite the contrary. For example, the most satisfying view for me regarding such considerations has crystallized around the idea that we, as a human species, are co-creators of the world with what Emerson called "the Oversoul." In this idea I am again influenced by my former colleague, Isidore Chein. In his book, he drew what he thought to be the appropriate image of humankind from a version of the Creation to be found in the rabbinic literature. On this view as God approaches the creation of humankind, he says, "We will make Man." This is the first time in the description of the Creation that a plural subject and a future tense are used. (The previous declarative form had been: "And God said, Let there be light: and there was light.") The "we" form is seen to indicate that God took human beings into partnership; the future tense indicates that this creation is far from completed. As Chein notes: "What more magnificent creation, short of the creation of the universe itself, can be attributed to God than a self-creating being?" (1972, p.42). This is a role we take on by purposefully engaging the circumstances of our living in mutually respectful partnership with our Creator and our fellow human beings all over the planet. I am quite satisfied that this qualifies as a religious *and* a humanistic perspective.

References

Atkinson, B. (ed) (1950) *The Complete Essays and Other Writings of Ralph Waldo Emerson.* New York: Random House.

Cameron, N. and Rychlak, J.F. (1985) *Personality Development and Psychopathology: A Dynamic Approach.* Boston: Houghton-Mifflin.

Chein, I. (1972) *The Science of Behavior and the Image of Man.* New York: Basic Books.

Cushman, P. (1995) *Constructing the Self, Constructing America: A Cultural History of Psychotherapy.* Reading, MA: Addison-Wesley.

Edelson, M. (1971) *The Idea of a Mental Illness.* New Haven: Yale University Press.

Ellison, R. (1952) *Invisible Man.* New York: Signet.

Ellison, R. (1964) "That same pain, that same pleasure: An interview." In R. Ellison *Shadow and Act.* New York: Signet.

Fay, B. (1996) *Contemporary Philosophy of Social Science: A Multicultural Approach.* Malden, MA: Blackwell.

Gurin, P. and Epps, E.G. (1975) *Black Consciousness, Identity, and Achievement.* New York: Wiley.

Guthrie, R.V. (1976) *Even the Rat was White: A Historical View of Psychology.* New York: Harper.

Holt, R.R. (1972) "Mechanistic and humanistic themes in Freud's thought." *Psychoanalysis and Contemporary Science 1*, 3–24.

Howard, G.S. (1991) "Culture tales: A narrative approach to thinking, cross-cultural psychology, and psychotherapy." *American Psychologist 46*, 187–197.

Jenkins, A.H. (1982) *The Psychology of the Afro-American: A Humanistic Approach.* Elmsford, NY: Pergamon.

Jenkins, A.H. (1989) "The liberating value of 'constructionism' for minorities." *Humanistic Psychologist 17*, 161–168.

Jenkins, A.H. (1990) "The dynamics of the relationship in clinical work with African American clients." *Group: Journal of the Eastern Group Psychotherapy Society 14*, 36–43.

Jenkins, A.H. (1992) "Hermeneutics versus science in psychoanalysis: A 'rigorous' humanistic view." *Psychoanalytic Psychology 9*, 509–527.

Jenkins, A.H. (1997) "Free will and psychotherapy: The enhancement of agency." *Journal of Theoretical and Philosophical Psychology 17*, 1–13.

Jenkins, A.H. (2001) "Individuality in cultural context: The case for psychological agency." *Theory and Psychology 11*, 347–362.

Jones, R. (ed) (2004) *Black Psychology*, 4th edn. Hampton, VA: Cobb and Henry.

Kagitcibasi, C. (1996) "The autonomous-relational self: A new synthesis." *European Psychologist 1*, 180–186.

Kohut, H. (1977) *The Restoration of the Self.* New York: International Universities Press.

Maslow, A.H. (1968) *Toward a Psychology of Being*, 2nd edn. New York: Van Nostrand Reinhold.

Mitchell, S.A. (1993) *Hope and Dread in Psychoanalysis.* New York: Basic Books.

Myers, L.J. (1988) *Understanding an Afrocentric World View: Introduction to an Optimal Psychology.* Dubuque, IA: Kendall/Hunt.

Rychlak, J.F. (1968) *A Philosophy of Science for Personality Theory.* Boston: Houghton-Mifflin.

Rychlak, J.F. (1976) "Is a concept of 'self' necessary in psychological theory, and if so why? A humanistic perspective." In A. Wandersman, P.J. Poppen and D.F. Ricks (eds) *Humanism and Behaviorism: Dialogue and Growth.* Elmsford, NY: Pergamon.

Rychlak, J.F. (1977) *The Psychology of Rigorous Humanism.* New York: Wiley.

Rychlak, J.F. (1979) *Discovering Free Will and Personal Responsibility.* New York: Oxford University Press.

Rychlak, J.F. (1994) *Logical Learning Theory: A Human Teleology and its Empirical Support.* Lincoln, NE: University of Nebraska Press.

Sampson, E.E. (1988) "The debate on individualism: Indigenous psychologies of the individual and their role in personal and social functioning." *American Psychologist 43*, 15–22.

Sarbin, T.R. (1977) "Contextualism: A world view for modern psychology." In A. Landfield (ed) *1976 Nebraska Symposium on Motivation.* Lincoln: University of Nebraska Press.

Sarbin, T. (1986) "The narrative as a root metaphor for psychology." In T.R. Sarbin (ed) *Narrative Psychology: The Storied Nature of Human Conduct.* New York: Praeger.

Schafer, R. (1976) *A New Language for Psychoanalysis.* New Haven, CT: Yale University Press.

Schafer, R. (1992) *Retelling a Life.* New York: Basic Books.

Thomas, A. and Sillen, S. (1972) *Racism and Psychiatry.* New York: Brunner/Mazel.

Tyler, L.E. (1978) *Individuality: Human Possibilities and Personal Choice in the Psychological Development of Men and Women.* San Francisco: Jossey-Bass.

Weinstein, A. (speaker) (1996) "American fiction and the individualist creed, Lecture 1." *Twentieth Century American Fiction.* (Cassette Recording, Course No. 231) Chantilly, VA: Teaching Company.

White, J.L. and Parham, T.A. (1990) *The Psychology of Blacks: An African-American Perspective,* 2nd edn. Englewood Cliffs, NJ: Prentice-Hall.

White, R.W. (1963) "Ego and reality in psychoanalytic theory." *Psychological Issues 3*, 11.

CHAPTER 11

On Growing Up as a "Premodernist"

Steen Halling

Several years ago, a good friend and colleague asked me if I considered myself to be a postmodernist. I replied that I had never quite subscribed to a modernist view of the world, and that consequently postmodernism did not seem compelling to me. Postmodernism, after all, has grown out of disillusionment with modernism, and thus is still significantly shaped by it (Halling, 1997). Perhaps, I said, I am more of a premodernist. I hope that the story of my life, as I tell it here, will make this statement more understandable. As I write this story, I am keenly aware that I have been shaped by my history and culture and yet that I (like everyone else) have responded to these circumstances from within myself; a self that is both a given and a work in progress; a self for which I have words but that is also something beyond what I can name or fully know.

I was born in Copenhagen, Denmark, in 1944, the last year of the German occupation. When I was about ten years old, I looked at a map that my father had kept in the basement of our house and on which he had marked the progress of the war (as reported by the BBC). I concluded that my parents decided to have a second child (my brother Jørgen was born in 1938) once it became apparent, by summer of 1943, that the Germans were losing the war. My explanation, true or not, showed a certain inclination toward thinking psychologically. Who, in their right mind would bring a child into the world without some sense of hope for the future?

My father was an architect specializing in the design of stores and had his own factory, so we were moderately well off. He worked long hours while my mother did not work outside of the home. I was closer to my mother than my father; in fact, I felt somewhat intimidated by his apparent certainty about things.

In 1956 my father immigrated to Canada, and my mother, my brother and I followed in January of 1957. My father's business had run into economic difficulties and he wanted to get a fresh start. Also, he was concerned, given the Suez Crisis of 1956, that there might be another war in Europe. It was a difficult change for my mother (my father was 50 at that time and my mother 46). She missed our family greatly and would frequently return to Denmark for visits until she was too frail to travel. I too missed our family and yet I was ready for a change.

Although I was sorry to say goodbye to my friends, I was glad to leave my school behind. It was a large regimented institution where physical punishment was used frequently and boys and girls were segregated even during recess. Even though this school (I assume) was like many others in Denmark at that time, I thought there was something "unnatural" about all of this. On Sunday evenings I dreaded the return to school the following morning. On occasion, I would tell my parents about some of the difficulties I had in school. While they expressed concern and tried to help, it did not seem that they understood what it was like for me and so I felt rather alone with my unhappiness. It is telling that for years I believed that the school building, constructed of yellow bricks, was gray in color.

The district where we lived when we first arrived in Toronto had a large Jewish population. As a Dane, I was welcomed to an extent that would not have been the case had I been from Germany, or even France. My fellow students knew little about Denmark, but they did know that the Danes had helped their Jewish countrymen escape to Sweden. Obviously, I had made no contribution to this rescue and yet was clearly a beneficiary, however undeserving, of what others had done. But here I was, an awkward and shy boy in a new country, having a limited grasp of English, and struggling with the advent of puberty. Had we not moved to Canada, and had I not received such a warm welcome to my new school, followed by encouraging experiences in subsequent schools, I would surely not have completed graduate studies and become an academic. In Denmark, my grades had fluctuated between good and mediocre and I had few positive associations with education other than the fact that I enjoyed reading.

As I have already suggested, circumstances do not by themselves fully account for the direction of one's life. Thus, I question the idea that the self is socially constructed, as if one is primarily a reflection of one's culture (Halling and Lawrence, 1999). I am more taken by Søren Kierkegaard's dictum that we are what we make of what we are made. A memory from my childhood in Copenhagen speaks to this point and is also revealing of another dimension of who I was (and am). Often I would play after dinner, typically alone, in the backyard of the house where we lived. The ringing of the nearby church bell at 7pm was loud and clear. This sound touched me in a way that I did not have words for then, and barely even now. It resonated with the loneliness I felt and it had a haunting and melancholic quality that pointed to something beyond the everyday world, something timeless. These were not feelings or reactions that I ever shared with anyone in Denmark.

Denmark was, and is still, not a country that is characterized by any great interest in spirituality, religion, or even introspection. In that context, I was an odd duck, or, in Jungian terms, an intuitive introvert. However attached I was to my family and home, I nonetheless felt out of place among my countrymen. The extent to which people find themselves at home in the culture in which they grow up varies depending upon their temperament, family, and social context. There is always a complex process of dialogue and negotiation between a person and his or her life circumstances.

Another memory foreshadowed some of my later interests and values. A friend told me that his biology teacher had explained to his class that the heart is basically a pump. Therefore, it would make as much sense to say that one loved someone with one's entire pump as to say that one loved the person with all of one's heart. Even at that tender age, I thought this was a silly and offensive thing to say, not because I was theoretically precocious but because the world and the people around me were so obviously real, as was my own emotional life. Whatever doubts and uncertainties I had, the lifeworld (as Husserl called it) was a source of both wonder and fear for me. Later, when I gained a greater understanding of science, I was daunted by its power and precision and curious about its history and application. But the notion that science could give us the truth about life never seemed convincing to me, nor did it seem plausible that everyday experience was an illusion, as some reductionists might claim. Instead, I assumed (or intuited) that answers to questions about our existence would be found within our experiences, not outside of them.

The perspective I developed was indebted to the views of my parents and yet was different from either one of theirs. My father, who was strong in math and science, often spoke of what amazing powers the brain had. I thought this was an odd way to speak of thinking (it is the person who thinks, not the brain). In this respect, I saw myself as being quite different in outlook from him. Yet, I gradually realized that architecture is not just a technical science but also a human science as it has to take into account human experience. In contrast, my mother took for granted the everyday world, the world I deeply value even as I have a lot of questions about it.

Gradually, as I became competent in English, I studied hard, and, to my amazement, succeeded academically. This success was at odds with my sense of myself as an average student, and so I was pleasantly surprised when I did well. Since my grades in science and math were not so impressive toward the end of high school, my self-doubts were not entirely unreasonable. But I excelled in history and English and had the good fortune to have several exceptionally able teachers (at Royal York Collegiate Institute and Leaside High School). Inspired by their example, I decided to become a high school history teacher, and applied for admission to the University of Toronto.

I spent a year at "U of T" in a liberal arts track called "Social and Philosophical Thought," and adjusting to the idea of being a university student. In Denmark universities were open only to a select few; this was much less the case in Canada. The University of Toronto was and is a great university, Canada's grandest. Even freshmen were taught by major professors, many of them excellent lecturers and scholars. I was, however, disappointed by my psychology course since it was taught in the 1960s tradition of scientific reductionism.

Even though I liked most of my classes, I was ready to move on at the end of my freshman year. I felt lost in the large lecture classes, and the categorical separation among disciplines did not make sense to me. As a result, I transferred to Glendon College, the founding college of the newly inaugurated York University. The vision at Glendon was that one should study the whole "man," and accordingly there was an emphasis on interdisciplinary courses and small seminars. Although this college was only a 15-minute walk from my home, I decided it was time for me to live on my own and so I moved into the dorm.

At Glendon, I started to break out of my relative isolation. Several of the people I met there are still among my closest friends. Here I also met one woman with whom I had a tumultuous relationship over a number of years, and another with whom I found, for all too short a time, a love beyond anything I had ever imagined possible. In the midst of studying history and political science with teaching in mind, something was nagging at me. I wondered if I should consider a vocation that would get me more closely involved with people.

Then in the spring of my sophomore year, I read about an innovative program at the Oak Ridge Division of the Penetanguishene Hospital, north of Toronto. Oak Ridge was the maximum security section, reserved for the "criminally insane." Dr. Elliott T. Barker, a psychiatrist who was the assistant superintendent at the hospital and had previously been a residence director at Glendon, was looking for students to participate in the program. Five or six of us went up to the hospital to meet the patients and staff, and to tour the facility. The summer "job" involved living on G ward, where Barker and a select group of staff and patients had developed an intensive treatment program for patients, many of whom had committed serious crimes. Most of the patients were diagnosed either as schizophrenic or psychopathic; all of them had volunteered to be on the unit.

Although daunted by what we saw (bars on the window and some patients who looked obviously disturbed), some of us nonetheless applied for the position, and that summer of 1966 Paul Rollison, Gordon West, and I moved onto G ward. The program was based on the therapeutic community model developed by Maxwell Jones, an English psychiatrist. Patients were expected to be actively involved in their own treatment and that of their peers. Martin Buber's notion of the healing power of dialogue was also an important influence on the program.

The patients had agreed to our becoming temporary residents on their ward, but they probably had as much trepidation about our stay as we did, wondering how they would be evaluated by three "sane" people. In turn, we were keenly aware that about a third of the patients had committed homicide, worried about to what extent they would accept us, and wondered how well we would cope with living in a prison hospital. Our reasons for taking part in this experiment were varied and complex. I wanted to learn more about mental health and psychotherapy as I was considering whether or not teaching was the right vocation for me. Indeed this seemed like a great opportunity to gain first-hand knowledge about a world that was largely unknown to me. I was also struggling with my own demons, including questions about my own sanity. From early on, I had been moody, introspective, and had struggled to find ways of feeling comfortable in relationships.

Our two-month stay in Oak Ridge profoundly affected us. The emphasis on speaking one's mind and the constant interaction with our fellow residents resulted in our becoming more emotionally expressive. It took some time for us to readjust to living outside of the hospital. Everyday social conversation seemed superficial and we were initially overwhelmed by the number of decisions required of anyone living "on the outside." The program also introduced me to the work of Martin Buber and Ronald D. Laing. Their approach had a deep resonance with my own experience. While I did not know it at the time, I was getting "hooked" on the existential and phenomenological tradition.

During the summer I had also come across a quotation from a personality theorist: "Any therapy worth its salt, increases your capacity to feel both joy and sorrow." This has been my guiding maxim since that time.

We developed relationships with a number of the patients, and came to see them as fellow human beings, however disturbed they might be, and however appalling were the actions that had brought them to this hospital. As we lived with these men 24 hours a day, we caught glimpses of their concerns, fears, and hopes. This was truly an unforgettable summer, one that changed my life and my vocational aspirations. By the time I returned to school in the fall, I had decided to become a psychotherapist, wanting to work with people diagnosed with schizophrenia, and accordingly changed my major to psychology and sociology. My earlier disillusionment with psychology remained but I knew that to get into a graduate program in psychology I needed to take courses in this discipline.

As a result of this summer at Penetanguishene, I was both more open and, as I was soon to discover, more vulnerable. Because of my greater openness, I continued to distance myself from the restrictive evangelical Protestant tradition with which I had been connected, even if ambivalently, during high school and my first two years of college. During my junior year, I became involved with Faith, a woman I had met during my sophomore year. This relationship was exciting but also very difficult. One of the obstacles to our relationship was her parents' opposition to our relationship – Faith was Jewish and I was not. But this was just one source of tension. We were both attempting to find our way in life, and in that process had all too many expectations of the other. At that time, I was confused about what was happening between us, or even within myself. My way of dealing with the hurt and rejection I felt as Faith ended our relationship was gradually "to shut down."

The following summer, I returned to Penetanguishene as an assistant to Dr. Barker. In that position, I read psychological evaluations of a number of the men on the unit. Although I did not doubt these reports had value, I was struck by how abstract they were – how little connection there seemed to be between my direct observations of the same patients and how they were portrayed in these evaluations. I was left wondering how such a gap could be overcome. Some years later, as a graduate student at Duquesne University, I was fortunate to take classes from Constance Fischer who had developed an individualized and phenomenological approach to assessment that overcame this gap.

As I started my senior year, my life was in turmoil. Having taken abnormal psychology and personality theory in my junior year, I now had to take the classes that emphasized quantitative research. At the beginning of the year, I struggled with these classes, even as I became more preoccupied and detached. When I withdrew from the university later in the fall, I wrote a letter to a university administrator explaining my disappointment with the narrowly defined experimental orientation of the department, one that had little relevance for psychotherapy.

One positive side of that fall was that I had signed up for an elective, the Idea of Nature in Western Thought, taught by Brayton Polka. Brady later became a friend and colleague. In his seminar, we learned to think seriously and carefully about human existence and were reminded of the power of good teaching.

There was another bright spot. One day, while meandering through the York Library, I found a description of a graduate program in phenomenological psychology at Duquesne University in Pittsburgh. As was true for many others who applied there, discovering a psychology program that matched my deepest hopes and aspirations was deeply encouraging. But I knew that a graduate program was not going to resolve my personal problems.

Several of my dreams reminded me of the ones R.D. Laing (1965) describes in his *The Divided Self*, a book about schizoid and schizophrenic phenomena. I was afraid I was heading down the road towards schizophrenia. In retrospect, I do not know whether my fear was justified, but this was by far the most difficult and frightening period in my life. A close friend affirmed my sense that something was quite wrong, and helped me to recognize that I needed to do something. Eventually, I decided to leave York University and become a childcare worker, thinking that the solution to my increasingly detached existence – one for which the "life of the mind" was anything but an antidote – was to take on the responsibility of working closely with others. I went to work for a branch of Warrendale, a private organization that provided treatment for emotionally disturbed children and adolescents, just outside Windsor, Ontario. Since I was in an honors program (requiring four years of study after the thirteen years of high school that was then the standard in Ontario), I could still graduate in spring with what in Canada is called a general BA.

The six months I worked as a childcare worker were extremely difficult. The treatment center, with residents ranging in age from six to eighteen, was located in a large house. Although many of the staff were very able, the center was chaotic and we were understaffed. The days were long and days off were rare. But I did the best I could and slowly became more effective in responding to the residents, and more engaged with the world around me. During the half year I was at this center, I saw how eager children were to connect with adults, and how positive change was possible for them.

During the winter, I started psychotherapy with a skilled psychiatrist who had been trained by Alexander Lowen, the founder of bioenergetics, an approach that emphasizes the connection between psyche and soma. This was my first exposure to psychotherapy and it taught me about the intimate connection between our psychological and our bodily experience, and it was a good introduction. I started to feel more rooted in my body within a relatively short time, and I also became more decisive. Soon I decided that I wanted to move back to Toronto. Having established relationships with staff and residents, I left feeling guilty but at the same time convinced that this is what I needed to do. I had learned a lot at Warrendale, especially about the healing power of relationships and the importance of understanding another from his or her point of view, a principle that was key in a publication 20 years later (Halling and Dearborn Nill, 1989). In the meantime, Duquesne University had accepted me as a graduate student and offered me an assistantship for the fall of 1968, which I was more than happy to accept.

When I returned to Toronto, I managed to secure a position as coordinator of staff education at a facility for the mentally retarded, just north of the city. I also started to pursue Faith, once again. Soon, Faith and I were engaged. We planned to get married before moving to Pittsburgh so I could start graduate school. It was early summer and life looked good, and yet whatever gains I had made during the previous half year had not gotten me on entirely solid ground emotionally. As the weeks passed, we had increasingly frequent arguments.

In the midst of one of our most intense arguments, which started as we were returning from a drive in the country, something unforgettable happened. Even now, more than three decades later, it sends a chill down my spine to think back to that evening. As the pitch of our argument increased in intensity, I felt very tense, almost as if I were going to explode. Then, suddenly I let go of something, and relaxed into the moment. Faith immediately noticed the change in me and she too relaxed. When I stopped the car in front of the apartment building where she lived, I looked at her and experienced a sense of awe and amazement – she was actually there, the world was actually there, I was actually there. It was as if I had suddenly landed in my own body, whereas previously I had somehow hovered above it. This was a sudden and remarkable experience of becoming fully present and open to the world around me. Something about this experience was familiar to me, but from such a distant point in my past that I thought it must have been in my preschool days.

Nonetheless, our arguments continued and toward the end of the summer we decided to end our engagement. We parted with great sadness, yet I also felt some relief since our conflicts had become so intense. As my relationship with Faith ended, I expected that the rest of the summer would be uneventful, and started to think about my move to Pittsburgh. I was excited about the Duquesne program, but the United States did not look like an attractive place in 1968. There had been riots in many cities, including Pittsburgh and Detroit, in 1967. Robert Kennedy was assassinated in the summer of 1968, and to most of us living in Canada the war in Vietnam was both pointless and horrifying. On the other hand, I would only stay in the United States long enough to get my MA, or so I thought.

Then something completely unexpected happened that touched me to the core of my being. I had planned to go to Montreal for a vacation toward the end of the summer. I mentioned this in passing to a woman with whom I had been friends for several years, and we agreed she would join me. Although I had been attracted to Heather (a pseudonym) since we first met, it did not occur to me that our relationship would change on this trip. Writing about this episode is particularly difficult since it was an intense and very personal experience. But along with my experience with Faith, what happened in Montreal profoundly influenced the direction of my academic as well as my personal life. For the sake of brevity, I will focus on the evening when, so to speak, heaven and earth moved.

We had gone to see the play *Man of La Mancha*. The performance was so compelling that I became completely caught up in the play. It took some time for me to recover myself and remember where I was when the performance ended. Metaphorically speaking, I had ended up "on stage" as Don Quixote pursued his impossible dream. His idealism and his madness resonated with something deep within me, and gave it back to me in such a way that I could own and appreciate it in a new way. Perhaps this is part of what Aristotle meant when he argued that a play could produce a "cathartic" experience in the audience. When we walked out of the theatre my demeanor had changed to the point that Heather was unsettled. For no apparent reason, I had changed from being reserved to being jovial and outgoing. After the play, we walked around downtown Montreal and watched the nightlife, allowing us to become more relaxed together.

Later, we drove up to a park overlooking the city. The park was beautiful and remarkably well lit even so late in the evening. As we walked around, I was struck by how completely peaceful I felt. I had the sense, as never before, that everything in the universe was just as it should be. We sat down on a bench and as I looked around me I experienced the world as alive, vibrating almost. There was a sense of presence all around me, a presence that transcended the distinction between the personal and impersonal. Again, as in my experience with Faith, I had a sense of having come home, but home to a place that I had not even imagined. Nothing I had read or experienced had prepared me for this evening and yet it was not as if I felt unprepared – there was nothing that I needed to do.

Subsequently, I looked for some literature that might address this experience, and discovered that Maslow's (1962) characterization of "peak experiences" closely coincided with what I had encountered that evening. As in his description, I felt so at home in the world, so awake, and so alive. Later, when we were sitting in the car, enjoying the view of downtown Montreal, Heather turned toward me and said, "You look so vulnerable." Then she took off her seat belt and starting kissing me.

The last few days of our trip to Montreal, and the time we spent together the last few weeks in Toronto before leaving for the United States, were unforgettable. But I was so caught up in the newness of this relationship and everything that surrounded it that I failed to grasp what was happening in any sort of reflective way. I did notice that everything around me was so alive, that kissing Heather was incredibly pleasurable, and that I had no interest in any other women. It took me months to realize I had come to love Heather wholeheartedly. Some years later I came across Max Scheler's (1970) assertion that the fullness of another is most deeply revealed in love because love takes in the other as a whole person rather than just his or her qualities, and I knew he was absolutely right. I did not lose sight of Heather's insecurities and limitations; this was not infatuation. Rather, I saw these, along with her strengths, as part of the totality of who she was.

The events of the summer of 1968 allowed me to see dimensions of reality or of the world that shaped my view of life in fundamental ways. I don't know that I ever subscribed to "subjectivism" (the notion that we live inside our own heads or personally constructed worlds), but these experiences made it plain to me that we live in the world, and that the world and our fellow humans vastly exceed our image of them.

The epiphanies of this summer also gave me the focus for my doctoral dissertation on "The Recognition of a Significant Other as a Unique Person" (Halling, 1976), and for a subsequent book chapter (Halling, 1983). They also set the stage for my research on other aspects of the interpersonal, such as forgiveness and disillusionment, and made me think twice about dismissing accounts of mystical or spiritual experiences.

The MA program at Duquesne was as exciting and as promising as I had hoped it would be. Since I ended up living with several other students in the program (all from Massachusetts), I felt like I had entered a community of scholars rather than just a graduate program, while also getting an interesting cross-cultural experience (the differences between Canada and the United States are quite real). The graduate program in phenomenological psychology was relatively new, and the students and faculty were passionate about this alternative approach. The chair of the department, Amedeo Giorgi, critiqued mainstream psychology and advocated for a paradigm shift in the discipline. I thought such a change unlikely, but his vision of a phenomenologically based psychology (Giorgi, 1970) was compelling. I was fortunate enough to have been given an assistantship to work with Rolf von Eckartsberg, a social psychologist and an inspiring teacher and scholar.

Although life at Duquesne was good, I was dismayed when Heather did not come to visit me as we had originally planned. She had reconnected with her former boyfriend. I had not assumed that she loved me in the same way that I loved her, even though I knew she was fond of me, but I was nonetheless taken aback. The shock of the loss of this relationship haunted me for years, but it did not deter me from becoming involved with other women, though I was more guarded.

Following the first year of the program, I returned to Canada to work at Whitby Psychiatric Hospital, near Toronto, for the summer. I had no idea that this was to be the last time I would work in Canada. When I returned to Duquesne in the fall, I started working at Dixmont State Hospital, west of Pittsburgh, and by the following summer I had transferred to Somerset Hospital, an hour and a half east of the city. Somerset was rated as one of the two best state psychiatric hospitals in Pennsylvania. The training I received in these two settings was invaluable. I gained experience in group and individual psychotherapy, psychological assessment, staff education, and eventually, administration and supervision when I was appointed co-coordinator of psychological services for one of the units at Somerset. The combination of graduate education and clinical work provided a healthy balance. My practical work was informed by theory, and my daily contact with patients and staff informed my studies.

Initially, I entered graduate school to become a psychotherapist and treat persons who were diagnosed with schizophrenia. Several years of work in psychiatric settings convinced me that while I might become a good psychotherapist, working with intensely psychotic patients was beyond my reach. I decided to apply to the doctoral program at Duquesne, and was accepted. I was really enjoying my academic work, and wanted to continue studying, but I did not have a specific career goal in mind.

In my first year as a doctoral student I took a course from Professor Charles Keyes, titled the Philosophy of Intersubjectivity. Psychology students at Duquesne could take some philosophy courses and have them count toward their degree requirements. Keyes's course introduced us to the philosophy of Emmanuel Levinas, through his recently translated *Totality and Infinity* (1969). This was a truly remarkable (and enigmatic) book, and a number of us were virtually transfixed as Keyes laid out Levinas's philosophy. I read Levinas's book more like a poetic exposition on human life than as an abstract philosophical text. Sections of it resonated deeply with dimensions of my own experiences the summer before I left Canada and helped me to place them within a broader context. Levinas wrote of how we totalize others by reducing them to our concept or image of who they are, even while we also know, at a deeper level, that the other – as genuinely other – eludes our grasp and our understanding. As I read his book, I thought of my encounters with Faith and Heather during those moments when I was truly open to them. The paper I wrote for this class, addressing the implications of Levinas's text for psychotherapy, was later published (Halling, 1975).

My doctoral dissertation was a qualitative investigation of related issues. I looked at "epiphanies" in close relationships, asking my research participants to describe a time "when you came to see someone of real significance in your life more as a real person in his or her own right" (Halling, 1976, p.66). It took me almost four years to finish this project.

By early 1972, I was becoming weary of the politics of the state hospital and started to think of other possibilities for work. My early enthusiasm for teaching returned as I believed that I had something to teach. As a doctoral student, with most of my course work behind me, teaching at college level seemed feasible. After several interviews, I was offered a full-time position at Seton Hill, a Catholic liberal arts women's college (now a university) in Greensburg, Pennsylvania. My initial thought was that I would try my hand at teaching for a couple of years. Aside from a post-doctoral internship (1978 to 1979) I have been teaching ever since.

In some ways Seton Hill was the hardest job I have ever had. Teaching four courses a semester, when some of them are courses you have never taken, and when your prior teaching experience is minimal, is demanding. For the first two years I worked about seventy hours a week, while also taking classes and working on my dissertation. But I was also very fortunate. The Sisters of Charity who ran the college were, in fact, quite charitable. Sr. Maurice

McManama, the chair of the psychology department, had reservations about phenomenology and, I suspect, about some of my teaching methods, and yet she was both appreciative and patient. Sr. Colette Toler, the academic dean, was incredibly supportive of faculty and became a dear friend over the years. Again, as in my early experience of schools in Canada, the kindness of those around me made a critical difference. The initial verdict on whether I was a good teacher was mixed, but after several years at Seton Hill, I was doing well overall, and I was starting to think of myself as a college teacher. I think back on Seton Hill and the faculty and students I met there with a strong sense of appreciation and gratitude.

In 1976, Amedeo Giorgi let me know of an opening at Seattle University, a Jesuit university where the chair, George Kunz, was planning to start a master's program in phenomenological psychology. The defense of my dissertation was close at hand, and the prospect of being involved in the development of a graduate program was very enticing, especially for someone who was just beginning his academic career. I was fortunate enough to be hired, contingent upon my having defended my dissertation before my contract started.

That I was able to complete my dissertation at this point was due to my own commitment to and passion for the topic that I was working on, but also in large measure to the members of my dissertation committee. Rolf von Eckartsberg, my chair, encouraged me to develop my own thinking while providing as much direction as I needed, and Frank Buckley, a true humanist and a wonderful friend, was truly supportive of me and my interests. Amedeo Giorgi, who is especially known for his work in the theory and methodology of phenomenological psychology, helped me to be more organized in my presentation. Along with many others, I was deeply saddened by the untimely deaths of Frank in 1982 and Rolf in 1993.

It was difficult to leave Seton Hill and my friends and colleagues in Pennsylvania, and also to move so far away from Toronto as my parents were getting older. Moreover, as I drove west the day after I successfully defended my dissertation, I wondered if I, like Don Quixote, was following an impossible dream; perhaps the idea of developing a graduate program in phenomenological psychology was unrealistic.

Seattle University did become my academic home. But that this was going to be the outcome was not so clear during my first few years there. The weeks upon weeks of overcast days and drizzle during the winter reminded me all too much of Copenhagen and I found, as have most other "immigrants" to Seattle, that making friends there is a slow process. On the other hand, my colleagues in the psychology department were collegial and there was strong interest in phenomenology among members of the philosophy department. I became involved in Matteo Ricci College, a new unit within the university that used an interdisciplinary approach to education, and had the opportunity to team teach, first with a philosopher and then a member of the English department.

An important impetus to my scholarly development came from outside the university. I was accepted into a National Endowment for the Humanities seminar on Sociology, Psychology, and Literature with Robert N. Wilson at the University of North Carolina, Chapel Hill, for the summer of 1977. We read and discussed the works of Hemingway, O'Neill, Samuel Beckett, John Barth and F. Scott Fitzgerald, among others. I had less background in literature than anyone else in this group, but once I got past feeling intimidated, this seminar provided me with a wonderful opportunity to enter the world of the creative imagination. It was also a delightful summer of reading, reflection, good conversation, and companionship. Robert Wilson encouraged us to pursue our own interests in relationship to the seminar, and I chose to work on "Eugene O'Neill's Understanding of Forgiveness" as my paper for the seminar, a revised version of which was published two years later (Halling, 1979).

My interest in forgiveness was based on an experience from the previous summer. I had become involved in a relationship that ended on a sour note, and I felt both angry and hurt, and was struggling, with little success, to come to terms with my very mixed emotions toward the woman with whom I had been involved. One summer evening I went for a walk and everything changed, at least for the moment. I wrote about this event some years later:

> My anger and hurt vanished as I was thinking about her, but this time as another human being who was struggling, and who basically did not mean me any harm. It is not accurate, I am realizing, to suggest that I just thought that; it was more like an image that emerged for me, an image that was not so much seen as felt. I felt healed, blame and anger vanished, and there was a larger dimension of this whole experience that I can only describe in religious language: a sense of transcendence, of the future opening up, of a sense of presence, not of a personal being, but of being connected to something larger than oneself and yet still having an experience of myself as me (Unpublished).

This first study of forgiveness led to a number of others over the next few years. One of the greatest benefits of being an academic is that one can study (at least in some departments and some universities) the topics that are closest to one's own heart and mind.

Back at Seattle University, a small group of us continued to work on making the master's program a reality. In late 1978, while I was away doing a post-doctoral internship at the Reading Medical Center in Pennsylvania, our group submitted a grant proposal to NEH. This proposal, for a pilot study for the MA program, was funded. At the federal level, psychology is defined as a natural science, but we were able to persuade NEH that phenomenological psychology was much closer to the humanities.

When I returned from Reading in 1979, I became the director of the pilot study, which allowed us to develop a curriculum, test out specific courses, get input from outside consultants on our conception of the program, and prepare to submit a proposal to the university. The graduate program was approved in 1980, and accepted its first students in 1981. Lane Gerber, who came to Seattle University in 1980, became the director of the graduate program. As the program developed, we developed a strong community in the department that provided support for our teaching and developing scholarship.

There was another significant change in my life around that time. In 1979, I married Mical Goldfarb. Mical, who was initially trained as a rehabilitation counselor, became a psychotherapist and a Focusing trainer. Focusing is an approach to personal growth and psychotherapy developed by Eugene Gendlin, a philosopher and psychotherapist. Mical and I learned a lot from each other over the years; she is a fine writer, and we co-authored several articles. One of the issues that we wrote about, and that has informed my subsequent work, is the relationship between experience and language, especially as presented in Gendlin's work (Halling and Goldfarb, 1991). While I have never been trained in Focusing, the basic philosophy behind it has informed my therapeutic work, teaching, and scholarship.

In 1984, my colleague Jan Rowe and I discovered that we were both interested in the topic of forgiveness. This discovery set us on the road to working together with small groups of graduate students for the next 20 years. Along with four very talented graduate students we decided to study the experience of forgiving another, and we proceeded to review the existing literature, write our own descriptions, and then interview people about their experiences. Our approach was informed by the phenomenological methods developed at Duquesne as well as the qualitative methods used by other researchers. We presented our findings at the International Human Science Research Conference at the University of Alberta, Edmonton, in summer of 1985, and published our study four years later (Rowe *et al.*, 1989). What we found was very much in line with what my own experience in 1976 had indicated. Forgiving another involves a healing of the self, a realization of the humanity of the other, a restoration of one's sense of being at home in the world, and the opening up of one's future. Since 1993, I have taught psychology of forgiveness as an undergraduate course, drawing extensively on our research. Seattle University is, as far as I know, the first university in North America to offer such a course.

As Jan and I reflected on the path we had taken with this first group of students, we realized that we had "invented" a new method that we called *dialogal phenomenology*. It is difficult to explain it in a few words; it certainly took us some time before we were able to articulate the essential dimensions of this approach (e.g., Halling and Leifer, 1991). My own understanding of it increased as I taught a graduate course at Duquesne University in the summer of 1987 and introduced the students to this method. In a recent publication on the experience of despair, we discussed how this method has dialogue at its core: among the researchers and between the researchers and the phenomenon. The direction of the research also arises out of dialogue and thus, in contrast to other methods, does not entail following predefined steps (Beck *et al.*, 2003).

Encouraged by the success of the first project, we subsequently started another group, on the elusive topic of self-forgiveness (Bauer *et al.*, 1992). In the summer of 2001, I approached Jan and asked if she might be interested in working on the topic of despair, a topic that became all too timely after the terrorist attacks on 9/11. Forgiveness is a topic that inspires people, whereas despair is a topic that we tend to avoid thinking or talking about. This time, again, four graduate students who were mature and thoughtful joined us. They endured the uncertainty and distress that is involved in using an open-ended method, especially when applied to a painful subject. As in the earlier studies, we started by sharing descriptions of our own experience with the phenomenon in order to ground ourselves in the reality we were studying and in order to identify some of the assumptions we brought to the research. We enjoyed our work together so much that after completing our first study on the experience of despair in everyday life (Beck *et al.*, 2003), we decided to continue for a second year. Having looked at what it is like for people to be in despair, we interviewed psychotherapists to find out how they dealt with this experience as it came up in their work with clients (Beck *et al.*, 2005). Both studies pointed to how despair, which often leaves us without words, can best be described in metaphors. We found that the presence of another can help to

ence appears, it talks back" (p.294). As experience has talked back I have made changes to take into account what I have heard and felt. At the end of this process, the feeling that predominates for me is one of gratitude. I am grateful for my friends and family, for my life with Kathryn, and for the multitude of people who have inspired and supported me during the past six decades. I am also grateful for the moments of grace in my life, the most influential of which I have attempted to describe here.

At the same time, there is much in human life and human history that is horrifying and, in my mind, largely incomprehensible. Yes, psychologists and other social and human scientists have made, and will continue to make, important contributions to our understanding of human beings. But I believe we can only rise above the "fray" in an incomplete and momentary way. Nonetheless, we also can take satisfaction in the value of our work insofar as it informs people's lives, helps to improve public policy, and heightens our appreciation of the gift of our humanity.

References

Bauer, L., Duffy, J., Fountain, E., Halling, S., Holzer, M., Jones, E., Leifer, M. and Row, J.O. (1992) "Exploring self-forgiveness. A dialogal research approach." *Journal of Religion and Health 31*, 2, 149–160.

Beck, B., Halling, S., McNabb, M., Miller, D., Rowe, J.O. and Schulz, J. (2003) "Facing up to hopelessness: A dialogal research approach." *Journal of Religion and Health 42*, 4, 339–354.

Beck, B., Halling, S., McNabb, M., Miller, D., Rowe, J.O. and Schulz, J. (2005) "On navigating despair: Reports from psychotherapists." *Journal of Religion and Health, 44*, 2, 187–205.

Gendlin, E.T. (1973) "Experiential phenomenology." In M. Natanson (ed) *Phenomenology and the Social Sciences*. Evanston, IL: Northwestern University Press.

Giorgi, A.P. (1970) *Psychology as a Human Science*. New York: Harper and Row.

Halling, S. (1975) "The implications of Emmanuel Levinas' *Totality and Infinity* for therapy." In A. Giorgi, C.T. Fischer and E.L. Murray (eds) *Duquesne Studies in Phenomenological Psychology*, Vol. 2. Pittsburgh, PA: Duquesne University Press.

Halling, S. (1976) "The recognition of a significant other as a unique person: An empirical phenomenological investigation." Doctoral dissertation, Duquesne University.

Halling, S. (1979) "Eugene O'Neill's understanding of forgiveness." In A. Giorgi, R. Knowles and D.L. Smith (eds) *Duquesne Studies in Phenomenological Psychology*, Vol. 3. Pittsburgh, PA: Duquesne University Press.

Halling, S. (1983) "Seeing a Significant Other 'As if for the First Time'" In A. Giorgi, A. Barton and C. Maes (eds) *Duquesne Studies in Phenomenological Psychology, Vol.3*. Pittsburgh, PA: Duquesne University Press.

Halling, S. (1997) "Truth in the context of relationship: The researcher as witness." In *Phenomenology and Narrative Psychology: The Fourteenth Annual Symposium of the Simon Silverman Phenomenology Center*. Pittsburgh, PA: Simon Silverman Phenomenology Center.

Halling, S. (2000) "Meaning beyond 'heroic illusions'? Transcendence in everyday life." *Journal of Religion and Health 39*, 2, 143–157.

Halling, S. and Dearborn Nill, J. (1989) "Demystifying psychopathology: Understanding disturbed behavior." In R.S. Valle and S. Halling (eds) *Existential–Phenomenological Perspectives in Psychology*. New York: Plenum.

Halling S. and Goldfarb, M. (2001) "Grounding truth in the body: Therapy and research renewed." *Humanistic Psychologist 19*, 3, 313–330.

Halling, S. and Lawrence, C. (1999) "Social constructionism: Homogenizing the world, negating embodied experience." *Journal of Theoretical and Philosophical Psychology 19*, 1, 78–89.

Halling, S. and Leifer, M. (1991) "The theory and practice of dialogal phenomenology." *Journal of Phenomenological Psychology 1*, 1, 1–15.

Laing, R.D. (1965) *The Divided Self.* Harmondsworth: Penguin.

Levinas, E. (1969) *Totality and Infinity*, trans A. Lingis. Pittsburgh, PA: Duquesne University Press.

Maslow, A.H. (1962) "Lessons from the peak experiences." *Journal of Humanistic Psychology 2*, 9–18.

Merleau-Ponty, M. (1964) "The philosopher and sociology." In *Signs*, trans R.C. McLeary. Evanston, IL: Northwestern University Press.

Rowe, J.O., Halling, S., Davies, E., Leifer, M., Powers, D. and van Bronkhorst, J. (1989) "The psychology of forgiving another: A dialogal research approach." In R.S. Valle and S. Halling (eds) *Existential–Phenomenological Perspectives in Psychology*. New York: Plenum.

Scheler, M. (1970) *The Nature of Sympathy*. Hamden, CT: Archon Books.

CHAPTER 12

Life Reflections of a Nomadic Subject

Tod Sloan

As a person trained in a field known as the "study of lives," which relies primarily on the analysis of autobiographical narratives gathered through depth interviews, I find it no simple matter to plunge into this task of intellectual autobiography. In the process of conducting the life history interviews for my doctoral dissertation and the book *Self-Deception in Life Choices* (Sloan, 1986), I learned that we can tell many different and often contradictory stories about the dilemmas and decisions that shape the course of our lives. Two years on the psychoanalytic couch in my late twenties convinced me that I was certainly no exception to the rule. The version of my story I might tell today for publication would be quite different from the one I would tell tomorrow to a new friend. This is not a problem. It is just a recognition of the slippery relation between the accounts we give and the "objective" time/space positions and actions of our bodies in relation to other bodies and places. Ideological processes saturate our self-stories extensively, which makes them interesting as cultural artifacts, but not especially useful if one aspires to objectivity. I believe ideology and reflexive subjectivity are related as a stormy ocean to a small boat. Only occasionally do the seas lift our boats high enough to glimpse how far we are from shore and then we are plunged into the trough again, pushed around by currents and swells over which we have little control.

This prelude is designed to account for why I might have trouble with questions about my identity and why it is difficult to answer questions suggested by the editors of this volume such as: "Who is Tod Sloan? What motivates him to do the work that he does in critical psychology?" I nevertheless believe it is important to give accounts of ourselves and have appreciated accounts given by others, so I accepted the editors' invitation without much hesitation.

The editors had seen my introductory biographical comments in *Critical Psychology: Voices for Change* and asked me to elaborate on them in response to a series of very thought provoking questions. So, to launch a new version of my account, I reproduce that text here and will refer to it as I try to give a fuller account:

> I suppose the beginnings of my critical bent could be found in the fact that my father's work took my family all over the world during my childhood, especially to Asia. These travels helped me see that there are different ways of organizing societies, with immense consequences for the well-being of their citizens, and also left me feeling quite alienated from my "own" culture in the USA, since I kept returning to it as an outsider every few years. Added to this was an element in my mother's faith, Mormonism, which spoke of the primitive communism and simple living practiced by the pioneers who crossed the North American plains to Utah. As a teenager, I wondered why the Mormons hadn't continued that noble experiment rather than sliding into individualistic and consumerist lifestyles. During high school, in late 1960s California, I witnessed from a distance the anti-war protests on campuses and in the streets, and learned vicariously that even if it is hard to change the order of things, one nevertheless has an ethical duty to speak out and work for change.
>
> I started college with the strange idea that I was supposed to be an engineer, but I gradually drifted toward the idea of helping people more directly (employing that common projective device that allows one to focus on how others need help when it is actually oneself who is feeling that need). As I saw it, clinical and counseling psychology offered the most obvious forms for helping individuals. I had received no political socialization to speak of, so I was unable to consider politics or law as possible paths, nor to imagine solutions beyond the individual level. So, I swallowed the standard psychology curriculum with glee and occasional boredom (in social psychology and experimental psychology in particular). I found myself especially attracted to personality theory, especially the existentialist versions, in part as a replacement for my rapidly crumbling religious worldview, but also because of their emphasis on human possibilities and agency. I wondered why more people were not able to explore their options and choose alternative modes of selfhood. But most of the answers to my questions, I now understand, were not to be found in psychology per se. Meanwhile, the

research training I received as an undergraduate left me cold. Not only were the questions addressed not very central to real problems in living, but it was also clear that the data could be used to buttress anyone's favorite idea. There was also very little one could point to as accumulated knowledge, especially in social and personality psychology. The field felt more like an ever-growing pile of concepts, with a bit of attached empirical support for each. This bothered me especially in my favorite subfield, personality theory. Chapter after chapter in the textbooks – on Freud, Jung, Maslow, Bandura, etc. – laid out a model and provided pieces of evidence for it. Textbook authors usually pointed to the strengths and weaknesses of theories as well as a review of the evidence for them, but something essential was missing. That something essential was the angle I would come to recognize as *ideology criticism*. But it would take me a few more years before I found that angle.

My first introduction to the practice of critique related to ideology criticism was during my doctoral studies at the University of Michigan in George Rosenwald's (cf. Rosenwald and Ochberg, 1992) course on personality theory in 1975. For the first time in my educational experience, I was asked to evaluate various core concepts in psychology on grounds other than empirical evidence. In the seminar, we examined ethical, political, practical, and aesthetic aspects of basic concepts like development, learning, identity, and were introduced to the emerging interdisciplinary *human science* perspective. I found this practice of *critique* very difficult because I had been taught to accept published facts, concepts, and constructs as established once and for all.

During the next few years, I began training as a psychotherapist and became increasingly aware of the critical potential of psychoanalytic theory and the practice of psychoanalysis. I suppose I might have even gone on to become a psychoanalytically-oriented psychotherapist had it not been for a fateful encounter with critical social theory, particularly the Frankfurt school, to which I was introduced by fellow graduate students, Randy Earnest and Gary Gregg. Earnest had come over to psychology from political science in order to do psychoanalytically-informed studies of ideology (cf. Earnest, 1992). Gregg had been reading widely in the anthropology of the self and brought a strong cultural and social class analysis to personality research (cf. Gregg, 1991). We were all doing dissertations based on depth-interviews, so we met to listen to interview tapes and to discuss our readings of Adorno, Foucault, Habermas, Deleuze and Guattari, and others. Gradually, I began to see the utter necessity of ideology criticism. For example, I had been infatuated with Heidegger for some time, especially with his concept of authenticity. While interviewing research participants about what they meant by authenticity as they made important life choices (cf. Sloan, 1996b), I ran across Adorno's *The Jargon of Authenticity* (1973). I finally understood that ideology is more than a set of values that keep us a bit off-track as we go through life. I glimpsed how profoundly social systems produce individual character structures and ideational patterns in a manner that makes it very difficult to imagine that a social order might be arranged in a less exploitative or oppressive manner. The concept of ideology, defined in this *critical* manner, became a compass for all my subsequent work, since it provided not only the method – ideology criticism – but also the purpose that was missing in the psychology I had previously encountered. That purpose is *to challenge and confront ideological processes and the unjust social orders that they sustain.*

At another point during my doctoral work, another Michigan faculty member, Barnaby Barratt, was extremely influential. Barratt was working out a critical epistemology for psychoanalysis (cf. Barratt, 1984, 1993) and required his students (in a Psychology course!) to wade through large chunks of Hegel, Husserl, Lévi-Strauss, Heidegger, and Lacan. My discussions with Barratt reinforced my interest in the connection between Adorno's negative dialectics and psychoanalysis. I have yet to find a combination that works as well as a basis for ideology criticism, although I sense that others get to roughly the same place through Foucault or Derrida (or even Lacan plus Marx and Hegel, as in the case of the Slovenian scholar Zizek).

Since those heady days, the question has been how to put these insights into practice. After finishing my PhD, I took a position as a psychology professor in Tulsa, Oklahoma, which cut me off from the progressive urban centers in the United States. I wandered for quite awhile. I did some local disarmament organizing, published a few articles on critical personality theory, and, looking for inspiration, traveled to meet Marxist theorists Lucien Sève, Gerard Mendel, and Slavoj Zizek in Paris and Klaus Holzkamp in Berlin. A bit later, in the mid-1980s, there was some obvious political work to do when Reagan's CIA was hurling the Contras against the fledgling socialist Sandinistas. That experience prompted a phase of work in which I tried to examine possible progressive roles for psychologists in the Third World (cf. Sloan and Montero, 1990). To make a long story short, I concluded that there is very little to be done as long as we continue to work within the framework of what is known as scientific psychology. There is, however, an immense challenge awaiting anyone who wants to work in solidarity with Third World struggles for democracy, human rights, and economic justice.

Over the past decade, I have been trying to learn from Latin American scholar/activists in social and community psychologists. I was fortunate to meet and learn from the examples of Ignacio Martín-Baró, the social psychologist who was assasinated by US-trained Salvadoran troops in 1989; Maritza Montero, in Venezuela, who exemplifies scholarly and socially committed community psychology; Ignacio Dobles and his colleagues in Costa Rica who deal with scarce resources and logistical nightmares to conduct psychosocial action research that really makes a difference for communities and influences public policy; and Elizabeth Lira and her associates in Chile who work tirelessly to develop psychological theory and practice that address the collective and individual suffering caused by state terrorism, torture, disappearances, and other human rights violations.

My Latin American colleagues have awakened me from a slumber induced by the relative comforts of academia and the absence of a vigorous progressive movement in the USA and helped me see that carrying critical psychology through to its practical implications is more a matter of courage and commitment than a matter of having obvious opportunities for action. Oppression and injustice are all around us, within a mile or two of our universities and clinics as well as in remote corners of the globe. (Sloan, 2000, pp.xxii–xxvi)

Now, five years after writing this account, I will try to tackle the questions offered by the editors of this volume in response to it. It is worth noting first, however, that in 2001 I resigned from my position as chair and professor of psychology at the University of Tulsa, where I had worked for 19 years, and set off to find work in the field of international development, particularly in poverty eradication through psychosocial and participatory interventions. Shortly after I arrived in Washington, DC to look for work along those lines, the attacks of September 11, 2001 occurred, funding for international development work shifted toward military and security efforts in the United States, and I did not find work. Through a fortunate connection, I was invited to start working part time as national co-coordinator of Psychologists for Social Responsibility in the fall of 2001. Since 1982, PsySR had been mobilizing psychologists to "build a culture of peace with social justice," especially in relation to nuclear weapons issues. This work took me to many campuses and cities across the US to help organize psychologists interested in political action. We have held several important conferences and accomplished quite a bit with scarce resources, but after I reached the limits of several credit cards, I began to look again for an academic position that would afford plenty of space of community organizing and social action. I fortunately encountered that position as chair of the department of counseling psychology in the graduate school of education at Lewis and Clark College in Portland, Oregon and began there in the summer of 2004.

Who is Tod Sloan? What motivates the work that you do in critical psychology?

I see both identity and motivation as potentially misleading concepts. Answers to questions about identity tend to be ideological, in the sense that we try to be consistent with affirmations about our identities, which reflect the intertwining of socialization, enculturation, and life history. The task is thus to dislodge facile identity proclamations, and expose contradictions, not in a quest for consistency, but for fuller appreciation of complex subjectivity. The same goes for motivations. I can nevertheless say that I prefer to think of personhood (identity, if you will) as an ensemble of projects/relations in various stages of development in different life spheres. To be as frank as possible, my projects connected to critical psychology draw on energies from deep friendships, aesthetic preferences in the intellectual realm, disappointment with the poverty of imagination in scientistic psychology in the United States, Oedipal impulses that inspire rebellion here and loyalty there, and narcissistic gratification from standing apart from the crowd in what I judge to be a more tenable discursive space. Having said this, I work for the advancement of critical psychology as a way of transforming the discipline of psychology from within, while not identifying with it, and from without, by bringing the values and perspectives of critical social theory to bear on the field. The point is to end psychology's collusion with corporate consumerist ideology and augment psychology's capacity to work as a de-ideologizing and de-colonizing force in the global struggle for social justice.

Partly because of my characterological mix of obsessive and impulsive tendencies, I have long been fascinated by the difficulty of teasing out sublimation from "acting out." When are our projects so overdetermined by unconscious motives that our conscious reasons are primarily untruths? How much should one worry about this dimension of living as opposed to, for example, the practical effects of one's actions, regardless of motives?

I tend to use the concept of ideology to begin to think this through, so we can turn to the editors' next questions.

Define ideology. What is it about mainstream psychology that does not allow for ideology criticism?
I prefer to employ the critical notion of ideology, as elaborated by Thompson (1984), as a system of practices and associated representations that sustain social relations of domination. It is pointless to use the term ideology if any and all representations or practices are deemed to be ideological. I understand that this is problematic for those who want to emphasize that no discursive position can be free of ideology. For strategic reasons, I think it is important to point to practices of de-ideologization, in which greater *intersubjectivity*, fuller participation, and deeper democracy can challenge and transform social relations of domination. Ideology criticism is the practice of engagement with and against ideological processes in efforts to expose how certain practices and discourses collude with racist, sexist, classist, and other oppressive social relations, with the aim of restoring power to those who have been subjected to domination. With this power, we can then practice alternative, less exploitative forms of decision making and action.

Mainstream psychology has not glimpsed the effects of ideology or the possibilities of ideology criticism because its objectivistic epistemology sees rational action as deriving from access to scientific knowledge. The scientific knowledge that mainstream psychology generates is itself produced within the ideologically constrained frames of individualism, objectivism, and neo-liberal political economics. It is thus unlikely to perceive how these frames guide assumptions about the causes of behavior and deflect attention from the underlying imperatives of corporate capitalist social relations. Ideology criticism thus does not imply, for example, providing data on the correlates of racial prejudice.

It is fairly clear to me that the system's rewards have made life comfortable for psychology professors who stay within liberal as opposed to radical frameworks. There are of course exceptions, but in general processes of editorial review and tenure/promotion decisions within APA-oriented departments exert a constraining effect.

What is scientific psychology? Does it occlude the necessary political work that you envision as necessary in the field of psychology?
By scientific psychology, I mean the set of concepts and practices that psychologists have developed as part of the science of human behavior. They begin by assuming that human action is lawful and that these laws can be discovered by observing and measuring patterns of association and cause and effect among human acts. The model underlying this approach is clearly that

of Newtonian physics. No acknowledgment is made of our ability to reflect on our actions, construct meanings, expand our horizons of understanding through dialogue, and so forth. Because of this, "evidence-based" interventions designed to change behavior patterns approach the individual as an object whose features (whether cognitions or behaviors) are to be manipulated by an outside, objective observer. I agree with Nicholas Rose (1985) that all this must be seen as the operating system of the vast psy-complex, an extension of the military-industrial-corporate complex of capitalist modernity. My book *Damaged Life* (1996a) attempts to lay out the psychosocial effects of this "colonization of the lifeworld," following Habermas's (1984) beautiful synthesis of Marx, Weber and Durkheim.

So, yes, scientific psychology is an expression of the ideology of scientism. When I hear terms like objectivity and value-neutrality used to justify certain practices, I tend to interpret them as masks for the interests of those who defend the socially unjust status quo.

Define critical psychology
I have come to see critical psychology as a critique of scientism and instrumentalist colonization of human action and as the expression within academic psychology of the contemporary global movement for human rights and social justice. Critical psychology coalesced in various places at different times (e.g., Berlin, London, Manchester, Ontario, El Salvador, Sydney) in response to currents that conjoined arrays of socialist, feminist, anti-racist, or anti-imperialist organizing with critiques of psychology's ideological complicity or strategic neutrality in these struggles. I was initially not especially conscious of the effects on critical psychology of the currents set up by social movements and political struggles of our times. I became more aware of how they connect with psychology and psychologists only when I stepped outside of academia a few years ago and traveled widely in the US attempting to organize psychologists for political work. In the United States, the attention of the few critical psychologists is only recently turning from critiques of the discipline to the task of developing radical forms of psychosocial praxis in light of critiques such as Fox and Prilleltensky's (1997) *Critical Psychology: An Introduction*. Many psychologists have been active in political movements in the US, but they have tended to apply mainstream psychology concepts and practices in their work (see the projects organized by Psychologists for Social Responsibility since 1982 at www.psysr.org).

What is it about critical psychology that offers you insight into the ideological and structural workings of an unjust world?
Most of the tools in the repertoires of critical psychologists are imported from other fields: psychoanalytic interpretation, discourse analysis, participant observation, ideology criticism, action research, and community organizing. These all have in common an interdisciplinary mixture of concepts or methods that afford a cultural, economic, historical or political perspective on the subjective processes to which psychologists regularly have access in clinical settings or research interviews. Among critical psychologists in the United States, there have been few chances for discussion about which of several contemporary epistemological or methodological frameworks might be most fruitful. Even the basic work of critique around the world has been done from many different angles, the most prominent probably being a blending of psychoanalytic feminism and poststructuralism. My point, in answer to this question, is that to the extent that critical psychology affords insights into social injustice it is due to our attempts to integrate the lessons of critical social theory in general. In North American critical psychology, most of the work lies ahead. We need to develop and share practices that move beyond academic exercises and begin to deliver on the promise of direct engagement in social transformation.

Does critical psychology offer a theory of the self? If so, how do you see your identity through this lens?
I have relied on a psychoanalytic Marxist view of self or personality amplified by postmodern considerations about the role of discourse in structuring available subject-positions. In others words, in relations with others over the years we develop fairly fixed modes of organizing affect, ideation, action and these modes can be seen as ideological structures in that they tend to play a part in sustaining social relations of domination (Sloan, 1997). These structures of "character" are later mediated by social and discursive relations that either reinforce ideological functions or negate them through the resymbolizing effects of intersubjectivity.

A bunch of jargon, right? I will try to explain this using a personal example. My socialization in a conservative American religion left me overly deferent to authority figures, but also critical of authority when it is wielded selfishly or abusively. Many local Mormon church leaders who taught me were grumpy, self-righteous men. This, combined with the dynamics of my own family, produced a character structure primed to interpret life scenes as being about being "good" or rebelling. The "compromise" position was to rebel indirectly or passive-aggressively. As I moved into my years at Brigham Young University and while serving as a missionary, I bent rules, associated with young men more directly rebellious than I, slacked in my church work, helped organize a magazine critical of church authorities, and so forth. I now see this compromise position as itself ideological. It permitted me to remain within the sphere of the church's authority and surveillance (through yearly counseling and confession sessions), but afforded room for partial gratification of my resentment about prohibitions on pleasure through minor indirect rebellion. Once the church's authority system became emotionally irrelevant to me in early graduate school, I ignored the rules entirely and was excommunicated for living with a woman to whom I was not married. I did not bother to attend the "trial."

That ideological structure of character persisted and found new scenes in which to play itself out, but in forms mediated by more complex self-reflection and dialogue with others. My choice of philosophical rather than scientific approaches within psychology reflected continuing issues with authority (many professors of the scientific bent were cranky and self-important). My mentor, George Rosenwald, supported philosophically minded graduate students and the study group I had with Gregg and Earnest, in association with Barratt, clearly served as a symbolic space for planning rebellious forms of critical psychology. Obviously, at the intellectual level we were convinced that we were on a better track and that those holding to the mainstream were deluded or coopted, but our critiques were energized by our diverse issues with paternal authority. The ideological apparatus functioned perfectly, however, to sideline our efforts to transform academic psychology. I took a job as a professor in a remote place and became isolated from other critical psychology projects. My comrades all soon left academia. It was not until ten years later that I was able to connect effectively with various strands of the international critical psychology movement. We now spend a lot of time reflecting on how to ensure that our "rebellious" projects are effective and not just forms of acting out that will be accorded space within the ideological system as a means of defusing their impact.

Explain how you enact the theory behind critical psychology? What is the material political content of your critical psychological praxis?
I sense that it has taken me 20 years to position myself to add material content to my critical psychological praxis. My critical-theoretical work (books and articles, presentations) has a certain materiality, of course, but it has mostly been promissory. My new academic position provides an ideal space for

beginning to realize the vision I have been developing. (More on this later.) Up until now, as a teacher, mentor, and organizer, I have emphasized dialogue, discussion, and self-reflection. I am uncomfortable speaking from the place of the "father who knows best." In my community consulting work, I avoid the position of the expert and simply try to participate as a co-worker in the improvement of program effectiveness. As chair of a psychology department, I emphasized democratic process and consensus decision making in a department that had had little practice with either.

What are the ethical and political implications of having chosen the self that you have chosen?
I understand that forms of selfhood are in a sense "chosen," but I prefer to see them as overdetermined. This does not mean that they are not mutable. Choosing a self is not like plotting a course on a map and then driving there. For me, it is like leaning in a general direction and hoping that shifts of underlying structure or position happen, and then being surprised when new capacities emerge. I do feel some strong ethical and political obligations and contradictions in association with the self I have become. Many of these are problematic because they feel too linked to character/ideological urges. For example, I feel uncomfortable with middle-class American consumption patterns, for all the obvious reasons. But I try to make sure I have a good sound system, television, and personal computer. For the last few years, I was relatively homeless and downsized extensively. I also went into debt as I self-financed work with PsySR and travel for organizing purposes. This lifestyle pattern was inconvenient and interfered with my effectiveness. Recently, as I began to set up a new living space in Portland, I was torn between taking advantage of inexpensive communal living opportunities or setting up a cool loft-type apartment of my own downtown. I opted for the latter after bargaining with myself about how I could avoid using a car and be more effective in my psychopolitical work from a more comfortable and ego-gratifying homebase. (I also planned to spend some time reflecting with colleagues and friends about how to deal with bourgeois guilt in the 21st century.)

Following on what I said earlier, I feel an obligation to work through remaining personal/ideological issues around authority and leadership, especially since I am again in an administrative position. My new colleagues and I are interested in exploring modes of shared leadership on campus and ways of connecting the department's work more effectively to disadvantaged communities, locally and internationally. Doing this well is going to require extensive collaborative work with people in powerful positions outside academia who control resources that are essential for building social justice. I feel a broadening of my sphere of action as time goes by and a clearer sense of what battles need to be fought and where. The battle for the hearts and minds of psychology is of much less interest to me now than the struggle for economic democracy and the eradication of global poverty. Given who I have been and what I know, my task now is to construct critical practice in the space between graduate psychology training and the global social justice movement.

If the self is an ideological construction, what makes the self that you have become (since critical psychology) any less ideological?
I hear this question often from people who have been reading Foucault and/or postmodern perspectives on the self. I prefer to believe that critique spawns important movements *away from* ideological positions and that actions related to these should not be called equally ideological. I recently read Badiou (2002) and found his call to be faithful to one's truth quite compelling. A "truth" would consist of intuitions that emerge as critique negates ideology, decentering identities and calling affirmative discourses into question. Rather than speak of an ideological self, I would prefer to counterpose ideological processes to intersubjectivity, by which I mean the expansion of horizons of understanding and action through deep dialogue and critical self-reflection.

In your introduction to Critical Psychology: Voices for Change *you state: "One nevertheless has an ethical duty to speak out and work toward change." What is the source of this "ethical duty"?*
Apart from a vague sense of the importance of prophetic voices in the Judeo-Christian tradition, I was especially struck by the example of the social psychologist and Jesuit priest Ignacio Martín-Baró, whom I met in 1985 and with whom I collaborated on several small projects. He served as a voice for the poor of El Salvador. Given the reach of the death squads there, he knew he was taking risks every time he spoke out against US support for the right-wing government or advocated peace talks with the guerrilla forces. He also conducted objective public opinion surveys to inform the country about the people's wishes. When he and his colleagues at the Universidad Centroamericana were assassinated in November 1989, six articulate voices for millions of struggling Salvadorans were silenced. Like a slap in the face, I woke up and understood how basic human rights such as freedom of speech, of the press, and assembly – that I had taken for granted and rarely used – must

be defended vigorously by all who seek to end oppression. Those who *can* speak and organize for social justice have an obligation to do so simply because they would be complicit with oppressors if they do not.

Where did your desire to help people stem from?
Briefly: my mother knew she was dying from the tumor in her brain. She continued to raise her children cheerfully and selflessly. My father spent his professional life quietly working to build a world with less poverty and more democracy. I know that I have been given much, led a privileged life, was educated at public expense. I don't know how it works psychologically, but I feel a compulsion to do work that contributes to the betterment of society. I originally defined this in individualistic terms and sought training in counseling and therapy. I later understood the need to work at the level of institutions and social systems affecting larger communities.

Again, in your introduction you mention that your religious worldview was crumbling. Would you describe yourself as "religious"? Do you see any ways that you might combine the revolutionary spirit embedded in certain ways of religiously being-in-the-world with your critical psychological approach?
I would say that I was more brainwashed than religious. I never had an intellectually elaborated or emotionally strong faith in a supreme being. My Mormon beliefs were easily supplanted by the more interesting and realistic frameworks I found when I started studying existentialism in late adolescence. I have been comfortably atheistic for 30 years. I understand that many people find it meaningful to employ a language of spirituality grounded in religious traditions and I think it is important to ally with them in the social justice work. I do occasionally wish that I had the willpower to develop a spiritual discipline such as Zen, and I may do so yet, but I have only dabbled in such things so far. (I could say the same for my lack of discipline with regard to practicing musical instruments.) From what I have seen in others, such practices can strengthen resolve, focus one's efforts on the essential tasks and augment agency, so they are indeed potentially revolutionary.

What keeps people from envisioning other forms of selfhood?
I have wondered about this a bit and even worked with a very dedicated doctoral student, Caroline Pyevich, who interviewed people who had managed to make radical lifestyle changes. One thing she found is that lifestyle changes were often associated with traumatic incidents or other suffering. For example, a couple who lost all their possessions in a fire adopted

a lifestyle of voluntary simplicity. Probably the main thing that loosened up my own sense of possible selves was living in several different cultural contexts while growing up. This does not mean that I am flexible about how I can live. I struggle to consider my objective options fully as much as anyone else.

Talk about the origin of your political consciousness.
My political consciousness is still fairly shallow compared to some lifelong leftist activists I have met. But to the extent that I am conscious about political dimensions of life, I would mark the beginnings of this in college when I was allowed, in my final year, to prepare and teach a six-session seminar on American utopian experiments. The idea for that must have come out of occasional references in Mormon history to early attempts to hold property in common. I was curious what other groups had tried to solve the problem of inequality. When I later found fellow graduate students working seriously to usher in economic democracy around the world, it rang a bell and critical social theory became the framework for my worldview.

What keeps you from becoming seduced by dominant forms of ideology that inculcate forms of false consciousness?
I am sure that I have been seduced in many ways. It is mostly in dialogue with others who are also questioning that I discover where I need to rethink things. In turn, I find that I try to raise questions about how we live and about what is happening around the world whenever I get the chance. I am not very good at small talk.

What exactly was it about Heidegger's discussion of authenticity that was so attractive to you? What was it about Adorno's work that shifted you away from Heidegger's language of authenticity?
Speaking of small talk, I remember being struck by Heidegger's idea that we all tend to get caught up in the idle chatter of society and become inauthentic in the sense that this makes us closed to all the possibilities of life. He suggested that a deep awareness of our finitude would move us toward a more authentic relation to our possibilities. Ironically, my book on self-deception started out as a study of authenticity in life choices. Adorno (1973) argues that Heidegger's talk of confronting death in order to live authentically was theological mystification that obscured the social, economic and political forces that make it difficult for the majority of humanity to get very far in actualizing life possibilities. Heidegger's call to authenticity still resonates as an ideal, but he provides no tools for getting there. So, adding this insight to

the basic concepts of psychoanalysis, I shifted the book's focus to how we tend to ignore both the characterological and the ideological forces that constrain decision making.

How does one successfully "challenge and confront ideology processes and the unjust social orders that they sustain?"
This is something we all need to work on together. One of the obstacles I have sensed lately is that mass demonstrations have little effect beyond the solidarity felt among participants. Organizers need to be much more creative and strategic as they lead social movements in the age of the internet and cable TV. Some of the internet-based movements like moveon.org have had impressive results, but I keep thinking that person-to-person, face-to-face work is ultimately the most important, especially if it takes advantage of the power of dialogue and leads to public deliberation and a deepening of democracy.

What sustains you in your quest for social justice? What are the values that help to sustain you?
Art and music nurture me. I wish I could participate more in their creation. Friendships are critical, both with fellow travelers and those who ask tough questions about my projects. Values? They are not things that need to be referred to outside the work itself. They are embodied in the work and can only be elucidated interpretively. But if I have a conscious motto related to values, it is that this is the only life I have to live and I have a responsibility to make my life meaningful and effective by leaving the world a better place. I guess if I believed in reincarnation I might relax and smell the flowers a bit more.

What are some of your current and future projects?
I have mentioned dialogue often in this piece and that is because I am eager to explore the potential of dialogue practices for a variety of purposes, ranging from personal development to deliberation in the public sphere. My interest in dialogue stemmed initially from my studies in critical hermeneutics, but was revived recently by the obvious polarization of citizens in the United States around issues connected with the attacks of September 11, 2001 and the subsequent "war on terrorism." It was very clear that neither side of the debate leading up to the military response to the attacks was able to hear the concerns of the other side. Several non-profit groups such as Study Circles and the Public Conversations Project offered free dialogue guides for families and

communities to use in the hopes that collective wisdom would emerge and guide foreign policy decisions. This is just one example of a role universities can play by offering open spaces in which citizens gather for deep dialogues about divisive social issues, find common ground, generate creative solutions, and contribute to the development of critical consciousness. I urge readers to visit the websites of the Co-Intelligence Institute (www.co-intelligence.org) and the National Council on Dialogue and Deliberation (www.thataway.org) to learn about the breadth and depth of the movement for deep democracy.

Some modes of dialogue practice may be problematic and we need to understand why. Critical psychologists can accompany these social innovations with action research, to evaluate them, and contribute to a repertoire of practices for deep democracy. We need to know what sorts of facilitation and communication arrangements dismantle ideological rigidity, foster critical self-reflection, augment creativity and cooperation, and ultimately lead to social transformation. Imagine how things would look if psychologists were involved in deepening democracy rather than helping individuals adjust to life in postmodern society.

In short, my next decade of work will contribute to a critical hermeneutics of dialogue and deliberation practices related to social justice issues. The main point of this work is to realize the potential of democratic society. Secondarily, it would contribute to the forging of effective roles for psychologists in the long struggle for social justice.

References

Adorno, T. (1973) *The Jargon of Authenticity*. Evanston, IL: Northwestern University Press.

Badiou, A. (2002) *Ethics: An Essay on Understanding of Evil*. London: Verso.

Barratt, B. (1984) *Psychoanalytic Knowing and Psychic Reality*. Hillsdale, NJ: Analytic Press.

Barratt, B. (1993) *Psychoanalysis and the Postmodern Impulse*. Baltimore, MD: Johns Hopkins University Press.

Earnest, W.R. (1992) "Ideology criticism and life history research." In G. Rosenwald and R. Ochberg (eds) *Storied Lives*. New Haven: Yale University Press.

Fox, D. and Prilleltensky, I. (1997) *Critical Psychology: An Introduction*. London: Sage.

Gregg, G. (1991) *Self-representation: Life Narrative Studies in Identity and Ideology*. New York: Greenwood.

Habermas, J. (1984) *Theory of Communicative Action*, Vol. 1. Boston: Beacon.

Rose, N. (1985) *The Psychological Complex*. London: Routlege and Kegan Paul.

Rosenwald, G. and Ochberg, R. (eds) (1992) *Storied Lives: The Cultural Politics of Self-understanding*. New Haven: Yale University Press.

Sloan, T.S. (1986) *Self-deception in Life Choices*. London: Methuen.

Sloan, T.S. (1996a) *Damaged Life: The Crisis of the Modern Psyche.* London: Routledge.

Sloan, T.S. (1996b) *Life Choices: Understanding Dilemmas and Decisions.* Boulder: Westview.

Sloan, T.S. (1997) "Theories of personality: Ideology and beyond." In D. Fox and I. Prilleltensky *Critical Psychology: An Introduction.* London: Sage.

Sloan, T.S. (ed) (2000) *Critical Psychology: Voices for Change.* London: Palgrave.

Sloan, T.S. and Montero, M. (eds) (1990) "Psychology for the Third World." *Journal of Social Issues 4*, entire issue.

Thompson, J. (1984) *Studies in the Theory of Ideology.* Berkeley: University of California Press.

CHAPTER 13

Autobiography

Ilene A. Serlin

The request to write an autobiography about oneself as a psychotherapist raises important questions about the nature of autobiography, the nature of the self, and the nature of therapeutic work. In this chapter, therefore, I will attempt to respond to each of these questions in turn by weaving together stories from my life with reflections on those stories.

It is only recently that the subject of women's autobiography, or women's *bios*, women's *aute*, and women's *graphia* has been a legitimate subject of critical or theoretical study (Smith, 1987, p.7). Psychoanalysts like Nancy Chodorow and Luce Irigay argue that men's autobiographies are individualistic and objective, while women's are relational and subjective (Gilligan, 1982). Women's stories retain the symbolic preverbal language between mother and infant, while men's stories reflect the Oedipal separation from the mother. It would follow that women's stories would not follow the male heroic stories of individuation, and indeed Carolyn Heilbrun (1988) shows that women authors tend to attribute their achievements to another person or to a force other than themselves.

Who is the "I" in a woman's narrative, therefore? Perhaps the "I" is more diffuse, multiple, and non-linear than the male "I." Is there an encapsulated self, or is the self created in a context of events and in relation with others? To what extent is the self influenced by gender and by personal history?

What does it mean to be a psychotherapist? Is it a profession or a calling? How is one's perspective as a psychotherapist affected by one's personal history and self? Is psychotherapy an objective scientific process based on prediction and control, or a subjective artistic process that uses the therapist's self as the primary tool?

The narratives that follow will focus on these questions through the themes of the self, gender, body, and spirit.

Who am I?

"I" was always a "we" and an "I." Born as the fraternal member of a set of triplets, my life has been shaped by my earliest experiences of being my own egg. That led to a lifetime of feeling different, longing for community but always being "on my own path"; profound loneliness and yet spirited independence; efforts to understand the meaning of the number "three," (archetypes of three sisters, three Furies, triple Goddesses); asymmetry as a model of change, instability with the potential for a greater dynamic stability, and appreciation for the paradox of belonging and not belonging. In my early memories, my sisters talked to each other at night while we all slept in the same room. Even though they were asleep, their nonsense talk was in perfect synchrony, with comments and pauses as if it were real conversation. I listened from the other end of the room, feeling out of the vibration, alone in an ancient way. And yet we were teased as we spoke of "our" mother. We were dressed alike until we were 12 years old, on all-triplet television shows *Name That Tune*, and *Merry Mailman*. We still confuse memories and identities ("No, that happened to me!"). Our mother taught English in the 1950s; we were taught to speak properly and politely to every stranger who accosted us, as we always were in public. We all performed well, and were always at the top in our classes. My sisters sang and I danced and drew. We played musical trios, and my sisters swapped lead roles in the camp plays. They were specimens in grade school biology class, demonstrating that as identical twins, one was right-handed, the other left-handed, one had a crooked tooth on the right side and the other on the left. We inevitably attracted attention; the most conspicuous outfits were three white bunny suits given to us by a business partner of my father. We still tell stories to each other about three little girls holding hands and wearing white fur coats, hats, and muffs on the New York City subway. On the one hand, we performed for the guests and were dolls ("poupée"), as Jean-Paul Sartre describes himself in his autobiography. On the other hand, we had extremely generous and supportive parents who encouraged us to individuate and believe in ourselves. Finally, my experience of being born into a "litter" gave me a very special bond with my sisters. We always trusted each other with our latest rebellions against the parents, as we still do with our secrets, dreams and fears. We learned a kind of loyalty that turned out to be unfortunately naive in terms of the rest of the world, and learning about betrayals and falseness came hard. Despite significant struggles, however, we did manage to create a very loving and close family.

My way has been a search for "authenticity" (Bugental, 1989), "sincerity" (Sartre, 1964), and some understanding about why I was put on this earth in this odd configuration.

Reflection

The theme of solitude is not common in the psychological literature, but it appears vividly in literature and philosophy. I think, for example, of the fundamental existential issues of facing one's aloneness, which I found in the writings of Albert Camus, Gide, Sartre and Simone de Beauvoir. Or in one of my favorite French writers, Colette, who wrote in *The Vagabond*: "Must I discover and perpetually renew in myself that rich fund of energy which is essential to the life of wanderers and solitaries? Must I, in short, struggle – ah, how could I forget it? – against solitude itself? And to achieve what? What? What?" (1955, p.121).

Clark Moustakas, a psychologist, bravely depicts loneliness in a heuristic essay and concludes: "No formula can predict the profound awakenings and discoveries that will occur in a person's inner searching. Nevertheless, inherent in loneliness as I have come to know it are guidelines to a new life" (1972, p.5). Irwin Yalom names aloneness as one of the four existential challenges of life (1980). For me, an existential approach to psychology is foundation to my theoretical approach.

Facing the existential void of our aloneness or mortality is, I think, the critical turning point in therapy and in life that lets us create in the face of this void. It gives us the freedom to create, and the motivation to be authentic. Performing for others as a child made me acutely conscious of acting, and of the roles played in everyday life. I had a tremendous longing for authenticity, which is why the work of Rollo May, James Bugental and other humanistic psychologists spoke so clearly to me (Bugental, 1989; May, 1975). I also enjoyed the Jungian concepts of persona and archetype (Jung, 1966), and therapies that use masks, create characters, and tell stories.

Finding a balance between unique and archetypal selves is not simple, and takes wisdom. While I do not believe that there is one "authentic" or monolithic self (Gergen, 1991; Hillman, 1975), I also do not think there are no essences or universals. In a therapeutic session, therefore, I might explore "subpersonalities" through verbal and nonverbal imagery, as well as universal constants like "love" and "compassion" and "home." I find it helpful, therapeutically, for a client to appreciate the absolute uniqueness of his or her experience in all its rich texture. At the same time, when appropriate, he or she can also see this experience in a larger context of cultural or historical patterns. The discovery that we share our most human dimensions with others is deeply therapeutic for many people.

Being a triplet has also influenced my therapeutic posture. I easily create sister transferential relationships, which obviously can be either helpful or problematic. I fantasize about writing articles on how the feeling of sisterhood is therapeutic in and of itself, and how in so many ways we are older and younger sisters to each other. Instead of "re-parenting" as therapists, we "re-sister." I often hear another kind of loneliness from a woman client who has never had a sister, and a lack of certain interpersonal "litter" social skills. I have clients who have never been teased as youngsters and need to learn. I have even tried to talk my sister into co-writing something with me, and she faintly agrees. So far we haven't done a thing.

Being so tuned into each other also gave me a very early experience of a nonverbal way of knowing. Nonverbal communication training helps me pick up on the nonverbal correlates of subgroup formation in a therapy group, for example. The work of Davis (1970), Scheflen (1973), and Birdwhistell (1970) helps me analyze group process or dyadic relationships. The experience of deeply felt implicit knowledge corresponds for me to the "personal knowledge" (Polanyi, 1958), or embodiment as "kinetic melody gifted with a meaning" (Merleau-Ponty, 1963, p.130). The effort to describe levels of meaning in nonverbal communication led me to the subject for my dissertation, which was a phenomenological study of what I called "Kinaesthetic Imagining," and published as an article (Serlin, 1996). It also led to a framework for understanding kinaesthetic transference and countertransference in psychotherapy (Serlin and Stern, 1998).

Psychology of women

As this form of knowing is the shadow side of the dominent culture's overt, verbal language, it tends to be more usual among women (Goldberger, 1996). Women's narratives are more likely to be personal, embodied, relational, and woven rather than linear (Plaskow and Christ, 1989). They may be, by their very nature, anti-authoritarian and anti-hierarchical. Smith calls this "an unspoken presence, that feminine unconscious repressed by the masculine logos, always threatens to disrupt the narrative order and to destabilize the fiction of identity the autobiographer inscribes" (Smith, 1987, p.41).

Women's narratives are related to nature in a creative collaboration. The sister theme in my own narrative takes me to ecofeminism as "a sisterly bond, a fundamental rejection of all forms of domination, whose necessary goal is diversity rather than dualism" (Gaard, 1993, p.7). This takes me to a feminist view of science: "The Feminine in each of us – the part that sees life in context, the interconnectedness of everything, and the consequences of our actions on future generations can help heal the wounds of our planet" (Shepherd, 1993, p.1).

I have been blessed with some extraordinary women mentors, and try to continue that tradition today with my students or supervisees. My advisor in the Honors Psychology program at the University of Michigan was Judith Bardwick, who was reading newly written chapters of her book on the psychology of women. I then apprenticed with Anna Halprin, who put together dance and movement with Gestalt therapy. With Anna, we did movement improvisations during rush hour traffic in San Francisco, and sunset rituals on top of Mt. Tamalpais. I feel it important to document these women's contributions to help balance the history of psychology and as a corrective to psychological theory. I interviewed Anna Halprin for an article published in the *American Journal of Dance Therapy* (Serlin, 1996). My first real therapist and wise old woman grandmother figure was Laura Perls. My therapy with her flowed into study at the NY Gestalt Institute in 1975 and then teaching with Laura and others. Trained as a concert pianist and dancer, Laura helped create Gestalt therapy as an "aesthetic philosophy" (Serlin and Shane, 1999), which provided a strong theoretical framework for me to conceptualize movement as meaning in process. I was with Laura, her daughter and granddaughter, when she died, and have made a videotape and written some articles that place her appropriately in the history of the development of US Gestalt therapy. As one of the founders of Gestalt therapy, she was not given credit. Her softer, more nuanced approach needs to balance Fritz's aggressive confrontational style. During this time, I also studied with Irmgard Bartenieff, one of the students of Rudolf von Laban, the grandfather of modern dance. Irmgard (Bartenieff and Lewis, 1980) taught us effort-shape analysis and space harmony, which were extremely sophisticated time–weight–flow analyses of movement. This system was applied to a wide range of issues, including the analysis of hospitalized psychiatric patients (Davis, 1970), workers in an assembly line, and cross-cultural dance. I wrote my master's thesis at Hunter College on the nonverbal correlates of valium on behavior and on couples in therapy. I still use effort-shape (Labanotation) in innumerable ways in my work; sometimes it is just a subtle recording of nonverbal behaviors during a verbal therapy session, to overt dances that are movement choirs with a Laban-based structure like Race for the Cure. In my writing, I have tried to find a verbal equivalent of a process language like Labanotation or Gestalt therapy as a language for psychotherapy that is based on the arts, and not a linear medical model (Serlin, 1989).

Finding one's voice as a woman was always a central area of my research and clinical interest. Simone de Beauvoir, Virginia Woolf and Mary Catherine Bateson were "sisters," and I built later courses on Women and Narrative on their theoretical foundations. I made pilgrimages to Virginia Woolf's house in London, and spent a day with Helaine de Beauvoir. I not only read Simone de Beauvoir's manifesto of the second sex, but I followed her footsteps through cafés and the student demonstrations in Paris, 1968. She and Sartre talked to a group of us students before we were tear gassed. I have explored and written about the voices of those women artists who commit suicide, and the dark side of creativity called "The Anne Sexton Complex" (Serlin, 1994). Students who take courses in Women and Narrative study the lives of women role models such as Marie Curie, and discover imagistic (rather than verbal) narratives in the lives of artists like Georgia O'Keefe. I may suggest that clients get in touch with the narratives of women in their family and cultural context. They may find inspiration in a family elder to guide them or discover their place within a family context or set of traditions. Or else they use narrative as a research methodology (Howard, 1991; Lieblich and Josselson, 1997; Polkinghorne, 1988).

I continue to stay interested in the psychology of women in many ways. I interviewed Aniela Jaffe about Jung and dancing (Serlin, 1992), co-wrote a chapter on Women in Humanistic Psychology for the *Handbook of Humanistic Psychology* (Serlin and Criswell, 2001), belong to Division 35 (Society for the Study of Women) and the Women's Caucus of the Council of Representatives of the APA. I currently supervise interns at a feminist clinic where we are developing a training program with a depth psychological perspective. Writing about women, creating curricula, getting involved in my professional association are all forms of social activism for me, of trying to walk my talk and embody my values.

It was Virginia Woolf who asked: "Who am I, what am I, and so on: these questions are always floating about in me" (Woolf, 1953, p.85). I find that many of my women clients suffer from various forms of social oppression, and finding their authentic voice is another keystone of their therapy.

Reflection

Both humanistic psychology and women's ways of knowing share values related to personal experience, tacit ways of knowing (Polanyi, 1958), the importance of finding one's authentic voice (Maslow, 1962), and a collaborative method of psychotherapy (Hare-Mustin, 1983). Women's ways of knowing include the following elements:

1. *Connectedness* – using empathy and intuition rather than argument and separation to seek collaboration with others.

2. *Social construction of methodologies* – seeking meaning rather than truth through descriptive and qualitative research (Howard, 1991; Polkinghorne, 1988).

3. *The Self* – known in relationship with others, demonstrates the "paradox of separateness within connection" (Jordan, 1991, p.69).

4. *Dialogical knowing* – transforming an "It" into a "Thou" (Buber, 1985; Friedman, 1985; Goldberger, 1996, p.221).

5. *Feeling* – that which is inseparable from thinking, allows us to feel ourselves into the world of the other (Goldberger, 1996, p.224).

A postmodern perspective shares an interest in "the situational and cultural determinants of knowing" and "the relationship between power and knowledge" (Goldberger, 1996, p.8). Feminist thought extends humanistic values to the "ecosocial matrix" (Spratnak, 1997) of body and earth.

The body

It is often through women's bodies that their voices come. The clinical work that I did with women who were living with breast cancer involves some of the most profound therapeutic experiences of my life. In 1995, I organized an Arts Medicine program at the Institute of Medicine and Philosophy at California Pacific Medical Center. I won three grants from the Susan Komen Foundation to organize 12-week Dance Medicine groups. We created imagery and healing rituals for each member as she dealt with mastomectomies and reconstructions (Serlin *et al.*, 2000b). We participated in the Annual Race for the Cure, and entered a collaborative art project created by the group into the Art.Rage.Us exhibit in San Francisco. We became activists in the Hike Against the Odds, and sat at tables distributing literature about resources. Doing therapy with this group is different from doing traditional psychotherapy, in ways noted by David Spiegel *et al.* (1989). This approach is congruent with a feminist approach to psychotherapy, which is collaborative and egalitarian (Hare-Mustin, 1983).

The power of dance to heal had early roots in my interest in folk dance. At age 14, I began folk dancing in Israel. This was followed by a small performance with my Zionist group in Carnegie Hall when I was 16, and years of Balkan dancing. I traveled through the Balkans during the summer of 1973, danced in small villages in Yugoslavia, and lived in Turkey for one month. I participated as a research assistant at Columbia University with Alan Lomax, the anthropologist who did cross-cultural field research in dance, using Labanotation to document patterns of simplicity and complexity across cultural traditions. I still use folk dance as a foundation for my work, whether in the "gerobics" groups I lead in nursing homes in Massachusetts or in the warm-up for the annual Race for the Cure.

The ancestors – What's in a name?

Being a triplet was rare. We heard figures of it being 1:10,000 in those days before any fertility medication. Nor was it part of our family history – it seems to have been a complete fluke. Although we were each full weight and full term, and my mother gained so much weight that she couldn't see her feet, she and my father said they believed their doctor who told them to expect one child. So my mother and father had one boy's name prepared. It was Eric, and so my middle sister got the name Erica. When the naming got to me as the last one, I got the fathers' names. For a girl to inherit the names of family men is unusual in a traditional Jewish family; however, the families of my parents were not traditional, and were involved in left-wing politics and labor unions, Yiddish music and culture.

I was named Ilene with the letter I for Isadore, my mother's father. She adored him, and was so desolate when he died that she promptly got pregnant – with us. The story about him is that he was a gentle and cultured soul who earned a basic living as a house painter in the Bronx ("when the Bronx still had potato fields"). He came from Russia with his young bride from Kamenetz Podolsky in Ukraine to New York City. We have a photo of him, small and dapper, with his blonde and pretty young bride, in a (probably) rented suit and stiff smile, taken in a Russian photography studio in New York in the early 1900s. My mother came very close to naming me Isadora, but was afraid that I would be called Izzy like her father. Nevertheless, I feel sure that the archetype of Isadora Duncan runs deep in my soul. I live in her hometown, and am working with colleagues on a chapter about her. Is she an image or template for me? I think so.

In a self-made coming of age ceremony at age 30, when I went off to graduate school in psychology in a new part of the country, I took again my given name Ilene. This was a change from my childhood tomboy nickname Leni, which close friends and family still call me. Taking on the full birth name with a conscious appreciation of the legacy it carried was an important part of my growing sense of identity during my middle years.

My middle name is Ava. I was probably 40 years old before I admitted this to anyone – the name always sounded so pretentious. In fact, I was actually named for my father's father Avraham, Abraham, or Avram. This grandfather, whom I never knew, was described by my father as a kind and scholarly man who earned a living with candy stores and as a tailor on the Lower East Side of New York. We knew that he had some siblings in the United States, but never knew that others did not come over from Poland and were sent to Treblinka. Two years ago some cousins and I discovered this family secret. We visited Bialystok, found the villages of these relatives, and said Kaddish in Treblinka.

Knowing about this part of my family has made an enormous difference in how I articulate my identity to myself. Now I understood some of the profound grief and survival experiences of my father and his family. I understood a great deal more about my father's expectations for his children, and the frustration of his having no male heirs to inherit the business he built. As the family tomboy, I carried the math, science, and sports role. Getting interested in poetry and French literature marked my initiation into my womanhood, as I fell in love for the first time in my late teens. Getting back to math and science has been a struggle since, although I found ways to call on my "inner tomboy" to help me pass the psychology licensing exam. I understood aspects of my sadness as carrying a cultural connection to the Holocaust. I am now focused on inner and outer psychological repair work, trying to find a way to help "repair the world": "Tikkun Olam." I am finding small ways to sustain family, like visiting my father's parents' graves in New York and cleaning and maintaining them. Seeing my own personal issues in the context of my family and world politics gives me an invaluable perspective on them and helps me find ways to move from grief to reconstruction.

Reflection

In my experience, many of us today are rootless, lost, and do not know who we are. The parents of baby-boomers tried to forget the pain of World War II and their immigrant pasts, and looked into the optimistic American future. Today we no longer have the family home where the photos and narratives are stored. We have intermarried, and are changing/losing traditions (Serlin et al., 2001a). I have found, in my own life and with my clients, that some form of creative recapulation and experiencing of family history can stabilize the personality and contribute to a sense of belonging and identity. We need to find a balance between getting stuck in a sentimentalized or literalized version of our stories and the freedom to create new ones. As we do this, we need to give voice to the different aspects of ourselves.

In one clinical case, for example, a young client had lost both her parents within a year, and suddenly found herself the new family parent. She was worried about the holidays and how she could now hold the family together. By creating a shared space where family members could bring their favorite Christmas mementos of the parents and family, they were able to talk about their grief and also begin a process of rebuilding.

I have also noticed that the breakdown of traditional religious guidelines on how to live have left many people with the task of creating their own system of morality or spiritual beliefs. They may come into therapy with a crisis of identity, or meaning and purpose. As I have written, I believe that psychologists should be prepared to deal with issues of religious and spiritual diversity in their training programs (Serlin, in press).

Articulating the self

I kept a diary from age nine. One entry at age ten showed a struggle with my anger toward my mother, who would not let me go barefoot outside because I had a cold. Looking at this entry 45 years later, I was surprised not only by the strength of my feelings, but also the moral dimensions of my questions; for example, I wrestled over whether it was wrong to be angry toward my mother. I had a private spot at a lake near our house where I hid my journals and communed with them while sitting on a tree; carving out private time within a strongly connected collective has always been an edge for me, never easy, but always essential. Asking myself questions about ethics, meaning, and motivation were natural. I think I was perhaps an "old soul."

But reflecting on the family, talking about family issues with each other and our friends was a natural path to psychology for all of us, and my middle sister is a family therapist. Although we picked a similar field, however, our different perspectives reflect our personality and birth order differences. She was the middle sister and known as the "Philadelphia lawyer" who mediated between her more hot-headed baby and older sister. Her PhD is from an APA approved clinical psychology program, while I was more attracted to the existentialist philosophers, dance and the arts, Gestalt, humanistic and Jungian psychology.

I do therefore think that one's choice of psychological or philosophical perspective is both a reflection of, and an influence on, one's personality. Yet the relationship between private experience and its public expression is complicated. One goal of therapy, I think, is to bring about a greater coherence among levels of cognitive and non-cognitive, rational and non-rational levels, individual and group, modes of experience and expression. Going beyond traditional dichotomies of mind and body, however, may mean going beyond Western, Cartesian psychology. For me, this was studying Gestalt theory and therapy with Laura Perls at the New York Gestalt institute as a kind of "applied philosophy," then Tibetan Buddhism, and phenomenological and archetypal psychology at the University of Dallas. I try to ground my observations in some form of political action; I got involved in Division 32 of the American Psychological Association, and as past-President and Representative to Council, I tried to represent a humanistic perspective in traditional psychology (Serlin et al., 2000a).

The early experience of being an observer in life was basic training for my becoming a psychologist. However, the questions I asked myself were not addressed by psychology, but rather by philosophy. I found in Gide my affirmation that one had to break out of the bourgeois family in order to find real authenticity and freedom ("only the bastard has a right to be free"). At the University of Michigan, a group of us created courses on humanistic and existential psychology, and interdisciplinary courses in French and psychology. We had student sit-ins and practiced activism, discussing our actions in our philosophy class on existentialism with Fritzhof Bergmann. I was seriously interested in issues of authenticity, family and government oppression, personal and political liberation.

Spirit and psyche

Finding coherence among all my parts was not as easy as it may have sounded above, and these parts were often in conflict. For example, the philosophical psychology at the University of Dallas was grounded in a conservative contemplative Catholic monastic tradition, and I was a Jewish dance therapist from New York. By experiencing the sometimes excruciating squeeze of a male authoritarian classroom and paper writing disciplines, I saw more clearly by contrast the world from which I came and took for granted. Yet it also propelled me into action to reclaim my own life. Having to consciously reclaim my Judaism led me back to temple and the mentorship of a far-thinking rabbi and philosophy professor. I was homesick in Dallas, not only for familiarity, immediate family and friends, but also for my tribe. A few years later, I went back to Israel to rediscover my Zionist roots, was able to balance the idealist image of Israel from my youth with the reality of the volatile country today, and come to terms with my having left Judaism. I studied for my Bat Mitzvah with a woman rabbi and group of women, and chanting the ancient melodies was a high point when I turned 50. Yet I continue to struggle with the role of women in Judaism, and try to find places to bring a feminist perspective into the tradition. For example, each year at Passover I offer a Miriam's dance at the place in the text where the Red Sea parts. Since Miriam's song is the first song in the Bible, the women play tambourines and dance in a serpentine line around the Passover tables in a tribute to the gifts of Miriam the Prophetess.

I rediscovered Judaism in the community. I spent Shabbaton with Chassidic families, danced all night with the Torah, and joined with Starhawk (1988), Ester Broner, and other Jewish warrior women to create an all-women's Torah Scroll that is now housed in the Jewish Women's Library in Los Angeles. I lived near and visited the Israel Levin Center on Venice Beach written about so movingly by Barbara Myerhoff, an anthropologist who lived with, loved, and wrote about these old Jewish people (Myerhoff, 1978). As Gelya Frank described Myerhoff's method: "Myerhoff's vision of the people at the Israel Levin Center was a form of redemption through historization. She assumed the role of a granddaughter who took time from her busy and successful life to give her 'grandparents' the recognition and respect they deserved" (Frank, 1995, p.209). Years later, I worked in nursing homes where I often experienced myself as their granddaughter, and was given a lot of love in return. It is a different form of transference, and the healing happens through this love.

My own path through spirituality is in some ways typical of others of my generation. Not finding a spiritual connection in the suburban reform Judaism of my childhood, I turned to Buddhism in my twenties. I became a student of the notorious Tibetan Chogyam Trungpa Rinpoche, and taught dance therapy at the Naropa Institute. Learning meditation has been another cornerstone of my therapeutic practice. It comes into play whether I am sitting in a therapeutic session, or teaching someone to center and focus. I have tried to write about bringing spiritual perspectives and practices into psychotherapy

(Serlin, in press), while also being cautious about spirituality sometimes being used as a defense against feeling. I have found the Buddhist Abhidharma to be an extremely sophisticated psychological system with a taxonomy of human thought, emotion and action based on thousands of years of meditation insights. It is another fluid, process-oriented language, very different from the more rigid Western systems that emphasize psychopathology. While I struggled for some years with not knowing whether I was Jewish or Buddhist, I found my way to "Ju-Bu" through Jungian analysis and writing about this experience (Serlin, 1986). To this day, I think of Buddhism as my spirit and Judaism as my soul.

These questions of soul and depth could not be found in Gestalt and humanistic psychology, and I began to delve into Jungian psychology. I studied with James Hillman during my graduate work at the University of Dallas, and entered Jungian analysis at that time. I did a pre-doctoral internship at the C.G. Jung Institute of Los Angeles, and studied in the sandtray room of the Children's Clinic. Jungian psychology gave me an archetypal and symbolic language system that was invaluable for depth therapy work, both verbal and dance. I taught in Zurich, where I experienced a more pure archetypal approach. I found the stories and myths enchanting, yet at times disembodied and forced. I was uncomfortable with discussions about Jung's relationship with the Nazi party, and found some traditions underlying classical Jungian theory to be socially regressive. I learned more about the feminine as an archetype and my own feminine side, while I also rebelled against it as dogma. My mentors in the Jungian world were primarily creative and nontraditional therapists on the fringes of the Jungian community, for example, Ernie Rossi, Marvin Spiegelman, James Hillman, and Andrew Samuels. To this day, however, I still feel very attracted to a Jungian depth perspective, and it informs my work thoroughly.

Reflection

Having a spiritual perspective in psychology raises a difficult question: To what extent is our identity that of our cultural and historical context, and to what extent is our real identity a spiritual essence? I once heard Jean Bolen say that from a spiritual perspective we are primarily spirits temporarily inhabiting this body in this time and place, whereas a humanistic perspective says that we are primarily humans in this time and place, but have spirituality in our nature. That definition has remained with me since then, and seems useful. I have believed both passionately at one time or another.

However, having a spiritual perspective on psychology can immensely broaden the clinical work. Echoing personal issues with cultural myths and universal energies can help a person emerge from the cocoon of a narcissistic preoccupation with self.

Conclusion

Selves are fluid and escape definition. However, over time my affiliations, writings, and clinical work have grown into commitment. This commitment has taken the shape of a perspective which is simultaneously humanistic-depth-feminist-somatic-artistic. What these theories share is the importance of personal experience, tacit ways of knowing, holism, and interconnectedness. These qualities are embodied through relationship, engagement with the world, and creative work as a psychotherapist. At the end, there is the question posed by the poet, Mary Oliver, about how each of us will live this one wild and wonderful life.

References

Bartenieff, I. and Lewis, D. (1980) *Body Movement: Coping with the Environment.* New York: Gordon and Breach.

Birdwhistell, R. (1970) *Kinesis and Context: Essays in Body Motion Communication.* Philadelphia: University of Pennsylvania Press.

Buber, M. (1985) *Between Man and Man,* trans R. Smith. New York: Macmillan.

Bugental, J. (1989) *The Search for Existential Identity.* San Francisco: Jossey-Bass.

Colette (1995) *The Vagabond.* New York: Farrar, Straus, and Cudahy Inc.

Davis, M. (1970) "Movement characteristics of hospitalized psychiatric patients." *Proceedings of the Fifth Annual Conference of the American Dance Therapy Association.* Columbia, MD: American Dance Therapy Association.

Frank, G. (1995) "The ethnographic films of Barbara Myerhoff: Anthropology, feminism, and the politics of Jewish identity." In R. Behar and D. Gordon (eds) *Women Writing Culture.* Berkeley: University of California Press.

Friedman, M. (1985) *The Healing Dialogue in Psychotherapy.* New York: Jason Aronson.

Gaard, G. (1993) *Ecofeminism: Women, Animals, Nature.* Philadelphia: Temple University Press.

Gergen, K. (1991) *The Saturated Self.* New York: Basic Books.

Gilligan, C. (1982) *In a Different Voice.* Cambridge, MA: Harvard University Press.

Goldberger, N. (1996) *Knowledge, Difference and Power: Women's Ways of Knowing.* New York: Basic Books.

Hare-Mustin, R. (1983) "An appraisal of the relationship between women and psychotherapy." *American Psychologist 8,* 593–601.

Heilbrun, C. (1988) *Writing a Woman's Life.* New York: Ballantine.

Hillman, J. (1975) *Re-visioning Psychology*. New York: Harper and Row.

Howard, G. (1991) "Cultural tales: A narrative approach to thinking, cross-cultural psychology, and psychotherapy." *American Psychologist 46*, 187–197.

Jordan, J. (1991) "Empathy and self-boundaries." In J.V. Jordan, A.G. Kaplan, J.B. Miller, I.P. Stiver and J.L. Surrey (eds) *Women's Growth in Connection: Writings from the Stone Center*. New York: Guilford Press.

Jung, C.G. (1966) *The Spirit in Man, Art and Literature*, trans R.F.C. Hull. Princeton: Princeton University Press.

Lieblich, A. and Josselson, R. (eds) (1997) *The Narrative Study of Lives*, Vol. 5. Thousand Oaks: Sage.

Maslow, A.H. (1962) *Toward a Psychology of Being*. New York: Van Nostrand.

May, R. (1975) *The Courage to Create*. New York: Bantam.

Merleau-Ponty, M. (1963) *The Structure of Behavior*. Boston: Beacon Press.

Moustakas, C. (1972) *Loneliness and Love*. New York: Prentice-Hall.

Myerhoff, B. (1978) *Number Our Days*. New York: Dutton.

Plaskow, J. and Christ, C. (1989) *Weaving the Visions: New Patterns in Feminist Spirituality*. San Francisco: Harper and Row.

Polanyi, M. (1958) *Personal Knowledge*. Chicago: University of Chicago Press.

Polkinghorne, D.E. (1988) *Narrative Knowing and the Human Sciences*. Albany: State University of New York Press.

Sartre, J.P. (1964) *The Words*. Greenwich: Fawcett.

Scheflen, A. (1973) *Communicational Structure: Analysis of a Psychotherapy Transition*. Bloomington: Indiana University Press.

Serlin, I.A. (1986) "Toward an erotic spirituality." In M. Spiegelman (ed) *A Modern Jew in Search of a Soul*. New York: Falcon Press.

Serlin, I.A. (1989) "Choreography of a verbal session." In A. Robbins (ed) *The Psychoaesthetic Experience: An Approach to Depth-oriented Psychotherapy*. New York: Human Sciences Press.

Serlin, I.A. (1992) "On meeting a remarkable woman." *Association for Transpersonal Psychology Newsletter*.

Serlin, I.A. (1994) "The Anne Sexton complex." In R. May and K. Schneider (eds) *The Psychology of Existence: An Integrative Clinical Perspective*. New York: Harper and Row.

Serlin, I.A. (1996) "Kinaesthetic imagining." *Journal of Humanistic Psychology 36*, 2, 25–35.

Serlin, I.A. (in press) "Spiritual diversity in clinical practice." In J. Chin (ed) *The Psychology of Prejudice and Discrimination*. Westport, CT: Greenwood.

Serlin, I.A. and Criswell, E. (2001) "Humanistic psychology and women: A critical–historical perspective." In K. Schneider, J. Bugental and J. Pierson (eds) *Handbook of Humanistic Psychology: Leading Edges of Theory, Research, and Practice*. Thousand Oaks, CA: Sage.

Serlin, I.A. and Shane, P. (1999) "Laura Perls and Gestalt therapy: Her life and values." In D. Moss (ed) *The Pursuit of Human Potential: A Sourcebook of Humanistic and Transpersonal Psychology*. Westport, CT: Greenwood Press.

Serlin, I.A. and Stern, E.M. (1998) "The dialogue of movement: An interview/conversation." In K. Hays (ed) *Integrating Exercise, Sports, Movement and Mind*. New York: Haworth Press.

Serlin, I.A., Aanstoos, C. and Greening, T. (2000a) "History of Division 32." In D. Dewsbury (ed) *History of Divisions*. Washington, DC: American Psychological Association Press.

Serlin, I.A., Classen, C., Frances, B. and Angell, K. (2000b) "Symposium: Support groups for women with breast cancer." *The Arts in Psychotherapy 27*, 2, 123–138.

Shepherd, L. (1993) *Lifting the Veil: The Feminine Face of Science.* Boston: Shambhala.

Smith, S. (1987) *A Poetics of Women's Autobiography.* Bloomington: Indiana University Press.

Spiegel, D., Bloom, J., Kraemer, H. *et al.* (1989) "Effect of psychosocial treatment on survival of patients with metastatic breast cancer." *Lancet 2*, 888–891.

Spratnak, C. (1997) *The Resurgence of the Real: Body, Nature, and Place in a Hypermodern World.* Reading, MA: Perseus.

Starhawk (1988) *Dreaming the Dark: Magic, Sex and Politics.* Boston: Beacon Press.

Woolf, V. (1953) *A Writer's Diary.* New York: Harcourt, Brace, Janovich.

Yalom, I. (1980) *Existential Psychotherapy.* New York: Basic Books.

The Contributors

Christopher M. Aanstoos received his PhD in psychology from Duquesne University in 1982. After having previously taught at the Pennsylvania State University, he accepted a position on the graduate faculty at the University of West Georgia, where he is now Professor of Psychology. He is a Fellow of the American Psychological Association and has served as President of the APA's Division of Humanistic Psychology, and editor of the journal *The Humanistic Psychologist*. He is currently on the editorial boards of several other journals, including *Journal of Phenomenological Psychology* and *Journal of Humanistic Psychology*. He has also served as Program Chair of the APA's Division of Theoretical and Philosophical Psychology, the Symposium for Qualitative Research in Psychology, and of the Human Science Research Conference. He has published more than eighty scholarly articles and chapters, and presented more than a hundred papers, examining issues concerning the conceptual and methodological foundations of psychology as a human science, and on the phenomenology of lived experience. His particular interest areas include: thinking, consciousness, lifespan development and potential and personal transformation.

Steen Halling, is a licensed psychologist and professor of psychology at Seattle University, Seattle, WA, where he teaches in the MA program in existential- phenomenological psychology as well as in the undergraduate program. The graduate program provides students with a solid foundation for the practice of therapeutic psychology. He received his PhD in clinical psychology from Duquesne University in Pittsburgh, and his B.A. in psychology from York University in Toronto, Canada. Since 1976, he has been at Seattle University where his research and publications have focused on topics such as psychology of forgiveness, phenomenological study of psychopathology, psychology of hopelessness, interpersonal relations, psychology of imagination, the history of phenomenological psychiatry and psychology, and qualitative research methods. He is editor of the International Human Science Research Conference Newsletter, and co-editor, with Ronald S. Valle of *Existential-Phenomenological Perspectives in Psychology* (Plenum, New York, 1989). He has been a visiting professor at Duquesne University and at Pretoria University in South Africa; he started his teaching career at Seton Hill University in Pennsylvania.

Lois Holzman is a founder and Director of the East Side Institute for Group and Short Term Psychotherapy, an international research and training center for new approaches to human development and community, located in New York City. In collaboration with Fred Newman, the creator of social therapy, she has advanced social therapeutic methodology as a cultural approach to human learning and development. Holzman's research involves studying educational, therapeutic, health, organizational and community development programs as well as exploring current trends in postmodern and critical psychology and education. Among the books Holzman has authored or edited are: *Psychological Investigations: A Clinician's Guide to Social Therapy*; *Postmodern Psychologies, Societal Practice and Political Life*; *Performing Psychology: A Postmodern Culture* *of the Mind*; *Schools for Growth: Radical Alternatives to Current Educational Models*; *Lev Vygotsky: Revolutionary Scientist*; and, *The End of Knowing: A New Developmental Way of Learning.* Holzman received her Ph.D. in developmental psychology from Columbia University, did post-graduate work with Michael Cole at the Rockefeller University's Laboratory of Comparative Human Cognition, and was on the faculty of SUNY's Empire State College for nearly two decades.

Adelbert H. Jenkins trained as a clinical psychologist at the University of Michigan and has been a member of the doctoral clinical psychology program faculty at New York University for over 30 years. He is a Diplomate of the American Board of Professional Psychology in Clinical Psychology and a Fellow of several Divisions of the American Psychological Association. He is past-President of Division 24 of the American Psychological Association (Division of Theoretical and Philosophical Psychology). His scholarly interests include teleologic philosophical issues in clinical psychology and psychoanalytic theory, and the application of humanistic perspectives on psychological agency to the consideration of people of color in America. The second edition of his book is entitled *Psychology and African Americans: A humanistic approach* (Allyn & Bacon, 1995). He has published in the journals: *Psychoanalytic Psychology*, *The Humanistic Psychologist*, and *Theory and Psychology*, among others. His recent writing attempts to complement the developing philosophically hermeneutic views in psychology with an emphasis on the relevance in all cultural contexts of a carefully constructed view of psychological agency.

David E. Leary has been University Professor at the University of Richmond in Richmond, VA, since 2002. Previously he was Dean of Arts and Sciences at Richmond for thirteen years, and before that he was Professor of Psychology, History, and the Humanities at the University of New Hampshire, where he co-directed the History and Theory of Psychology Program for twelve years. A fellow of the American Psychological Association as well as the American Psychological Society, he has focused his research on the history of psychology, and especially on the impact of the humanities (e.g., art, literature, religion, and philosophy) on the development of modern psychology. He is also interested in the converse influence of modern psychology upon culture, especially in the United States. The author of more than forty articles and chapters, including "William James and the Art of Human Understanding" (1992), he co-edited the award-winning *A Century of Psychology as Science* (1985, reissued 1992), which contains "The Cult of Empiricism in Psychology, and Beyond" (co-written with his teacher, the philosopher Stephen Toulmin) and *Metaphors in the History of Psychology* (1990), which contains his seminal chapter on "Psyche's Muse: The Role of Metaphor in the History of Psychology." He is currently directing his attention to the influence of literature on the life and work of William James.

Dan P. McAdams is Professor of Psychology and Professor of Human Development and Social Policy at Northwestern University, Evanston, IL. He received his BS from Valparaiso University in 1976 and his PhD in 1979 from Harvard University in Psychology and Social Relations. Honored as a Charles Deering McCormick Professor of Teaching Excellence at Northwestern, Professor McAdams teaches courses in Personality Psychology, Adult Development and Aging, Theories of Human Development, and the Literatures of Identity and Generativity. Professor McAdams is also the Director of the Foley Center for the Study of Lives, a research enterprise at Northwestern dedicated to the study of adult personality and social development, with an emphasis on prosocial aspects of adult functioning. His research examines the concept of generativity – an adult's concern for and commitment to the well-being of future generations – and the ways in which adults construct narrative identities (life stories) to provide their lives with meaning and purpose. His most recent book on these topics is *The Redemptive Self: The Stories*

Americans Live By (Oxford University Press, 2005). Professor McAdams is the winner of the 1989 Henry A. Murray Award from Division 8 of the American Psychological Association for his work on personality and the study of lives.

Gerald Monk is a professor at San Diego State University and teaches courses in conflict resolution, marriage and family therapy, and multicultural counseling approaches. He has worked as a mediator and family therapist over the last twenty-five years. His specialty areas focus upon family mediation and divorce mediation utilizing narrative mediation approaches. Gerald is also a trainer in conflict resolution and mediation for the Training Institute of the National Conflict Resolution Center (NCRC). He is internationally known for his work with the development and application of narrative approaches to therapy, mediation, and conflict resolution and has taught numerous workshops on this subject in United States, Canada, Mexico, Austria, Iceland, England, Cyprus, Australia, and New Zealand. He has written numerous articles and co-authored three books on narrative approaches to therapy and mediation.

Theodore R. Sarbin is currently Emeritus Professor of Psychology and Criminology at the University of California, Santa Cruz, and Senior Research Psychologist at the Defense Personnel Security Research Center in Monterey, California. Following the completion of his work for the PhD from the Ohio State University in 1941, he held a two-year Research Training Fellowship awarded by the Social Science Research Council. During the period, 1943–49, he held various posts as a clinician and part-time instructor. In 1949, he was called to the University of California where he spent the rest of his career; twenty years at the Berkeley campus, the remainder of the time at the Santa Cruz campus. During the latter part of his career he was Professor of Psychology and Criminology. He has held a number of fellowships: Senior Fulbright Award at Oxford University, 1961–62; Guggenheim, 1965–66; Wesleyan University Center for the Humanities, 1968–69. He was the recipient of the Henry Murray Award from the American Psychological Association in 1995. His bibliography lists over 250 books, research articles, reviews, and critical essays dealing with deviance, hypnosis, clinical inference, emotional life, metaphor, imagination, narrative, and dramaturgy.

Karl E. Scheibe was born in Belleville, Illinois in 1937. He graduated from Trinity College in 1959, and received his PhD in Psychology from the University of California at Berkeley in 1963. From 1963 to the present he has been on the faculty of Wesleyan University and has been Professor of Psychology since 1973 – with several interruptions for visiting professorships in Brazil and in California. He has twice been a Fulbright Fellow to the Catholic University in São Paulo in, 1927–72 and in 1984. He was also Professor at DUXX, Graduate School of Business Leadership, in Monterrey, Mexico from 1995–2002, and is a psychotherapist in private practice and Executive Director of the Saybrook Counseling Center. He is author of four books, *Beliefs and Values* (1970), *Mirrors, Masks, Lies and Secrets* (1979), *Self Studies* (1995), and *The Drama Of Everyday Life* (2000) and co-editor of *The Social Context Of Conduct* (1982) and *Studies In Social Identity* (1983), and scores of articles in psychological journals on topics in personality and social psychology. He has a special interest in utilizing the perspectives of theater for psychological issues and topics.

Ilene A. Serlin is a licensed psychologist and a registered dance/movement therapist. She is a Professor of Psychology at Saybrook Graduate School and Research Institute in San Francisco, founder of the Arts Medicine Program at the Institute of Health and Healing at California Pacific Medical Center, and Director of Union Street Health Associates, Inc. Dr. Serlin is past-President of Division 32 of the American Psychological Association, Council Representative from Division 32, and has served on the Editorial Boards of The *Arts in Psychotherapy*, *Journal of the American Dance Therapy Association*, and the *Journal of Humanistic Psychology*. She has taught and consulted around the world, and has been exploring since 1971 how the arts in psychotherapy bring together body, mind and spirit.

John Shotter is Emeritus Professor of Communication in the Department of Communication, University of New Hampshire. His long-term interest is in the social conditions conducive to people having a voice in the development of participatory democracies and civil societies. He is the author of *Images of Man in Psychological Research* (Methuen, 1975), *Human Action and its Psychological Investigation* (with Alan Gauld, Routledge, 1977), *Social Accountability and Selfhood* (Blackwell, 1984), *Cultural Politics of Everyday Life: Social Constructionism, Rhetoric, and Knowing of the Third Kind* (Open University, 1993), and *Conversational Realities: the Construction of Life through Language* (Sage, 1993). In 1997, he was an Overseas Fellow at Churchill College, Cambridge and a Visiting Professor at The Swedish Institute of Work Life Research, Stockholm, Sweden. He now works as a consultant with the KCC Foundation, London. Recently, he has begun to look beyond current "linguistic" versions of Social Constructionism toward the surrounding circumstances making such a movement possible. He calls his current approach a social ecological one. See his homepage: http://pubpages.unh.edu/~jds

Tod Sloan completed his doctoral work in personality psychology and clinical counseling at the University of Michigan in 1982. He was a professor of psychology at the University of Tulsa (Oklahoma) from 1982–2001. He is the author of *Life Choices: Understanding Dilemmas and Decisions and Damaged Life: The Crisis of the Modern Psyche*. Later, he edited *Critical Psychology: Voices for Change*. Sloan served as a Fulbright visiting professor in Venezuela and Nicaragua, and has also taught in Costa Rica, Brazil, Mexico and Canada. In 2004, Sloan became professor and chair of the Department of Counseling Psychology at Lewis and Clark College in Portland, Oregon. Since 2001, he has also worked as national co-coordinator of Psychologists for Social Responsibility (www.psysr.org). His current research and action interests include dialogue practices and social movements related to consumerism and the development of globally sustainable lifestyles.

Hendrika Vande Kemp earned her BA from Hope College (1971) and her MS (1974) and PhD (1977) in clinical psychology from the University of Massachusetts/Amherst. From 1976–2001, she was on the faculty of the Graduate School of Psychology at Fuller Theological Seminary, where she taught courses on family psychology, family therapy, interpersonal psychology, the history of psychology, the integration of psychology and theology, grief and mourning, and dream interpretation. She is the co-author with Barbara Eurich-Rascoe of *Femininity and Shame: Women and Men Giving Voice to the Feminine*; editor of *Family Therapy: Christian Perspectives*; and compiler of *Psychology and Theology in Western Thought 1672–1965: A Historical and Annotated Bibliography*. She is currently in private practice as a clinical psychologist and family therapist in Annandale, Virginia.

Subject Index

"action language" 201
action research 159–60, 232, 236, 243
actions 25, 31, 68, 75, 151
    accountability for 77, 161
    and behavior 161, 162, 164, 234, 235, 236
    and "inner voices" 92
    intentional 16, 21, 200–4
    and role of language 17
    see also interactions; role taking
adolescence, identity formation during 121–3
African-Americans 1, 126, 191–2, 196–9, 202, 204
agency 41–2, 151, 175, 181, 185, 187, 229
    control of 161–2
    and power 123–4, 126
    social context of 203–4
    theory of 199–200
    see also voice
aloneness 175, 247
All Stars (youth development project) 107
Alzheimer's disease 24
American Dream 192, 195
American Journal of Dance Therapy 249
American Scholar, The 49
ancestors, importance of 252–4
anti-Semitism 32, 213, 255
Aotearoa (New Zealand) 74–5
archetype 247, 252, 257
argumentation 159, 163
Asian spiritualism 142, 143
Association of Black Psychologists (ABPsi) 196–7
authentic voice 250–1
authenticity 231, 241, 247, 255
authority 181–6, 236–8
autobiography 10, 13, 31, 117, 127, 224, 228, 245
autonomy 75, 123, 163, 181–3, 203–4
    see also ego autonomy
awards 33, 42–3, 66, 262–4

Battle for the Bible, The (Lindsell) 178
behavior 79, 157
    action, distinct from 161–2, 164
    intentional 16, 21, 200–4
behaviorism 16, 31, 139, 140, 186, 194, 199
Being-as-a-whole 143–4, 146–7
believed-in imaginings 19, 27
belonging 133, 159, 163, 246, 254
Beyond Belief (Pagels) 40
biographical methods 9, 23, 116, 128
    see also narratives

biological functioning 90
body language 159, 167
bonding 246, 249
Brazil 47–9
Buddhism 134, 144–5, 256–7

cartesian paradigm 19, 30–1, 151, 157–8, 255
Catholicism 55–6, 58–9, 255
cause and effect 156, 234
Century of Psychology as Science, A (Koch and Leary) 65
characteristic adaptations 119
chess playing 139–40
child abuse 178
children
    affected by war 110, 156
    "competence" learning 198
    emotionally disturbed 214–5
    language development 102–3, 104–7, 156, 160
    literature for 176
    self-concepts of 120
Christianity 45–6, 87, 175, 177–8, 184, 185
citizenship 126, 163
Civil Rights Movement 56, 59, 196
Civilization and its Discontents (Freud) 115
class
    elitism of therapists 195–6
    hidden injuries of 152–3
    see also social class
clinical inference 15, 28, 264
Co-Intelligence Institute 243
Cognitive Psychology (Bloom, Lightbrown and Hood) 105
collective stories/voice 78–9, 81
collectivism vs. individualism 92, 203–4
communication 57, 154, 163, 167, 169, 243
    nonverbal 87, 248
    see also body language; dialogue
communion/intimacy, life-story theme 123–4
community 71, 183, 185, 218
    building of 110–11
    distancing from 196
    narratives circulating in 86–8
    organizing 100, 108, 111, 233, 236
    religious 58, 175
    scientific 118, 138
    sense of 67, 222, 246
    therapeutic 212
compassion 146, 247
"competence" 197–8, 202, 203
computer simulation 139, 158, 160
Concept of Mind, The (Ryle) 31
connectedness 181, 251
connections 54, 55, 60, 62, 71, 168
conscientious objection 58, 61
consciousness 120, 127, 131, 140, 160, 167
    see also identity; "presences"; self;
constructionism 19, 154, 200
    see also social constructionism

context 100
    cultural 127, 250, 257
    family 250, 253
    historical 10, 248, 257
    and identity 14, 30–1, 58, 81–2, 99
    and language development 106
    personality constructs 119
    religious 204
    social 10, 88, 124, 196, 204, 210
    socio-cultural 58, 125, 132
contextualism 19, 29–30, 42
conversation 40, 88, 91–2, 104, 181
    see also dialogue; discourse
Conversational Realities (Shotter) 166
counseling 61–2, 83, 91, 199, 229, 240
countertransference 248
Creation, the 205
creativity 60
    in drawing 110
    in dreaming 177
    in speaking 102, 104
    in writing 221, 225
critical psychology 228–39
Critical Psychology: An Introduction (Fox and Prilleltensky) 235
Critical Psychology: Voices for Change (Sloan) 229
critical social theory 230, 233, 236, 241
critique, practice of 162, 198, 230, 235, 236, 239
Crossing the Unknown Sea: Works as a Pilgramage of Identity (Whyte) 40
cultural differences 203, 224
Cultural Politics of Everyday Life (Shotter) 152
cultural politics 152, 159, 162

Damaged Life (Sloan) 235
dance therapy 251–2, 256–7
De Anima (Aristotle) 115
de-ideologization 234
death and dying, course on 179
deconstruction 91–2, 163
democracy 231, 234, 239–43
demonstrations, mass 242, 250
despair 40, 116, 223–4
diagnosis, psychiatric 16, 19, 21, 22, 26–7, 166
dialectical thinking 104, 200, 201, 202–3
dialogal phenomenology 141, 143, 223–4
dialogical approach, to social scientific research 166
dialogue 238, 239, 241
    and healing 212
    and identities 14, 28
    as research method 166, 223
Dialogue and Development (Gustavsen) 166
disability 180
discourse 87–8
    constructionist 83
    deconstructive 91–2
    and identity 81, 88–9
    liberal humanist 75–80
    personality 118–9
    and power 89
    see also conversation; dialogue
discrimination, racial 32–3

dispositional traits 119
distinctive features theory 160
Divided Self, The (Laing) 136, 214
domestic violence 178
dominant narratives 86–7
domination 234, 236, 249
Don Quixote 24, 216, 220
Drama of Everyday Life, The (Scheibe) 40, 49
dramaturgical psychology 21, 26, 29, 30, 33
dreams 23, 40, 117, 177, 181, 194, 214
Duquesne project 137–8
duty, ethical 229, 239
dyadic relationships 185, 248

ecological validity 100, 106
economic democracy 239, 241
effectance behavior 198
ego 118, 120, 123
ego autonomy 195, 202, 203
ego functioning 194, 202, 203
ego psychology 194–5, 197, 201
El Salvador 239
emotional life 19, 25–6, 30, 102, 210, 264
emotions 25–6
    development of 110
    expression of 201, 212–3
empirical research 39, 48, 70, 125, 137–8, 157, 230
emptiness 144–6
Encounter Group Movement 57, 59
Enlightenment 79, 154, 163
epiphanies 217, 219
Escape From Freedom (Fromm) 185
essentialist view 25, 83
eternal life 51–2
ethics 100, 109–10, 177, 229–30, 238–9, 254
Etruscan artefacts 37–8, 49–50
Eurocentrism 78–9
existence, meaningfulness of 71, 131, 210, 214
existential phenomenology 136–7, 142
existentialism 135, 212, 229, 240, 247, 255
experiences 44, 85, 210, 217
    expression of 69
    holistic nature of 157
    and narratives 9, 225
    subjective 194
experimental psychology 106, 137–8, 162, 213, 214, 229
Explorations in Personality (Murray) 116
Expression of Emotion in Man and Animals, The (Darwin) 40

factory workers, treatment of 153
false memory syndrome 26–7, 29
family therapy 173, 176, 180, 181, 184, 186
fantasy 24, 176, 180
feminism 172, 178–9, 185, 249–52
Focusing therapy 222
forgiveness 217, 221–4
Franciscan Order 55–9
free will 183, 201–2

freedom of speech 109, 239
fugue states 17–18
fundraising 107–8

gender 78, 178, 245–6
generativity 117, 118, 119, 124, 126
genetic epistemology 175
German Ideology, The (Marx) 112
Gestalt therapy 249–50, 255
God 56–7, 158, 173, 175, 180–2, 187, 193, 205
gratitude 126, 174, 220, 226
Great Depression 14, 32
group therapy 57, 102, 218, 248

Handbook of Humanistic Psychology 250
Handbook of Social Psychology (Lindzey) 20, 29
healing 177, 179–80
    using dance 251–2, 256–7
    by dialogue 212
    by forgiving 223
    and relationships 215
    and truth 181
hermeneutical approaches 129, 161, 242
history of psychology 60–7, 176, 177, 178, 249
hospitalization 21, 22
Human Development and Social Policy (HDSP) program 124
human rights 231, 232, 235, 239
humanism 76–7, 198, 199, 202–4, 205
Humanistic Psychologist, The 142
humanistic psychology 77, 137, 139, 142, 191, 251, 257
Humanistic Psychology Movement 57, 59
humiliation 152, 156
hypnosis 17–19, 31
Hypnosis: A Social Psychological Analysis of Influence Communication (Sarbin and Coe) 28
hypothetico-deductive methods 23

I–Thou relationship 181, 182, 251
identity 120, 163, 228, 233, 257
    change, death–rebirth metaphor 28
    and context 81–2
    and discourse 88–9
    formation of 14, 20, 28, 117, 121–3
    loss of 17
    as product of interactions 39–40
    stories as source of 24
    see also life stories; self
ideology criticism 230–43
Images of Hope: Imagination as Healer of the Hopeless (Lynch) 61
Images of Man in Psychological Research (Shotter) 161
imagination 60, 61, 200
imaginings 13, 18–19, 24, 27
imagoes 124
imitation, in language learning 105–6
independence 75, 203
individual differences, assessment of 124

Individual Differences in Conscious Experience (Kunzendorf and Wallace) 44
individualism 173, 193, 195
    vs. collectivism 92, 203–4
inequality 106, 241
injustice 151, 155, 196, 232, 236
"inner speech" 165, 168
interactions, and identity 39–40
interbehaviorism 16, 31
interpersonal
    behaviors 181
    language 159
    power 187
    psychology 185
    relationships 123, 173, 187
interpretations 26, 38, 60, 101, 161–2, 167
intersubjectivity 234, 236, 239
interviews 123, 126, 128, 166, 175, 228, 230
intimacy motivation 116–19, 123, 125
introspective view 191, 200, 203
Investigations (Wittgenstein) 168
Invisible Man (Ellison) 202
Israel 252, 256

Jargon of Authenticity, The (Adorno) 231
"joint action" 157, 162
Judaism 255
Jungian psychology 40–2, 247, 255, 257
justice, social 61, 232, 233, 235, 239–40, 242–3

kinaesthetic transference 248
knowing, women's ways of 251

Labanotation 249–50, 252
laboratory experiments 16, 18, 23, 106–7, 116, 125
Lamp Post, The 176
language 17, 91, 103, 159
    computer simulation of 158, 160
    development of 102–6
    expressing oneself 71, 84, 153–4
    symbolic 245, 257
    see also narrative
Latin America 232
leadership 66–7, 238
liberal humanism 75–6, 80, 83
Life and Story: Autobiographies for a Narrative Psychology (Sarbin) 13
life choices 227, 231, 241
    see also positioning theory
life stories 122–9
lifestyle changes 240–1
linguistics 100, 105, 160
literature 59–62, 68, 176, 194, 221
logical learning theory (LLT) 191, 200
love 184, 217, 247, 255
loyalty 39, 233, 246–7

mainstream psychology 137, 185, 218, 234–5
Man as Male and Female (Jewett) 178
Man's Search for Himself (May) 136
Maori culture 74, 79
marital therapy 180
Meaning and Myth in the Study of Lives: A Sartrean Perspective (Charme) 122
mechanistic paradigm 16, 33, 139, 151, 154–5, 157, 199
medical model of mental illness 21–2, 28–9
meditation 144, 175, 255
Memories, Dreams and Reflections (Jung) 40
memory 27, 33, 40, 51–2, 138–9, 179
  see also false memories
mental health 90
metaphors
  constructionist 88–90
  and despair 223
  narrative 28–9, 82–6, 91
  role of 66, 68–9, 70–1
Metaphors in the History of Psychology (Leary) 66
Metaphors We Live By (Lakoff and Johnson) 70
metapsychology 199
Mirrors, Masks, Lies and Secrets (Scheibe) 40
modernism 76, 80, 208
"moral ecology" 162
morality 21–2, 24, 161, 163, 254
Mormonism 229, 236, 240, 241
mortality 234, 247
motivation 125–6, 198, 204, 233
  see also intimacy motivation
multiple personality 26–7
multiple selves 80
music 9, 43–4, 59, 176–7
mystical experiences 69

names, importance of 47
narrative psychology 13, 23–33, 39, 40, 42, 84
Narrative Psychology: The Storied Nature of Human Conduct (Sarbin) 25
"narrative repair" 34
narrative therapy 85–7, 91
narratives 23–31, 74–91, 123–7, 129, 249–50
  see also life stories
National Service 155–6
Nature 160
near-death experiences 224
nonconformance 19–21, 31–2
nonverbal communication 87, 248, 249

objectivity 200, 228, 245
Oedipal impulses 194, 233
On Being Human (Kinget) 136
Open Door: Thoughts on Acting and Theatre, The (Brook) 40

pain 179–80, 102, 103, 110, 253–4
Pakeha (non-Maori) 80, 81, 85, 87
paranoia 15–16

participant observation 236
peak experiences 217
personal agency 185, 187
personal authority 181–4
personal constructs 41, 161
personality 76–7, 117–8
  assessment of 29
  authoritarian 185
  disorder 173–4
  and narrative identities 119–21
  research 117–20, 125, 230
  theory of 194, 229–31
  traits 116, 118–9, 173
personhood 163, 203, 233
phenomenological psychology 137, 214, 218, 220, 222
phenomenology 135, 137, 138, 141, 142–3, 177
philosophy of psychology 60–2, 64–5
political action 33, 101, 232, 255
political consciousness 241
political movements, US 235
positioning theory 88–9
positivism 15, 135
postmodernism 79–80, 142, 143, 172, 208
poverty 56–7, 232, 239, 240
power 89, 91, 123, 153, 157, 183
Power, Intimacy and the Life Story (McAdams) 123, 124, 125
"presences" 164
Principles of Psychology, The (James) 68
proactivity 203–4
  see also agency
problem solving, strategies for 160
psychoanalysis 17, 139, 194, 201, 230
psychological agency 199–202, 203
Psychologists for Social Responsibility (PsySR) 232, 235, 238
Psychology and Theology in Western Thought 177
psychopathology 174, 178, 194–5, 257
psychosomatic studies 16–17
psychotherapy 166, 175, 212–3, 230, 245
purposeful behavior 16, 191, 200, 201

Quixotic principle 24

racism 32, 106, 134, 192, 196, 198, 203, 234
radical psychology 100, 108, 234, 235
"real presences" 159
rebellion 233, 237, 246
recovered memory 27
redemption 126, 129, 180, 256
"redemptive self" 126–8
Redemptive Self, The (McAdams) 127
relational responsiveness 99, 100, 111, 159
"relational selves" 80
relationships 212–3, 215, 248
religion 44–5, 55–9, 61–2, 175–8, 193, 204–5, 236–7, 240
"reminders" 165, 168

Republic (Plato) 115
Review of Existential Psychology and Psychiatry 136
rhetoric 66, 68, 163
role taking 15–16, 19–20, 28–9, 186–7
Royal Air Force (RAF) 155–6

sanity 212
Saybrook Counseling Center 43
schizophrenia 21, 22
Schizophrenia: Mental Diagnosis or Moral Verdict? (Sarbin) 22
schizophrenia 212, 214, 218
scientific psychology 65–6, 137–9, 157, 231, 234–5, 245
scientism 233, 235
scientist–practitioner model 180
self 39–40, 68, 70–1, 120, 202, 251
    and identity 39–43, 80–1, 120–1
    theory of 236
    understanding of 65
    see also identity; redemptive self
Self Studies (Scheibe) 40–1
self-concept 120–1, 202
self-deception 228, 241
Self-Deception in Life Choices (Sloan) 228
self-determination 163, 187
self-forgiveness 223
selfhood 65, 70, 83, 120–1, 229, 238, 240–1
self-reflection 237, 238, 239, 243
September 11th 223, 232, 242
    see also terrorism
Seven Psychologies (Sarbin) 14
sexual abuse 27, 79
Social Accountability and Selfhood (Shotter) 151
social class 196, 203, 230, 238
social constructionism 29, 79, 82–4, 150–1, 158, 166, 251
social ecology 151, 158
social identity 13, 29
social interaction 82, 125
social justice 80, 235–6, 239, 242–3
social movements 235, 242
social psychology 19–21, 83, 120, 232
social roles 42, 119
social self 20, 29, 73
social therapy 100, 102–3, 109
Society for Personology 117
solitude 175, 247
speech 104, 156
    see also freedom of speech; "inner speech"
spirituality 191, 204–5, 217, 240, 254–8
spontaneous responsiveness 151, 157, 164, 167
stories *see* life stories; narratives
Stories We Live By, The (McAdams) 70, 125
storytelling 22, 26, 43, 84–5, 97, 116, 127–9, 246–7
"street performance" 107, 111
Studies in Social Identity (Sarbin and Scheibe) 29
subjectivity 120, 194, 200, 228, 233, 236, 245
subject–object dualism 145
suffering 126, 136, 145, 179, 232, 240–1
sunyata (emptiness) 144–6

Sybil (Schreiber) 26
symbolic interactionism 82, 186

teaching 62, 64–7, 219
teleological behavior 191, 200, 201
terrorism 223, 232, 242
Thematic Apperception Test (TAT) 116, 123
theology 172, 176, 178
    see also God; religion
therapeutic communities 212
Thinking and Speech (Vygotsky) 104
thinking, study of 39, 104, 139–40
Third World 231
Thought and Language (Vygotsky) 106, 160
Tibetan Buddhism 144, 255
To Know As We Are Known (Palmer) 184
Totality and Infinity (Levinas) 219
transcendentalism 193, 225
transference 248, 256
trauma, dealing with 179–80, 180, 240–1
truth 181, 182, 225, 239
    attainability of 67, 69
    and culture 78–9
    and knowledge 83
    and love 184, 187
    and music 176–7
    regimes of 77–8
    and science 79, 155, 210, 225

Ultimate Fitness (Kolata) 40
utopia, American experiments 241

Vagabond, The (Colette) 247
Varieties of Religious Experience (James) 44
Vienna Circle 135
Vietnam War 48, 56, 58, 61, 216
voice
    authentic 250–1
    collective vs. individual 73, 81–2
    feminist 179
    in therapy 91–2
    see also agency
vulnerability 213, 217

Walden Two (Skinner) 115
Western beliefs/culture 76–8, 84, 177, 197, 203, 255, 257
women
    courses on 178, 250
    psychology of 248–50
    role models 250
    stories by 245
    ways of knowing 251
World Hypotheses (Pepper) 29
World War II 47, 156, 208

zones of proximal development (ZPDs) 102, 106, 160, 164

Author Index

Aanstoos, C.M. 131–49, 261
Adler, A. 178
Adler, N. 28
Adorno, T. 230, 241
Alinsky, S. 57
Allen, V. 29, 42
Allport, G. 26, 33
Andersen, M. 28
Anderson, R. 180
Argyle, M. 21
Aristophanes 117
Aristotle 24, 26, 39, 216
Arons, M. 141, 142
Asch, S. 39

Badiou, A. 239
Bahktin, M. 91–2
Bailey, D. 29
Bakan, D. 175
Baker, G. 103
Baker, K. 63
Bakhtin, M. 157, 159, 163, 166
Barber, T. 28
Bardwick, J. 249
Barker, E.T. 212, 213
Barr, C. 180
Barratt, B. 231, 237
Barrett, F. 30
Barrett, J. 155
Bartenieff, I. 249
Barth, K. 176–7
Bates, M. 60
Bateson, M.C. 250
Baumrind, D. 177, 178
Beauvoir, S. de 247, 250
Beckett, S. 155
Beethoven, L. van 176
Benjamin, L.S. 178, 181, 182
Berger, P.L. 82–3
Bernal, G. 180
Bernstein, B. 156
Billig, M. 159
Birdwhistell, R. 248
Bloom, L. 100
Boisen, A. 175
Bolen, J. 257
Bonaparte, M. 38
Boszormenyi-Nagy, I. 175, 180
Bradburn, N. 63
Bregman, L. 179
Brentano, F. 175

Broner, E. 256
Brook, P. 40
Broughton, J. 103
Bruner, E. 85–6
Bruner, J. 23, 160
Brunner, E. 173, 174, 182
Buber, M. 115, 175, 180, 181, 186, 212
Buckley, F. 220
Bugental, J. 247
Burgess, E. 17
Burke, K. 186

Cameron, N. 15–16, 175, 186
Camus, A. 134, 247
Carlson, R. 122
Carney, R. 30
Caruso, I. 175
Cashdan, S. 186
Cassirer, E. 156, 164
Chandler, M. 30
Charme, S.T. 122
Chaves, J. 28
Chavez, C. 57
Chein, I. 199, 205
Chinnici, J. 58
Chodorow, N. 245
Chomsky, N. 105
Chun, K.T. 29
Coates, T. 58
Coe, W. 28
Coffin, W.S. 204
Cole, M. 100, 106
Colette, S.G. 247
Cooley, C.H. 39
Cooley, C. 174
Council, J. 28
Craik, K. 29
Crites, S. 30
Curie, M. 250

Darwin, C. 40, 117
Davies, B. 88
Davis, M. 248
Deleuze, G. 230
deRivera, J. 27
Derrida, J. 231
Descartes, R. 16–17, 26, 135, 151, 157
Dewey, J. 70, 161, 162, 185
Dillard, A. 49
Dobles, I. 232
Dooley, T. 133
Dostoyevsky, F. 116, 117, 129
Dreyfus, H.L. 161, 162
Dunbar, F. 178
Duncan, I. 252
Dykstra, D.I. 185

Earnest, W.R. 230, 237
Ebner, F. 175
Edelson, M. 200
Eliott, R. 28
Ellison, R. 202
Emerson, R.W. 40, 191, 193, 205
Epps, E.G. 204
Epstein, S. 120
Epston, D. 85
Erikson, E. 116, 117, 118, 120, 121, 125
Escoffier, J. 81
Eurich-Rascoe, B. 172, 179

Fant, C.G.M. 160
Festinger, L. 39
Fischer, C. 213
Fishman, H.C. 173
Foucault, M. 77, 89, 230, 231
Fowler, J. 123
Fox, D. 235
Francis of Assisi, St. 54
Frank, G. 256
Freud, S. 38–9, 115, 116, 117, 120, 122
Friedlander, J.W. 17
Friedman, M. 175
Fromm, E. 185
Frost, R. 40

Gadamer, H. 157
Gadlin, H. 177
Gandhi, M. 117
Gauld, A. 161
Geertz, C. 75
Gendlin, E.T. 222, 225
Gerber, L. 222
Gergen, K.J. 83, 99, 111, 165
Gergen, M. 111, 165
Giddens, A. 121
Gide, A. 247, 255
Ginsburg, G. 30
Giorgi, A. 136–8, 218
Giori, A. 220
Giroux, H.A. 77
Goethe, J.W. von 54, 63–4
Goffman, E. 20–1, 30, 39, 42, 120, 122
Goldfarb, M. 222
Goldstine, D. 28
Goodman, P. 134
Gorman, G. 180
Gough, H. 29
Greenfield, N. 28
Gregg, G. 230, 237
Guattari, F. 230
Guerreiro Ramos, A. 49
Guntrip, H. 175
Gurin, P. 204

AUTHOR INDEX

Gustavsen, B. 166

Habermas, J. 230, 235
Hadley, S. 9, 13, 96
Halle, M. 160
Hallie, P. 30
Halling, S. 208–27, 261
Halprin, A. 249
Hanh, T.N. 145
Hankiss, A. 122
Harr, R. 80, 88, 166
Hayes, L. 29
Hayes, S. 29
Hegel, G.W.F. 231
Heidbreder, E. 14
Heidegger, M. 131, 135, 230, 231, 241
Heilbrun, C. 245
Helson, R.M. 28
Hempel, C.G. 135
Hermans, H.J.M. 31, 80
Heschel, A.J. 184
Hilgard, J. 28
Hillman, J. 257
Hocking, W.E. 175
Holt, E.B. 175
Holzkamp, K. 231
Holzman, L. 96–113
Horgan, P. 30
Hozman, L. 262
Hull, C.L. 157
Hulst, W.G. van de 176
Husserl, E. 135, 138, 231

Ingleby, D. 103
Irigay, L. 245

Jaffe, A. 250
Jakobson, R. 160
James, W. 39, 51, 67–70, 120, 122
Jeeves, M. 172
Jencks, C. 79
Jenkins, A.H. 191–207, 262
Jewett, P. 173, 178, 182
Johnson, M. 70
Johnson, P. 175
Jones, D. 156
Jones, E. 38–9
Jones, M. 210
Josselson, R. 129
Juhasz, J. 28
Jung, C.G. 40–2, 122, 175, 182, 250

Kagiticibasi, C. 204
Kant, I. 63
Kantor, J.R. 16–17, 28, 31, 32
Katz, A.M. 166

Keen, E. 30
Kelly, G. 161
Kelsey, M. 175
Kempen, H.J. 31, 80
Kennedy, R. 48, 134, 216
Keyes, C. 219
Kierkegaard, S. 115, 129, 135, 175, 209
King, M.L. 48, 134
Kinget, M. 136
Kitsuse, J. 29
Koch, S. 65, 66
Kohut, H. 120
Kolata, G. 40
Krieger, L. 63
Kroger, R. 29
Kuhn, T. 135
Kunz, G. 220
Kunzendorf, R.G. 44

Laban, R. von 249
Lacan, J. 231
Laing, R.D. 136, 175, 184, 212, 214
Lake, F. 175
Lakoff, G. 70
Lannamann, J. 166
Leary, D.E. 54–72, 262–3
Lee, D.J. 13, 31
Levin, H. 24
Levinas, E. 219
Levy-Bruhl, L. 164
Lewin, K. 39
Lewis, C.S. 174, 176
Lewis, J. 18
Lieblich, A. 129
Lightbrown, P. 105
Lightfoot, C. 30
Lim, D. 28
Lindsell, H. 178
Linehan, C. 88
Lira, E. 232
Loevinger, J. 120
Loman, W. 155
Lomax, A. 252
Lowen, A. 215
Luckman, T. 82–3
Luria, A.R. 156
Luther, M. 117
Lynch, W.F. 61

McAdams, D.P. 70, 114–30, 263
McCarthy, J. 88
McCormick, B. 59
McDougal, W. 26
McKechnie, G. 29–30
MacLeod, R. B. 177
McManama, Sr. M. 219–20
Macmurray, J. 161, 173, 175
McNamee, S. 99, 111, 166
McPherson, M.W. 177

Maddi, S. 63
Magaret, A. 175, 186
Mancuso, J. 22, 29
Martn-Bar, I. 232, 239
Marx, K. 100, 112
Masek, B. 141
Maslow, A. 57, 142, 217
May, R. 57, 136, 247
Mead, G.H. 17, 19, 20, 39, 82, 156, 159, 174, 186
Meehl, P. 15
Mendel, G. 231
Merleau-Ponty, M. 135, 157, 159
Milgram, S. 39
Miller, A. 155
Minuchin, S. 173
Monk, G. 73–95, 263
Montero, M. 232
Moreno, J.L. 29
Mouffe, C. 89
Moustakas, C. 247
Mozart, W.A. 43–4, 176
Murray, H.A. 116, 117
Myerhoff, B. 256

Nagarjuna 145
Nagel, G. 180
Nagel, T. 167
Newcomb, T. 20
Newman, F. 97, 100, 109, 111
Newton, I. 135
Nietzsche, F. 135, 182
Nixon, R.M. 135
Nouwen, H. 175, 184
Nucci, L. 28

O'Brien, P. 59
O'Keefe, G. 250
O'Toole, P. 155
Ognjenovic, V. 110
Oliver, M. 257
Orne, M. 27, 29, 37, 46
Ortega y Gasset, J. 40
Orwell, G. 40

Pagels, E. 40
Palmer, P. 184
Parker, L. 90
Pavlov, I. 16
Pedersen, P.B. 80
Pelligrini, R. 30
Pel 37, 47–8
Pepper, S. 29
Perls, F. 57, 142
Perls, L. 249, 255
Piaget, J. 100, 105, 121
Plato 117
Plutchik, R. 26
Polanyi, M. 135

Polka, B. 214
Popper, K.R. 135
Popplestone, J. 177
Prilleltensky, I. 235
Pruyser, P.W. 175, 176
Pyevich, C. 240

Rabinowitz, S. 49
Richards, R. 63
Ricoeur, P. 142
Rogers, C. 57, 136, 142
Rose, N. 235
Rosenberg, M. 30
Rosenwald, G. 237
Rossi, E. 257
Rotter, J. 46
Rudeman, J. 9
Rychlak, J.F. 191, 198, 200–1
Ryle, G. 31

Samuels, A. 257
Sarbin, T.R. 13–35, 37, 42, 46, 263
Sartre, J. 115, 122, 134, 135, 246, 247
Saxton, C. 178
Sayers, D. 174
Schaeffer F.A. 176
Schafer, R. 201
Scheflen, A. 248
Scheibe, K.E. 29, 36–53, 264
Scheler, M. 217
Seidman, S. 79
Serlin, I. 245–60, 264
Seve, L. 231
Sexton, A. 250
Sexton, V.S. 177, 178
Shakespeare, W. 54, 59, 117, 155
Shaw, G.B. 155, 156
Shawver, L. 111
Shideler, M. 177
Shotter, J. 80, 92, 150–71, 264
Sloan, T. 228–44, 265
Smith, H.N. 30
Smith, S. 248
Snow, C.P. 138
Spanos, N. 28
Spiegel, D. 251
Spiegelman, M. 257
Stanton, F. 14–15
Steele, R. 122
Steiner, G. 164
Stocking, G. 63
Strachey, J. 116
Sullivan, H.S. 173–4, 177–8, 187
Sutton-Smith, B. 25
Swift, J. 60

Taft, R. 28
Taylor, C. 161
Thompson, C. 178
Thompson, J. 234
Tillich, P. 175
Toler, Sr. C. 220
Tolkien, J.R.R. 174
Tomkins, S.S. 26, 122
Toulmin, S. 63, 69, 135
Tyler, L. 199

van Vuuren, R. 224
Vande Kemp, H. 172–90, 264
Vico, G. 157, 159
Voloshinov, V. 157
von Eckartsberg, R. 220
Vygotsky, L. 100–5, 110, 157–9, 161–2, 164–5

Walkerdine, V. 103
Wallace, B. 44
Watson, J.B. 16, 194
Watts, A. 134
Wertz, F. 138
White, H. 30
White, M. 85, 91
White, R. 197
Whyte, D. 40
Williams, C. 174, 176, 177, 183–4
Williams, R. 159
Williamson, E.G. 28
Wilson, R.N. 221
Winnicott, D.W. 175
Winston, A. 32
Wittgenstein, L. 103, 105, 157–9, 164–6, 168
Wood, D. 160
Woolf, V. 250
Wordsworth, W. 40

Yalom, I. 247
Yancy, G. 9, 13, 96
Yeatman, A. 79
Yeats, W.B. 40
Young, I.M. 89

Zizek, S. 231